Routledge Revivals

The Market in History

First published in 1986. The free market is often associated with liberty and individualism, and this connection has been made for more centuries than is generally realised. The essays collected in this book trace the development, importance and influence of the market as a dominating component of the shared human life from classical antiquity to the present. The authors, from various backgrounds, keep constantly in view the moral and political questions raised by the role of markets, as well as laying out succinctly what can be known or deduced about the actual operation of the market in Western and other cultures. This book will be of interest to students of economics and history.

The Market in History

Papers presented at a Symposium held 9-13 September 1984 at St George's House, Windsor Castle, under the auspices of the Liberty Fund

Edited by
B.L. Anderson and A.J.H. Latham

First published in 1986
by Croom Helm

This edition first published in 2016 by Routledge
2 Park Square, Milton Park, Abingdon, Oxon, OX14 4RN
and by Routledge
711 Third Avenue, New York, NY 10017

Routledge is an imprint of the Taylor & Francis Group, an informa business

© 1986 B.L. Anderson and A.J.H. Latham

All rights reserved. No part of this book may be reprinted or reproduced or utilised in any form or by any electronic, mechanical, or other means, now known or hereafter invented, including photocopying and recording, or in any information storage or retrieval system, without permission in writing from the publishers.

Publisher's Note
The publisher has gone to great lengths to ensure the quality of this reprint but points out that some imperfections in the original copies may be apparent.

Disclaimer
The publisher has made every effort to trace copyright holders and welcomes correspondence from those they have been unable to contact.

A Library of Congress record exists under LC control number: 86002658

ISBN 13: 978-1-138-65019-0 (hbk)
ISBN 13: 978-1-315-62543-0 (ebk)

THE MARKET IN HISTORY

EDITED BY B. L. ANDERSON and A. J. H. LATHAM

Papers presented at a Symposium held 9–13 September 1984 at St George's House, Windsor Castle, under the auspices of the Liberty Fund.

CROOM HELM
London • Sydney • Dover, New Hampshire

© B. L. Anderson, A. J. H. Latham and Contributors, 1986
Croom Helm Ltd, Provident House, Burrell Row,
Beckenham, Kent BR3 1AT

Croom Helm Australia Pty Ltd, Suite 4, 6th Floor,
64–76 Kippax Street, Surry Hills, NSW 2010, Australia

British Library Cataloguing in Publication Data

The Market in history: papers presented at a symposium held 9–13 September 1984 at St. George's House, Windsor Castle, under the auspices of the Liberty Fund.
1. Markets—History
I. Anderson, B. L.   II. Latham, A. J. H.
381'.18'09   HF5471

ISBN 0-7099-4120-X

Croom Helm, 51 Washington Street, Dover,
New Hampshire 03820, USA

Library of Congress Cataloging in Publication Data

The market in history.

Includes index.
1. Markets—history—congresses. I. Anderson, B.L. (Bruce Louis) II. Latham, A.J.H.
III. Liberty fund.
HF471.M37   1986   381'.18'09   86-2658
ISBN 0-7099-4120-X

Phototypeset by *Sunrise Setting*, Torquay, Devon
Printed and bound in Great Britain by Mackays of Chatham Ltd, Kent

CONTENTS

List of Figures	vi
List of Symposium Members	vii
Introduction	1
1 Labour, Property and the Morality of Markets *Robert Sugden*	9
2 The Development of the Market in Archaic Greece *James M. Redfield*	29
3 Early Fairs and Markets in England and Scandinavia *Peter Sawyer*	59
4 Markets and Freedom in the Middle Ages *A. R. Bridbury*	79
5 Early Modern English Markets *Eric Kerridge*	121
6 Entrepreneurship, Market Process and the Industrial Revolution in England *B. L. Anderson*	155
7 Markets and Development in Africa and Asia *A. J. H. Latham*	201
Notes on Contributors	221
Index	225

LIST OF FIGURES

3.1: Coin Finds, Alvastra Monastery	70
7.1: Cross River Economy	203
7.2: Rice Trade *c.* 1910	211

LIST OF SYMPOSIUM MEMBERS

The editors wish to thank the Liberty Fund for their generous support in underwriting the Symposium, and General Sir Hugh Beach and the staff of St George's House, Windsor Castle, for arranging the proceedings. The editors would also like to thank all the Symposium members for their contribution to the discussion of the papers, and Tim Fearnside for preparing the drawings for this volume.

B. L. Anderson
A. J. H. Latham

B. L. Anderson (University of Liverpool)
A. R. Bridbury (London School of Economics)
C. E. Challis (University of Leeds)
S. Fenoaltea (Bryn Mawr College)
D. K. Fieldhouse (University of Cambridge)
R. M. Hartwell (University of Oxford and University of Sydney)
K. Hopkins (Brunel University)
E. Kerridge (University of Wales, Bangor)
A. J. H. Latham (University of Wales, Swansea)
D. N. McCloskey (University of Iowa and University of York)
D. C. North (University of Washington)
J. Redfield (University of Chicago)
P. Sawyer (University of Leeds)
H. K. Schneider (University of Indiana)
B. Shosan (Hebrew University, Jerusalem)
R. Sugden (University of East Anglia)

In attendance:
A. N. McLeod (President of the Liberty Fund)

INTRODUCTION

Theories about how societies change over time have frequently arisen in response to changes in societies themselves. All such theories, whether of an economic, social, anthropological, or other character, have been and remain highly problematical to test effectively and conclusively; so there is always need for considerable scepticism about how much confidence can be placed in them. Nevertheless, as the generation and utilisation of such theories has developed, some concepts have tended to exhibit a greater survival value than others. This may be only because they have provided more regularly fruitful insights into the functioning of societies, or organising principles for the empirical evidence to sustain them, than could be obtained without making use of them.

An example of this, of what might be called the phenomenology of social explanation, is the way the idea of the Market has become a part of common usage across the social sciences. Ideas of this type it seems, whilst often associated with particular 'schools of thought' or subject categories, have often proved to be separable from the particular area of investigation in which they originated. In the process it seems quite possible, even likely, that those who make use of them in different fields of research will come to understand them differently. The Windsor Symposium was organised with the object of bringing together representative speakers and discussants from the fields of economics and economic history, sociology and anthropology, as well as of history at different periods, to explore the idea of the Market in terms of their own thought and work. There was no presumption that all or any of the participants attached more or less importance to the concept of the Market among the range of ideas each of them worked with, merely that all had found it useful or were currently making use of it.

The Windsor Symposium was openly exploratory and the participants, including the editors of the collected papers, neither anticipated being able to draw up settled conclusions about the nature of the Market across so many different areas of application, nor do they believe that it would be useful to do so. However, it is clear that a few central themes reappeared in different forms in most if not quite all of the papers, that they also figured prominently in the discussions that followed them, and that they provide the basis for such unity as a volume of collected conference papers can hope to achieve.

Sugden's contribution addresses one of the central questions of debate over the moral bases of market versus non-market arrangements in the ordering of societies. What criterion of justice is most appropriate to the distribution of property? At least since Locke there have been two broad kinds of answer offered, what may be called the classical or entitlement, and the end-state. In recent years these different positions on the problem have been the objects of important restatements and extensions in the works of Rawls and Nozick, which have led to them being much more widely discussed.[1] The chapter suggests that human nature is not well served by adopting the utilitarian position that just rules offer the highest average utility possible to a society's members. This is because societies evolve just rules primarily in order to avoid conflict between their members. The utilitarian approach, by in effect conflating society's members to a single entity, assumes a degree of impartiality that is unnatural in a socially engaged human being. Instead, a social order based on reciprocal advantage is to be preferred. Extending the argument, the question is posed if a theory of justice needs to be compatible with human nature does this entail that the distribution of property in society be made on a basis of equal division? The conclusion arrived at is that an equal division would give rise to conflict and that a rule allowing each party to retain the produce of his own labour would be preferable. Being found uniquely appropriate in different circumstances over time, such a rule would tend to become customary among self-interested individuals lacking formal laws.

Redfield's chapter traces the historical emergence of the market among the Greeks in the two centuries after 800 BC. Here, too, the emphasis is on the market as an ethical as well as an institutional phenomenon. The chapter reveals an aspect of the market form that has been an important feature of its operation in society ever since. This is its tendency to come into conflict with, or at least exert tensions on, the polity. In Archaic Greece these tensions were manifested in the contrasts between traders whose status was low and who made their way by bargaining and trade, and the heroes whose status was high and who maintained their position by gifting and raiding according to circumstances. The action of the market is to be seen in a shift from redistributive institutions to exchange, or from an alternative perspective, from status to contract. This is exemplified in the substitution of fixed payments like rents for honour gifts of surplus production. In the seventh century BC the encroachment of exchange produced a new problem of agricultural indebtedness. Greek society accommodated this, not without difficulty, by moving the onus of redistribution on to the state. The tensions between market and polity remained, with the former becoming a 'repressed fact' and the latter retaining its ethical dominance. The paper concludes that these ambiguities have had a continuing influence in the Western tradition.

The chapter by Sawyer deals with a similar phenomenon in a Dark Age context. It shows how markets, which in many cases had been held '. . . from before the time of memory', were gradually brought within the permit of central and local authority in pre-Conquest England. When the royal power and its agents began to assert itself some two centuries after the end of Roman administration in the fifth century, it appears that many customary market tolls, rights and other impositions which almost certainly predated even the Roman occupation were simply taken over. Thus in their turn the Normans gained control of a country that was already well used to having its exchange activities taxed and monitored. Following Christianisation the spate of church building was an important encouragement to the spread of market places, with Sunday trading being commonplace. But markets are to be found at many other different kinds of places, especially court venues, but also wherever regular gatherings occurred. The provision of more fortified places, with the entrenchment of royal power later, combined to produce a situation where most of the larger market centres were operating under royal charter by the thirteenth century. Earlier attempts to contrive this, for example during the reign of Athelstan, seem to have failed. However, throughout the period local unregulated markets appear to have operated beyond the reach of authority regardless of the condition of the monarchy at any given time. This was especially so in areas of the North where controls were always less effective than in the heartland. Thus the earliest medieval markets were a natural growth in response to local requirements and were not just outgrowths of existing long-distance trades. Early English internal trade seems not to have depended on a prior network of coastal trading centres that had continued to function after the end of Roman dominion in the West.

Bridbury views the idea of the market in medieval society from a distinctly non-teleological perspective. He finds a pervasive 'changelessness' in the economic and social conditions of the medieval world; the theme is one of change without development. Within a social order originating in military landlordism, markets functioned in thickets of restrictions and the action of competition was ultimately contained within the franchise of lordship. Even the royal power was in the end a private dispensation because medieval society lacked a public law in the modern sense. Consequently the medieval society lacked a public law in the modern sense. Consequently the medieval idea of freedom was very different from our own, and '. . . when medieval people spoke of freedom, particularly in connection with trade, they meant what we should mean by privilege'. With a significant intermission in the fifteenth century as a consequence of the longer-run impact of the Black Death, markets remained largely fragmented during the long Middle Ages from the eleventh to the seventeenth centuries. This was not because medieval peoples were innocent of acquisitive instincts or eschewed pecuniary gain, nor because they were incapable of scientific speculation and rational thought, but because their attitudes to authority and order maintained and were maintained by a polity that was more occupied with the distribution than the creation of wealth.

In the next chapter Kerridge's focus is on the securing of rights of freedom of property as the essential prerequisite of continuous market growth. In early modern England, he suggests that freedom of trade was an ideal firmly rooted in the common law, whose maintenance was derived from the Scriptures in what was an overwhelmingly Christian country. In this sense the law was God-given and in accordance with a higher or Natural Law. There is an interesting contrast between this conception of the law and that described in the previous chapter. It is one that reflects two long-standing and quite different ideas about how law evolves. In one, the law is regarded as the specific creation of government or a ruler; in the other, it is seen as something existing independently of an individual's will, or a ruler's power. On the one hand legislation for particular purposes is viewed as being one of the competences of government in the same way as its administrative function; on the other, governments are only capable of discovering the Law, or of restoring original law which has perhaps been violated or allowed to lapse. Looking at Europe in general, Bridbury's chapter sees the extensions of freedom resulting from population reduction in the late fourteenth and fifteenth centuries as essentially a false dawn separating an earlier period of feudal imposition on society from its reassertion in the sixteenth and seventeenth centuries. Kerridge's perspective on the early modern centuries is a different one; it indicates that there may have been a divergent evolution of the idea of law in England from that occurring on the Continent where the rise of absolutism in government tied the business of making law closely to the supremacy of the ruler. It may be that because the common law became well entrenched in England during the medieval centuries, and perhaps also because the older Greek conception of law as a barrier to unlimited power survived the later Roman influence, early modern England possessed the elements of a legal tradition that enabled it to resist the impact of the rise of absolute power in seventeenth-century Europe. This may help to explain why the constitutionalism of Hale and Harrington was effectively deployed at the end of the period against the *Leviathan* of Hobbes.

It would clearly be wrong to see pre-modern societies as incapable of generating considerable market activity and on occasion quite long periods of sustained economic growth. Equally it does seem that such instances were exceptional, and that when the output growth of these societies did exceed their population increase, the process was regularly checked, and often reversed, by the ability of their governments and *élites* to channel the surpluses of their populations into tax revenues rather than permitting them to go for investment and income growth. There is a very widely held view that what distinguished these societies from those which underwent industrialisation first in Western Europe, and then elsewhere in the last two centuries, was their failure to produce a critical scientific ferment of the kind that we characterise as the intellectual revolution wrought by Galileo and Newton. The tensions generated in the symbiosis of the political and economic spheres in traditional societies appear never to have proved powerful enough to break the mould of their values. For this to happen it is said what is required is a major shift in the technological limitations on such societies, a drastic alteration in the parameters of what was possible, before they could release themselves from the essentially zero sum game of circular change which constrained their transition to sustained development. As Rostow expresses it:

What we would now call basic science, in the traditional world, did not inspire in political rulers or merchants, bureaucrats or landowners, a view of their physical environment that led them to believe it was comprehensible and subject to systematic, creative and profitable manipulation. Traditional science suffered another narrower weakness: by and large its practitioners did not link their work to the tasks of technology.[2]

The chapter by Anderson suggests that a further dimension has to be accounted when seeking explanations for the phenomenon of modern economic growth. The argument of the chapter is that the market process, being essential to any society which provides for its members by specialisation, operates on the basis of entrepreneurial competition. Since complete knowledge is not given to human beings in any situation in which they find themselves entrepreneurship, or the perception of gainful opportunity, must act to exploit the possibilities inherent in our ignorance as well as those offered by what we think we know. An attempt is made to apply this approach to several sectors of the English economy on the eve of industrialisation. The conclusion is that the scope for entrepreneurial action was an important aspect of the shift towards sustained economic growth, and that it is possible to point to some of the conditions that are essential for an entrepreneurial culture to continue.

Latham's study of the action of the market in modernising African and Asian economies in the late nineteenth and early twentieth centuries reveals similar tensions developing between the power of governments and the working of markets to those displayed in other contributions. The paper shows how these come to be played out on a much broader canvas, as a result of the growing unity of the world markets in basic food grains, during the decades between the World Wars. The continuing output growth of rice in the countries and regions of South Asia, and of wheat in the lands of recent European settlement produced mounting gluts from the mid-1920s and led to the world-wide agricultural depression of the 1930s. The collapse of basic grain prices produced sharp reductions in incomes and demand in the Western industrial countries and brought about secondary depression in the demand for industrial raw materials. The conclusion is that interventions and market manipulations of a variety of forms, together with protectionist policies on the part of governments, prolonged the depression by retarding or suspending altogether market responses from among grain- and raw-material producers themselves.

The problems that have afflicted the working of the international economy since the onset of the 1970s, the growth of protectionism and cartelisation among advanced and less developed countries alike, and the breakdown of international financial co-operation, may suggest that a re-examination of the function of the Market is overdue. Among the advanced countries, many of which have come to a better understanding of the limits of economic policy in general, and macroeconomic policy in particular, there has been a renewal of interest in the micro-foundations of their economic and social life in recent years. This has been prompted by the need to comprehend why so many of them have experienced diminished incentives to taking risks and investing capital, poor productivity growth, and sluggish labour markets. Whatever a renewal of interest in the idea of the market may bring, however, it seems unlikely to remove an enigma at the centre of the idea. The market diffuses information in the form of prices that enables men to obtain the maximum possible satisfaction of their wants from the circumstances of their current situation, the facts of their present condition. These circumstances have been shaped in the past, yet the tastes, values, and aspirations which men seek to impose on them look to the future; hence the relations between them seem destined to remain as elusive to Man's grasp as the following studies indicate they have ever been.

Notes

1. J. Rawls, *A Theory of Justice* (Oxford University Press, London, 1972); and R. Nozick, *Anarchy, State and Utopia* (Basic Books, New York 1974).
2. W. W. Rostow, *How It All Began. Origins of the Modern Economy* (Methuen, London, 1975).

1 LABOUR, PROPERTY AND THE MORALITY OF MARKETS

Robert Sugden

Though the Earth, and all inferior Creatures be common to all Men, yet every Man has a *Property* in his own *Person*. This no Body has any Right to but himself. The *Labour* of his Body, and the *Work* of his Hands, we may say, are properly his.

John Locke, *Two Treatises of Government* (1698), Book 2, Chapter 5, § 27

The property which every man has in his own labour, as it is the original foundation of all other property, so it is the most sacred and inviolable. The patrimony of a poor man lies in the strength and dexterity of his hands; and to hinder him from employing this strength and dexterity in what manner he thinks proper without injury to his neighbour is a plain violation of this most sacred property.

Adam Smith, *The Wealth of Nations* (1776), Book 1, Chapter 10

The institution of property, when limited to its essential elements, consists in the recognition, in each person, of a right to the exclusive disposal of what he or she have produced by their own exertions, or received either by gift or by fair agreement, without force or fraud, from those who produced it. The foundation of the whole is the right of producers to what they themselves have produced.

John Stuart Mill, *Principles of Political Economy* (1848), Book 2, Chapter 2, §1

These three quotations, spanning a century and half, express a common idea: that each person has a right to the produce of his own labour. For Adam Smith this was a principle that opposed legislative interference in the workings of the market. (The passage I have quoted forms part of an attack on 'impertinent' and 'oppressive' laws regulating apprenticeships.) For John Locke, a man's right to his own labour was more fundamental than any landowner's claim to a portion of the earth, since the earth was naturally common to all men; it was only by mixing his labour with a piece of land that a man could acquire rights over it. John Stuart Mill used a similar principle to distinguish between the claims of workers and landowners: the worker was entitled to the produce of his own labour in a way that the landowner was not entitled to the 'raw material of the earth'.[1] In the late nineteenth and early twentieth centuries this distinction was an important part of socialist and populist thinking; the idea that the expenses of government ought to be met from the proceeds of a land tax — a logical development of Mill's own thinking — was widely held after it was popularised by Henry George in *Progress and Poverty*.[2]

Nowadays it is rare for anyone to make the full-blooded claim that each person is entitled to the produce of his own labour. In modern industrial economies, by far the greatest part of national income derives from labour. The major programmes of redistribution carried out by the state do not, on the whole, transfer income from non-workers to workers; they transfer income from well-paid workers to less-well-paid workers, and from workers to non-workers (the old, the sick, the unemployed, etc.). On the left of the political spectrum, people demand *more* redistribution of this kind. On the right it is often argued that this would kill the goose that lays the golden eggs: if instead tax rates on higher incomes were lowered, more able people would work harder, more wealth would be created, and ultimately the poor would benefit too. But there is a marked reluctance to suggest that the better-paid workers have a special entitlement to their higher incomes, simply because these incomes derive from *their* labour. National income seems to be thought of as a common pool; the object of economic policy is to make the pool as large as possible and to distribute it as fairly as possible — with 'fairness' interpreted in a way that takes no account of the origin of income.

In my own discipline of economics, this way of thinking is now firmly established. Only a tiny minority of modern economists, I suspect, would acknowledge the principle of property invoked by Locke, Smith and Mill. In this chapter I shall discuss this marked shift in the way economists think about the morality of markets, and argue that we ought to take this earlier view of property more seriously.

Non-economists, particularly those who work in the other social sciences, often suppose that economists have a professional commitment to the market system, and that economics is a system of thought that attempts to justify capitalism and *laissez-faire*. The truth, however, is that modern economics is extremely muted in the support it offers the market; it is much more concerned with why governments *should* intervene in markets than with why they should not.

It is true that theoretical economists take a great deal of professional pride in the Walrasian (or Arrow-Debreu) general equilibrium model of the market economy, which shows that a competitive equilibrium is Pareto-efficient. (That is, it is a state in which it is impossible to make anyone better off without making anyone else worse off.) Kenneth Arrow is speaking for many fellow economists when he writes — referring, I take it, to the work of his predecessors, and not to his own major contributions — that 'The [price] system itself is certainly one of the most remarkable of social institutions and the analysis of its workings is, in my judgement, one of the more significant intellectual achievements of mankind.'[3]

Nevertheless, this analysis of competitive equilibrium is not usually taken seriously at the practical as opposed to the theoretical level. Few economists are brave enough to claim that any modern industrial economy organised on *laissez-faire* principles would work much like the Walrasian model, and, in particular, that it would settle down in a state that was at all close to Pareto-efficiency. It is more usual to say that the Walrasian analysis shows what kinds of conditions must hold if a market economy is to achieve Pareto-efficiency and then to say that, of course, many of these conditions do not hold in reality. The Walrasian model, it is said, is still very valuable as a benchmark or limiting case; it provides a framework for thought. Certainly, most economists *do* use some such framework: we tend to view the realities of economic life as divergences from an ideal Walrasian model. (That is why we use such expressions as 'market failure' and 'government intervention': the *theoretical* norm is a perfect market system and a *laissez-faire* government.) But the prevailing view is that these divergencies are many and significant: 'market failure' occurs in most areas of economic life, and 'government intervention' is therefore required.

Arrow's own work provides a good example of the mixed feelings that economists have for the Walrasian model. He has, of course, contributed greatly to the theoretical analysis of general equilibrium in an ideal competitive economy. He has also written a very influential paper on the economics of medical care in which he argues that the medical-care industry is far removed from the theoretical norm of the competitive market.[4] He presents a long list of ways in which reality diverges from the ideal model. For example: people are concerned about one another's health, so that one person's consumption of health care confers benefits on his caring neighbours; insurance markets do not function well because of moral hazard and adverse selection; there is an asymmetry of information between physician and patient; and so on. Arrow concludes by remarking that this kind of analysis 'force(s) us to recognise the incomplete description of reality supplied by the impersonal price system'. The medical-care industry is perhaps an extreme case, but there can be few real-world markets in which economists have not diagnosed some kind of market failure and prescribed some kind of government intervention.

Quite apart from the problems of market failure, most welfare economists see the redistribution of income as a proper function of government. An ideal competitive economy — the kind represented in the Walrasian and Arrow-Debreu models — would generate a Pareto-efficient outcome; but what is good about Pareto-efficiency? The usual answer to this question is to assert the *Pareto value judgement*: any change that makes at least one person better off, in his or her own estimation, while making no one worse off is a good thing. Welfare economists usually claim that this value judgement is 'weak', 'reasonable' or 'appealing'; it is one that they themselves would make and that (they believe) almost everyone else would too. Accepting this value judgement for the sake of the argument, it is clear that a Pareto-*in*efficient state of affairs is *un*desirable in the sense that it can be improved on. A Pareto-inefficient state is one from which it is possible to make a move that benefits at least one person and harms none, and such a move, according to the Pareto value judgement, is a good thing.

But this does *not* mean that Pareto-efficient states *cannot* be improved on. Suppose, for example, that two people, A and B, are together on a life raft, and that the only food they have is four tins of corned beef. If both individuals are selfish, *any* division of the beef is Pareto-efficient. But are all divisions equally good? The Pareto value judgement does not say so, and a claim that they *were* all equally good would not strike most people as either reasonable or appealing. Nor is it clear that every efficient state is better than every inefficient one. Let X be the state in which A gets four tins and

B none, and let Y be the state in which A gets two tins, B gets one, and one is thrown away. X is efficient while Y is not, but we might well believe that Y was better than X. No doubt we can all agree that Y can be improved on: it would be better to give the fourth tin of beef to one or other of the individuals than to throw it away. But to say that it would be a good thing to move towards *some* Pareto-efficient state is not to say that it would be a good thing to move towards *any* such state. For this sort of reason, most welfare economists would follow Amartya Sen in denying that Pareto-efficiency (or 'Pareto-optimality') is necessarily a good thing:

> An economy can be optimal in this sense even when some people are rolling in luxury and others are near starvation as long as the starvers cannot be made better off without cutting into the pleasures of the rich. If preventing the burning of Rome would have made Emperor Nero feel worse off, then letting him burn Rome would have been Pareto-optimal. In short, a society or an economy can be Pareto-optimal and still be perfectly disgusting.[5]

What is clear is that, if we accept the Pareto value judgement, we must conclude that Pareto-inefficient states can be improved upon. To put this another way, we may disagree about which of all the conceivable ways of organising our society would be best, but for each of us the best state of affairs would be one of the Pareto-efficient ones. This allows us to make use of another theorem about the competitive economy of the Walrasian model. The theorem states that *every* Pareto-efficient allocation of resources is a competitive equilibrium for *some* initial distribution of property rights. Thus if I accept the Pareto value judgement, I accept that the allocation of resources I believe to be best can be reached through the workings of a competitive market — provided that initial property rights are distributed appropriately. The same is true for you; but your notion of an appropriate distribution of property rights may be different from mine.

The conventional view, then, is that a policy of *laissez-faire* is not necessarily justified even for the ideal competitive economy of the Walrasian model. In order to maximise welfare it is necessary that property rights are distributed in the appropriate way, and there is no obvious reason to suppose that this distribution would come into existence of its own accord in a society in which the government's only function was that of the night-watchman. In particular, there is no reason to suppose that welfare will be maximised if each person is assigned full property rights in the proceeds of his own labour.

Among welfare economists there is a clear consensus in favour of the Pareto value judgement. There is much less agreement about distributional questions; no one has yet come up with an uncontroversial system of values for comparing different Pareto-efficient distributions of income — and probably no one ever will. However, a number of alternative approaches have found some favour. I shall begin by describing two of the most common approaches — neither of which has any room for the idea that the individual has an entitlement to the produce of his labour. The first of these is *utilitarianism*.

There was a time when 'utilitarianism' was something of a dirty word among economists, but now there seems to be a growing tendency for utilitarians to come out of the closet. Welfare economists are beginning to recognise that they are using a system of analysis that was constructed by classical utilitarians and that, in its fundamentals, remains utilitarian — despite some cosmetic changes initiated in the 1930s in response to the criticisms of logical positivists and behaviourists. I shall take as my example the work of J. A. Mirrlees — partly because his analysis of the problem of 'optimal taxation' has been enormously influential and partly because his utilitarianism is unusually explicit.[6]

Mirrlees starts from the proposition that 'utility must be given meaning, if at all, in terms of individuals' preferences'.[7] The essential idea is that an individual derives more utility from one thing than another if and only if he prefers the former to the latter. For any individual, Mirrlees argues, it is possible to construct a *utility function* giving a utility value to every possible state of affairs; this function describes not only the individual's preference *ordering* of these states but also the *strength* of his preferences between them. Mirrlees presents a procedure or mental experiment by which any individual could, in principle at least, construct such a utility function for himself.

Mirrlees makes it clear that he is concerned not with the morality of individual behaviour but with 'the evaluation of the outcomes of public policy'. In this context, he argues, moral judgements must be universalisable and impartial. In a society of identical individuals, therefore, there is no reason to treat an outcome experienced by one person any differently from the same outcome experienced by another person:

> Roughly speaking, the totality of all individuals can be regarded as a single individual. Therefore total social utility, the sum of the total utilities of the separate individuals, is the right way to evaluate alternative patterns of outcomes for the whole society. That should be the view of any individual in the society, and therefore also of the outside observer.[8]

It would be easy to say that all of this has no bearing on the world in which we live, since individuals are *not* identical. However, if we are to make sense of something as complicated as an economy, we *must* use simplified models; there is, as far as I can see, no alternative. When an economist tries to predict what the effect of a particular economic policy will be, or to discover after the event what its effect has been, he does so in the framework of some theory about how the economy works. (Notice that a statement about the effect of a policy, even after the event, cannot be simply a report of observable facts; it involves some comparison between what has actually happened and what would have happened in the absence of the policy.) Thus when the welfare economist evaluates the effects of a policy, he too is working within the framework of an economic theory. It may be that for some problems it is appropriate to *assume* that individuals are identical; if so, a system of evaluation designed for societies of identical individuals is not useless.

The problem that Mirrlees is concerned with is that of income taxation: what is the optimal structure of income tax rates? On the face of it, *differences* between individuals — particularly differences in ability or productivity — are central to this problem. But here Mirrlees has a trick up his sleeve, which he calls *isomorphy*: 'it is possible to regard individuals who are, by reason of age, skills, sex, strength or culture, apparently very different, as nevertheless identical for the purposes of social judgement'.[9]

For the problem of optimal taxation, Mirrlees supposes that for every individual there is an index of 'labour efficiency', n. Essentially, n represents the amount of money the individual can earn from a unit of effort; so if z stands for the individual's labour earnings, z/n is a measure of the effort he expends. For any individual n is given; individuals with higher values of n are more able or more productive. (It may help to think of n as the wage rate at which the individual can sell his labour and z/n as the hours he works; but Mirrlees is not committed to measuring effort in terms of hours and labour.) Then Mirrlees assumes that each individual's utility is a function of his after-tax income, x, and the effort he expends, z/n. (Income is a source of utility and effort of disutility.) Given this framework, it is possible to assume that all individuals have identical utility functions, even though their values of n differ. In other words, all individuals are assumed to have the same preferences over combinations of after-tax income and effort, even though some people's efforts are more highly rewarded in the market than other people's.

According to Mirrlees, income tax systems should be evaluated against the criterion of total social utility. Mathematically, a society is modelled as a set of people with identical utility functions but different values of labour efficiency; the objective is to design a tax system to raise a given amount of revenue in a way that maximises the sum of individual's utilities. Two conflicting considerations have to be balanced against one another in this maximisation problem. On the one hand, Mirrlees assumes that the marginal utility of income falls as income increases; thus a sacrifice of £1 by a relatively well-off person involves less loss of utility than the same monetary sacrifice by a poorer person. This provides a reason for requiring people to pay more tax the more they earn. On the other hand, income taxes distort individuals' choices between income and leisure (that is, the opposite of effort). The higher is the marginal rate of income tax, the more distortion there is; because of this, the cost in terms of utility of raising an extra £1 of tax revenue from a given person tends to rise as tax rates rise. (There may come a point at which the cost becomes infinite: increases in tax *rates* may actually decrease tax *revenue* because of the extent to which individuals substitute leisure for income.)

Mathematically this is a remarkably difficult problem, and Mirrlees's solution to it is a considerable intellectual achievement.[10] For my purposes, however, it is less important to ask how he solved the problem or what solution he found, than to ask why he chose to formulate it in this particular way.

Notice that there is no place in Mirrlees's analysis for the idea that the individual has a special claim to the proceeds of his own labour. If the 'optimal' system of income tax rates allows individuals with greater labour efficiency to finish up better off than their fellows, this is because of the essentially *practical* problem of the disincentive effects of income taxation. If it was possible to make pure lump-sum transfers of income from the better off to the less well-off, Mirrlees's analysis would recommend such transfers as a means of maximising total utility. What matters for Mirrlees — and for utilitarians in general — is that economic goods should go where they give most utility. At the level of principle, it is simply irrelevant whose labour produced these goods.

Many economists have been influenced by John Rawls's monumental work *A Theory of Justice*.[11] For economists, Rawls's work has a professional appeal, quite apart from its moral and philosophical content. As Rawls says, his contract doctrine 'conceives of moral philosophy as part of the theory of rational choice';[12] it thus provides a route by which economic reasoning can arrive at moral conclusions.

Rawls's conception of justice is based on a form of social contract theory:

> the guiding idea is that the principles of justice for the basic structure of society are the object of the original agreement. They are the principles that free and rational persons concerned to further their own interests would accept in an initial position of equality as defining the fundamental terms of their association.[13]

Rawls separates himself from earlier contractarian thinkers by the way he defines 'equality' in the 'original position'. In order to compel his contracting parties to arrive at what he sees as an impartial conception of justice, he drastically restricts the information available to them:

> The original position is not, of course, thought of as an actual historical state of affairs, much less as a primitive condition of culture. It is understood as a purely hypothetical situation characterised so as to lead to a certain conception of justice. Among the essential features of this situation is that no-one knows his place in society, his class position or social status, *nor does anyone know his fortune in the distribution of natural assets and abilities, his intelligence, strength and the like.*[14] [my italics]

Rawls repeatedly stresses the importance of his contracting parties being ignorant of their natural endowments. He says that he is looking 'for a conception of justice that nullifies the accidents of natural endowment . . . as counters in the quest for political and economic advantage', and that the distribution of natural endowments is one of 'those aspects of the social world that seem arbitrary from a moral point of view'.[15] Or again, if the original position is to yield arguments that are just, 'the arbitrariness of the world must be corrected for'.[16]

However, Rawls's contracting parties are remarkably restrained in the extent to which they plan to correct the arbitrariness of the world. Summarising his theory of justice in a paragraph, Rawls writes:

> As a first step, suppose that the basic structure of society distributes certain primary goods, that is, things that every rational man is presumed to want. These goods normally have a use whatever a person's rational plan of life. For simplicity, assume that the chief primary goods at the disposition of society are rights and liberties, powers and opportunities, income and wealth. [Later Rawls will treat self-respect as an additional primary good.] These are the social primary goods. Other primary goods such as health and vigour, intelligence and imagination, are natural goods; although their possession is influenced by the basic structure, they are not so directly under its control. Imagine, then, a hypothetical initial arrangement in which all the social primary goods are equally distributed: everyone has similar rights and duties, and income and wealth are evenly shared. This state of affairs provides a benchmark for judging improvements. If certain inequalities of wealth and organisational powers would make everyone better off than in this hypothetical starting situation, then they accord with the general conception [of justice].[17]

The final three sentences of this quotation encapsulate Rawls's 'maximin' theory of distribution: there is a presumption that income and wealth should be distributed equally among individuals, but if inequalities can be shown to benefit everyone, they should be permitted. In practical terms, Rawls is requiring a 'social minimum' financed by a system of income (or expenditure) taxation. Leaving aside some complications involving Rawls's concept of just saving, it would seem that the objective is to set the social minimum as high as possible. That, at any rate, is how economists have usually interpreted Rawls.

It is significant that Rawls distinguishes between two sorts of primary goods — the 'social' and the 'natural'. Social goods are *at the disposition of society*; natural goods belong to particular individuals. Rawls's contracting parties reach agreement about the distribution of the stock of social goods; the distribution of natural goods is treated as entirely external to their deliberations.

Obviously, we should not expect the contracting parties to regard the natural primary goods as *literally* at the disposition of society. If we do not indulge in science fiction, and if we leave aside the sinister possibility of arriving at equality by levelling down (maiming the vigorous, disfiguring the beautiful?), we must accept that some highly desirable personal attributes are the product of inheritance or chance, and are not transferable. However, there seems nothing to stop the contracting parties deciding on an unequal distribution of income and wealth that *compensates*, to some degree, for inequalities in natural endowments. Take, for example, the problem of the physically disabled. There can be little question that, on any moderate level of income, the life of a sighted person is normally more desirable than that of a blind person, nor that the blind person's life would be made more pleasant by additional income. Why, then, do the contracting parties not make sure that blind people receive extra income? From the viewpoint of the original position, this would be a form of insurance, since the contracting parties are supposed not to know whether they are able-bodied or handicapped; and Rawls insists that it is rational for them to be extremely cautious about taking risks with their life prospects.[18] This point has been made forcefully by Brian Barry,[19] and, in a more tongue-in-cheek fashion, by Antony Flew,[20] who wonders why the contracting parties do not agree on any rules of justice to compensate the plain for the disadvantages they suffer in relation to the beautiful.

Yet in Rawls's theory of justice there is no place for such compensatory payments. The 'benchmark' that Rawls chooses for 'judging improvements' in society is the state of affairs in which income and wealth are equally shared, and natural endowments are not. I think we must treat this as axiomatic in Rawls's theory: Rawls *presupposes* that natural endowments are a kind of personal property while income and wealth are at the disposition of society. Thus, for Rawls, *the distribution of income and wealth lies within the scope of* the theory of justice while the distribution of natural endowments lies outside it.

If we accept that income and wealth belong to a common social pool on which no one has any prior claim, it is indeed natural to treat an equal division as a benchmark. As a mental experiment, consider the following game. A group of, say, ten people are brought together in a room. They are told that a sum of money — say £1,000 — has been donated to them, but on one condition: they must reach unanimous agreement on how to divide it among themselves. It is open to everyone to try to hold out for the largest share in the £1,000, but, I suggest, it seems highly likely that the ten players would eventually settle for an equal division as the only acceptable way of avoiding a deadlock. As Rawls puts it when describing how any one of his contracting parties would view the problem of distribution:

> Since it is not reasonable for him to expect more than an equal share in the division of social goods, and since it is not rational for him to agree to less, the sensible thing for him to do is to acknowledge as the first principle of justice one requiring an equal distribution. Indeed, this principle is so obvious that we would expect it to occur to anyone immediately.[21]

This argument would surely apply to *any* common stock of goods that had to be divided by unanimous consent. If everyone's natural endowments were regarded as elements in a common pool, along with income and wealth, there would be a presumption in favour of an equal division of *this* pool — which would imply, of course, that those with the poorest natural endowments should be given more income in compensation. Conversely, if income is *not* viewed as a common social pool, the presumption in favour of an equal distribution vanishes. The principle that each person has a special claim to the produce of his own labour denies that income is a common pool; it requires that we treat the produce of a person's labour in the same way that Rawls treats natural endowments themselves — as already spoken for. Rawls's theory of justice, I suggest, does not provide a *justification* for rejecting this principle; his denial of the principle is an *axiom* of his theory, not an *implication* of it.

Neither the utilitarian theory of distribution nor Rawls's theory has any place for the idea that the individual has a special entitlement to the produce of his own labour. That idea — *the labour theory of property* — is currently at a low ebb, at least among economists and political theorists. The prevailing view seems to be that the labour theory of property is an essentially arbitrary belief about people's entitlements, and one which lacks the impartiality and deductive logic of the utilitarian and Rawlsian approaches. Can it still be defended?

I shall suggest that the germ of a defence can be found in Rawls's own writing. Rawls sees his theory of justice as an alternative to utilitarianism; utilitarianism, he says, is objectionable because it 'does not take seriously the distinction between persons'.[22] However, as he has to concede, a utilitarian conception of justice might seem to have a strong appeal to the contracting parties in his original position. If we assume that any one of the contracting parties has an equal chance of becoming any of the individuals in the society at the other side of the 'veil of ignorance', we might suppose that it would be rational for the contracting parties to choose whichever rules of justice promised the highest *average* utility. If the number of people in society is taken as given, this amounts to the classical utilitarian prescription of maximising total utility. This line of argument for utilitarianism has been deployed by a number of economists, including myself.[23]

Rawls's most telling objection to this argument deserves to be quoted at length. He starts from the principle that the contracting parties must act in good faith; they must not make commitments that, in the event, they would be psychologically unable to honour. Thus they should steer clear of principles of justice that may turn out to make extreme demands on them. They should, if at all possible, opt for a 'stable' conception of justice:

> A conception of justice is stable when the public recognition of its realization by the social system tends to bring about the corresponding sense of justice . . . [The] principle of utility seems to require a greater identification with the interests of others than the two principles of justice [that is, Rawls's own conception]. Thus the latter will be a more stable conception to the extent that this identification is difficult to achieve. When the two principles are satisfied, each person's liberties are secured and there is a sense defined by the difference principle in which everyone is benefitted by social co-operation. Therefore we can explain the

acceptance of the social system and the principles it satisfies by the psychological law that persons tend to love, cherish, and support whatever affirms their own good. Since everyone's good is affirmed, all acquire inclinations to support the scheme. When the principle of utility is satisfied, however, there is no such assurance that everyone benefits. Allegiance to the social system may demand that some should forgo advantages for the sake of the greater good of the whole. Thus the scheme will not be stable unless those who must make sacrifices strongly identify with interests broader than their own . . . We are to accept the greater advantages of others as a sufficient reason for lower expectations over the whole course of our life. This is surely an extreme demand. In fact, when society is conceived as a system of co-operation designed to advance the good of its members, it seems quite incredible that some citizens should be expected, on the basis of political principles, to accept lower prospects of life for the sake of others . . . Looking at the question from the standpoint of the original position, the parties recognise that it would be highly unwise if not irrational to choose principles which may have consequences so extreme that they could not accept them in practice. They would reject the principles of utility and adopt the more realistic idea of designing the social order on a principle of reciprocal advantage.[24]

What Rawls is saying is that utilitarianism treats society as a single entity whose overall good is to be maximised. As Mirrlees put it in a passage I quoted earlier, 'the totality of all individuals can be regarded as a single individual'. This is undoubtedly an impartial view of society; but it is a kind of impartiality that does not come naturally to human beings. Utilitarianism demands that we should be prepared to sacrifice our own interests and aspirations, no matter how important they may be to us, whenever such sacrifices are required for the good of the whole. But it is just not natural for us to think like this. We identify with our own interests, and with those of our immediate family and friends; we are not psychologically constituted to think of our own lives as insignificant components in some greater social scheme. Our ideas of justice — and here I mean the principles on which we are prepared to live our lives, and not the more elevated ones we may profess on public occasions or in intellectual debate, when our own interests are not seriously at stake — are grounded more on notions of *co-operation* and *reciprocal advantage* than on an impartial benevolence for all sentient beings.

This, I suggest, is not an accident of history, or a peculiarity of a particular social system or state of development. David Hume was surely right when, almost 250 years ago, he declared:

> Here then is a proposition, which, I think, may be regarded as certain, *that 'tis only from the selfishness and confin'd generosity of men, along with the scanty provision nature has made for his wants, that justice derives its origin.*[25]

There is such a thing as human nature — the modes of thought and feeling natural to the human species — and any realistic account of human nature would recognise the significance of selfishness and 'confined generosity' (that is, a limited sympathy for particular people). Because of developments in the science of biology, we now know much more than Hume did about *why* the characteristics of each species are as they are; it is now quite obvious why human beings are not naturally inclined to impartial benevolence.

It is equally obvious that human life as we know it would be impossible without social co-operation. Our fundamental ideas of justice must, as Hume argues, have *evolved* out of the necessity for individuals to learn to live together without constant conflict. (Like Hume, I am speaking of social and not genetic evolution.) This is why we think it 'extreme' that we should be expected to be willing to sacrifice our strongest interests for the good of society, but are more inclined to bear with restrictions that are part of a system of co-operation that advances our own good. Rawls's argument is that a theory of justice must be compatible with what we know of human nature. This seems to me to be a much more sensible position than the utilitarian one — that human nature is essentially irrelevant to the theory of justice, and if necessary is to be changed by enlightened education. (This aspect of utilitarian thinking has been powerfully challenged by Bernard Williams and Mary Midgley.[26])

Now let me return to the game in which ten people have to agree on a division of £1,000. This game, I have suggested, can be regarded as a simple model of Rawls's conception of the problem of distribution. Suppose that the ten people differ in age, sex, income and family circumstances. Some are indisputably better off than others, but no one is in desperate need. No one has any prior claim on the £1,000, which is effectively common property. If anyone is to gain, everyone must co-operate. Then, I suggest, each person will expect to receive something in return for his co-operation. Further, it will be difficult for anyone to accept that he should receive less than anyone else: why should he sacrifice his interests for those of other people? There is, surely, something natural about an equal division of the money that makes this solution stand out from all the other ones that might be proposed.

Exactly why this solution stands out is hard to explain, but its 'obviousness' seems to be more a matter of symmetry than the produce of any prior notion of fairness. Consider another example. When oil and gas reserves were discovered under the North Sea the problem arose of who had the right to exploit them. The potential claimants were nation states. Given the power of most nations to inflict harm on most others, it was important to find some way of dividing up the reserves that would be generally acceptable. The solution was to allocate each portion of the sea-bed to whichever country happened to be nearest. In terms of any abstract theory of justice, this seems completely arbitrary. Why, for example, should Norway and the United Kingdom gain so much more than Denmark and West Germany? Why, for that matter, should the share-out be restricted to countries with a North Sea coastline, with nothing being given to countries as desperately poor as Bangladesh or as overwhelmingly powerful as the USA and the USSR? But this division of the sea-bed seems to have been accepted as natural by all parties.

Here is another example, invented by David Hume:

> Suppose a *German*, a *Frenchman*, and a *Spaniard* to come into a room, where there are plac'd upon the table three bottles of wine, *Rhenish*, *Burgundy*, and *Port*; and suppose they shou'd fall a quarrelling about the division of them; a person, who was chosen for umpire, wou'd naturally, to shew his impartiality, give every one the product of his own country.[27]

Again, there is one solution that seems to stand out from the others, despite having no apparent basis in a general theory of justice.

Now consider a problem more closely related to the subject matter of this chapter. Imagine a society with no formal system of property, and no police, courts or rulers to enforce settlements when individuals cannot agree. Most individuals have the ability to inflict considerable harm on most others, should they choose to do so. In such a society there will be many circumstances in which two or more individuals come into conflict over the use of resources. For example: person A has gathered a pile of wood for a fire. Person B arrives on the scene and wants the wood for himself. If A and B are fairly evenly matched, we may suppose that neither of them wants a fight: if it came to the point, they would both prefer to go without the wood. But B may be tempted to threaten to fight if A doesn't hand over the wood; and if B looks like making such a threat, A may be tempted to make the counter-threat that he will fight rather than give up the wood he has gathered. In effect, then, the two individuals must reach some accommodation about the disposition of the wood if they are to avoid the outcome they both regard as the worst of all. Is there an 'obvious' or 'natural' solution to this problem?

All of these problems or games are ones in which there is an incentive for the parties concerned to reach an accommodation: almost any agreement is better than none at all. If one party is convinced that the others will settle only on one particular set of terms, then that party can do no better than to agree to these. Thus each party has to consider what terms are likely to prove acceptable to the others. An 'obvious' solution is one that everyone believes everyone else would think obvious. This sort of problem has been analysed with great insight by Thomas Schelling (1960), who argues that human beings have a remarkable ability to converge on particular solutions even in cases where no discussion is possible.[28]

Although it is difficult to produce a complete theory of 'obvious' solutions, at least one general principle can be recognised. As Schelling shows, 'obviousness' is often connected with *uniqueness*. If a number of alternative principles could be brought to bear on a problem, a principle that yields a unique solution is likely to be favoured over one that is more ambiguous. In the case of the £1,000, the principle of equal division gives a unique answer to the question of how much money each person should get. It might seem fairer to take some account of the income of the individuals concerned, and to give the largest shares of the £1,000 to the poorest people; but there is no obvious way of deciding on the precise scale of payments. Because of this it may be much easier to get agreement on an equal division than on any particular unequal one — even if, in the circumstances, an equal division seems morally arbitrary. (Indeed, the arbitrariness of the 'obvious' solution may be a positive advantage in securing agreement, since it provides so few footholds for counter-argument and special pleading by aggrieved parties.)

Notice, however, two special features of the £1,000 game that ensure that the rule of equal division is unambiguous. First, the resource that has to be divided is *homogeneous*: everyone knows what a tenth of £1,000 is. This, we may suppose, is also true of the pile of wood; but it is certainly not true of the resources at stake in the other two examples. In Hume's case, we must (I take it) treat each bottle as an indivisible unit. Then the problem is that the rule of equal division is indecisive; it tells us that each person should have one bottle, but not which bottle should go to which person. Similarly in the case of the North Sea: prior to detailed exploration, no one knew for sure which areas of the sea-bed were most valuable, but some good guesses could be made. There was no unambiguous unit of quantity or value.

The second special feature of the £1,000 game is that the set of potential claimants is clearly defined. Thus we can talk sensibly about giving each claimant an equal share. The same is true of Hume's example, which, like the £1,000 game, is contrived. But consider the North Sea case. Of all the nations in the world, which ones should be considered claimants to the oil and gas under the North Sea? With a rule of equal division, *every* nation would want to be a claimant. (Nations might even try to split themselves up to establish greater claims; the United Kingdom, for example, might try to claim separately for England, Scotland, Wales and Northern Ireland.) But if not all nations are to be allowed to claim, where should the line be drawn? Countries with a North Sea coastline? European countries? Countries with any coastline? Countries with oil-exploiting industries? In contrast to all these problems of interpreting the rule of equal division, notice the neatness of the rule of geographical closeness, which assigns every portion of the sea-bed to a unique country.

Similar problems would arise if the problem of the wood was to be resolved by equal division. With just A and B on the scene, it would be easy enough to give half the wood to each person. But if equal division was the rule, anyone who devoted his labour to amassing anything of value would immediately be surrounded by a swarm of claimants. It seems much more plausible to suppose that people would recognise as the 'obvious' solution the rule that everyone keeps what his own labour has produced. This rule, like the rule of geographical closeness in the previous example, can provide a unique resolution to a wide range of problems of conflict.

An important characteristic of the kind of game I have been considering is that the more often a particular solution is adopted, the more likely it is to be adopted again. Suppose you live in a society of the kind I described when presenting the problem of the wood. Sometimes you find yourself in a position of person A, having devoted your labour to gathering or producing something of value, and being confronted by someone else demanding a share. Other times you are in the position of person B, hoping to induce someone else to give you a share of the proceeds of his labours. If, in your experience, most B's back down when A's refuse to hand over the produce of their labour, it will be in your interest to stand your ground when you are an A. Conversely, if it is your experience that most A's stand their ground, it will not be in your interest to press your claim when you are a B. Thus once a convention begins to emerge, everyone acquires an interest in keeping it. This may help to explain why some apparently arbitrary rules strike us as 'natural' or 'obvious' solutions to problems of conflict. Once established, such rules have a life of their own; we learn them by experience and extend them by analogy.

The labour theory of property, I suggest, is a rule of this kind. It is a convention that would be very likely to evolve out of the interactions of self-interested individuals in any situation in which they were unconstrained by formal laws. This convention *has* evolved, and we have inherited it — just as we have inherited the convention that the 'natural' division of a fixed stock of goods among a fixed group of claimants is an equal division and the convention that geographical closeness can establish a claim to an item of property. We cannot easily unlearn it.

Rawls, I have argued, is right to see justice in terms of cooperation and reciprocity, and to reject as unrealistic any theory of justice that requires people to sacrifice their life prospects for the general good. But we cannot talk about 'sacrifice' without having in mind some benchmark of entitlement or expectation. Rawls asks us to accept as a benchmark the state of affairs in which income and wealth are equally divided among individuals. Or, more fundamentally, we are to take the state of affairs in which income and wealth constitute a common pool on which no one has any prior claim. There would seem to be at least as strong a case for taking as our benchmark the state in which everyone receives the proceeds of his own labour. To do this is to make the individual's entitlement to the produce of his labour once again part of the theory of economic justice.

Notes

1. J. S. Mill, *Principles of Political Economy* (London, 1848), Book 2, Chapter 2, p. 5.
2. H. George, *Progress and Poverty* (New York, 1881).
3. K. J. Arrow, 'Values and Collective Decision Making' in P. Laslett and W. G. Runciman (eds), *Philosophy, Politics and Society* (Blackwell, London, 1967), p. 221.
4. K. J. Arrow, 'Uncertainty and the Welfare Economics of Medical Care', *American Economic Review*, vol. 53 (1963), pp. 941–73.
5. A. K. Sen, *Collective Choice and Social Welfare* (Oliver and Boyd, Edinburgh, 1970), p. 22.
6. J. A. Mirrlees, 'The Economic Uses of Utilitarianism' in A. K. Sen and B. Williams (eds), *Utilitarianism and Beyond* (University Press, Cambridge, 1982).
7. Ibid., p. 67.
8. Ibid., p. 71.
9. Ibid., p. 70.
10. J. A. Mirrlees, 'An Exploration in the Theory of Optimal Income Taxation', *Review of Economic Studies*, vol. 38 (1971), pp. 176–208.
11. J. A. Rawls, *A Theory of Justice* (University Press, Oxford, 1972).
12. Ibid., p. 172.
13. Ibid., p. 11.
14. Ibid., p. 12.
15. Ibid., p. 15.
16. Ibid., p. 141.
17. Ibid., p. 62.
18. Ibid., pp. 150–61.
19. B. Barry, *The Liberal Theory of Justice* (Clarendon Press, Oxford, 1973).
20. A. Flew, *The Politics of Procrustes* (Prometheus Books, Buffalo, New York, 1981), pp. 102–3.
21. Rawls, *Theory of Justice*, pp. 150–51.
22. Ibid., p. 27.
23. J. C. Harsany, 'Cardinal Utility in Welfare Economics and in the Theory of Risk Taking', *Journal of Political Economy*, vol. 63 (1955), pp. 309–21; W. Vickrey, 'Utility, Strategy and Social Decision Rules', *Quarterly Journal of Economics*, vol. 74 (1960), pp. 507–35; P. K. Pattanaik, 'Risk, Impersonality and the Social Welfare Function', *Journal of Political Economy*, vol. 76 (1968), pp. 1152–69; R. Sugden and A. Weale, 'A Contractarian Reformulation of Certain Aspects of Welfare Economics', *Economica*, vol. 46 (1979), pp. 111–23.
24. Rawls, *Theory of Justice*, pp. 177–8.
25. D. Hume, *A Treatise of Human Nature* (London, 1739), vol. 3, part 2, section 2.
26. B. Williams, 'A Critique of Utilitarianism' in J. J. C. Smart and B. Williams (eds), *Utilitarianism: For and Against* (University Press, Cambridge, 1973): M. Midgley, *Beast and Man* (Harvester Press, Brighton, 1970).
27. Hume, *Treatise of Human Nature*, vol. 3, part 2, section 3.
28. T. Schelling, *The Strategy of Conflict* (Harvard University Press, Cambridge, Mass., 1960).

2 THE DEVELOPMENT OF THE MARKET IN ARCHAIC GREECE

James M. Redfield

The free market is often associated with liberty and individualism; I need not remind this audience why this should be so. The market is often also associated with rationality — or with reason's poor relation, rationalisation. Liberty and individualism — not to mention rationality — are often held, not without some plausibility, to be specifically Western values. The moment when the West developed the free market therefore has some claims to be considered the moment when the West became Western. I shall be sketching that moment here. I call it a 'moment' even though the story I shall tell stretches over some 200 years, from the early eighth century to the early sixth century BC; the arrival of the market can well be considered an event, but it is an event, in my view, best understood by an enquiry into the stages of its happening.

The market, like other aspects of civilisation, was not a European invention, but was imported from the East; like other aspects of civilisation it was, however, transformed in the transmission. I shall be examining that transformation. I shall speak of the market as an institution and as an ethic, as a specific form of social interaction which prescribes roles and transforms people's expectation of themselves and of others, which shapes life-chances and life-orientations. This transformation needs to be set in the context of wider social and political transformations. The 200 years in question were the centuries during which the Greeks were developing their characteristic form of socio-political organisation, to which they gave the name of *polis*. The *polis*, as we shall see, was a form of organisation which responded to market conditions and at the same time aimed to limit the effects of the market. This tense relationship generated ambiguities in our Western tradition which persisted, and to some extent still persist.

In the historical account that follows I shall be drawing on Homer; I therefore need to set the epics in their historical context. The *Iliad* and the *Odyssey*, in my view, were composed very nearly in the form in which we have them during the Late Geometric, in the second half of the eighth century BC. They are traditional poems, telling old stories about old times in a traditional poetic language, but in the form in which we have them they are characteristic of their own period; in the Late Geometric the poets told the stories in the way most interesting to that audience, and were therefore responsive to current concerns. This does not mean that the epics are a naturalistic account of the Late Geometric or of any other period. The heroes are provided with vast and sometimes magical resources: huge households, great fleets, immortal horses, the privilege of conversing with the gods. At the same time the heroes are denied certain resources which the audience possessed; iron weapons, for instance, and literacy. A hero is different from ordinary people and inhabits a different world; that is the point of him, in a way. At the same time these heroes are *for* ordinary people, and the themes of ordinary life are explored in the epics through epic amplifications and deletions.

One of the most strikingly deleted items is market exchange. The heroes do not buy and sell — except perhaps to purchase a slave, as Laertes had purchased Eumaios and Eurycleia. Commerce is carried on only by the disreputable Phoenicians, 'tricksters, dealing in countless trinkets' (xv. 416); these are like stereotypical Gypsies, mysteriously appearing and disappearing, seducing women and stealing babies. Odysseus in *Odyssey* 14 tells the story of the Phoenician who proposed taking him to Lybia as his business partner, but whose real intention was to sell Odysseus into slavery. This type of commerce is presented as poisoned with guile, fraud and moral danger; a hero acquires commodities respectably, by gift and theft. When Odysseus is reassuring his wife about the restoration of their fortunes he refers to the flocks which the suitors have consumed; they will all be replaced: 'I myself shall carry off many by raiding, and the Achaeans will give others, until all the pens are full' (xxiii. 257–8).

Oddly enough the only trader in the epics — apart from the shadowy anonymous Phoenicians — is the goddess Athena, or rather the parts she plays. Posing as Mentes, king of the Taphians, she says that she is travelling to 'alien peoples, to Temesa for bronze, dealing in shining iron' (i. 183–4); later, posing as Mentor of Ithaka, she says she must travel to the Kaukones, 'where a debt is owed me — not a recent one, mind you, nor small' (iii. 387–8). She then makes nonsense of this explanation and reveals her divine identity by turning herself into a bird and exiting through the smoke-hole. Athena in the *Odyssey* likes to tease her audience; when she takes on a mortal shape it is something less than respectable. As Mentes she says that her father gave Odysseus poison for his arrows although another had refused him 'since he felt the force of the moral disapproval of the gods' (i. 263). These Taphians are presented as a kind of Greek Phoenician; it was Taphians who kidnapped Eumaios' Phoenician nurse and sold her for a 'fit price' (xv. 424); this in turn led to the Phoenician kidnapping of Eumaios. Since Athena has the unquestioned status of god she can afford to play at a relatively marginal status.

The contrast between low-status trader and high-status hero is most explicitly stated by the young Phaeacian who taunts the still-disguised Odysseus:

Stranger, you do not look like a man of any skill
In games, in any of the varieties people have.
You look rather like someone who sticks close to the
    many-oared ship he goes about in,
A commander of sailors and of those who are traders,
Worrying about his wares and with an eye out for goods
    he can acquire in exchange
And whatever profit he can snatch. You look like no athlete.
                                                        viii. 159–64

In the Late Geometric, when these lines were composed, long-distance trade was already an important aspect of Greek society, at least in some districts. If we did not know this from the archaeological record we could deduce it from this passage, with its well-developed commercial vocabulary: there are words for trader (*prētēr*), profit (*kerdos*), the wares one puts in the boat for sale (*phortos*, cf. xiv. 296 quoted above), and the wares one brings back on the return journey (*hodaia*, cf. xv. 445). The heroes may have nothing to do with trade, but the poet obviously knows a lot about it.

The exclusion of trade from the epics is thus a specific literary strategy — which, paradoxically, implies the importance of trade in the world of the poet. In a time when traders were beginning to transform society the poet looks back to a simpler and (from his point of view) cleaner world when violence was preferred to bargaining; the epics are not about gain but about honour. In this sense the epics are a depiction of a pre-market society. They need not be an accurate description; as the epic looks back it to some extent projects a reaction against current conditions, with the schematic unreality of nostalgia. On the other hand it is probable that this picture (allowing for epic amplification and deletions) is also based on fact, not so much on accurate memory of the past as on accurate observation of the more old-fashioned parts of the present. As market behaviour and more civil forms of life developed gradually and locally the market and pre-market societies coexisted. Thucydides after all, 300 years after Homer, remarks that just as raiding was in heroic times a respected form of behaviour, so in the backwoods of Greece, 'in Ozolian Locris and Aetolia and Acarnania' it still is (I.5.3). Nor is it only the respectability of raiding that makes the fringe areas seem heroic; there is a pervasive 'Homeric' tone out there. Consider, for instance, Thucydides' story of Themistokles' asylum in Molossia; received by the king's wife he sits on the hearth with the king's child in his arms, and thus receives hospitality from his enemy (I.136). In the following century Xenophon, cast adrift in the interior of Thrace, finds it still a world of kings, heroic feasts, and formalised gift-giving (*Anabasis* VII, iii. 15–33). In Homer's time such behaviour was much closer to home. I take it that Homer had a clear understanding of how a premarket society was supposed to work, and that this understanding was not entirely unrealistic; in what follows I shall be using Homer as a kind of commentary on the archaeological evidence, as a source from which we may draw detail and concrete and human reality to fill out our imaginative picture of the past.

Let us pick up our story c. 850 BC, at the beginning of the pottery series called Middle Geometric One. Greece at this time was inhabited in villages on a basis of agricultural autarky; each community more or less produced what it consumed. Although by this period there had been substantial recovery from the radical depopulation of the Greek Dark Ages, communities remained small — to be counted in the hundreds rather than the thousands, and more often in the scores rather than the hundreds. Nevertheless we have some evidence, in the form of a few 'prestige' burials, for social differentiation; a typical example is the well-known woman's grave from the Athenian agora, well furnished with jewellery and including a pottery box with five model granaries on the lid.[1] We may presume that at this period some families controlled the land and labour of others.

The epics, particularly the *Odyssey*, provide us with a sense of how this was managed. Society there is divided between the leading households, those of the *basileis*, and the rest, the *plēthus*. The epic picture of this society is skewed by the narrative interests of the epics, which tell stories about the *basileis*. Such low-status characters as appear in the epics are the personal dependants of *basileis*, usually purchased slaves. The *plēthus* remains in the shadowy background. Nevertheless it is clearly assumed that there are people outside the 'heroic' leading households; these are the people who fill up the ranks on the battlefield, who provide the mass from which the leading warriors, the *promachoi*, emerge to engage in significant single combat; these are the people who assemble in the *agora*, the open meeting of the whole community, to provide an audience for debates between the *basileis*. Their relation to the households of the *basileis* remain obscure.

The household of Odysseus, for instance, includes besides the family of the *basileus*, a number of persons directly dependent on that family: there are the senior unmarried women who manage the household, Eurycleia and Eurynome; there is Eumaios, who keeps pigs for the great house, and was purchased as a child; there is Dolios, who had formed part of Penelope's dowry and keeps the farm where Odysseus' old father has retired to avoid the suitors, and there are Dolios' children, some of whom work on the farm with him, while one, Melanthios, keeps goats for the great house, and another, Melantho, works in Odysseus' house under the supervision of Penelope. These people are named, and they all 'belong' to the *basileus*. There are, however, many other persons who are mentioned, although they generally remain anonymous, and are not much dramatised as characters. There are many other girls working for Penelope; there are a number of young men working under Eumaios' supervision. The *thêtes te dmōes te*, hired men and bondsmen, of Odysseus are numerous, sufficient to man a ship without drawing on the general population of Ithaca (iv. 643–4). Telemachus says that it would take a long time to visit all the *dmōes*, spread out as they are through the fields and farmsteads (xvi. 309–20).

It seems to me clear (although the poet does not quite tell us so) that primary productivity in this society is in the hands of low-status families working small farms, called in Homeric Greek *klēroi*, allotments. These families are dependent on some *basileus*, and therefore are called *dmōes*, bondsmen. They 'honour their lord with gifts' and are expected to fight under his command if needed. Nevertheless they are more independent than chattel slaves; the *klēroi* in a certain sense belong to them. I would imagine that to evict such a family and sell its members abroad would be (if not absolutely impossible) savage and cruel behaviour, unworthy of a *basileus*. And the *basileis*, for all their overbearing ways, know that if their behaviour is sufficiently outrageous they may find the folk rising against them and casting them out (xvi. 424–30).

Dmōes, then, are dependants, but in this sort of society to belong *to* someone is to belong *in* the society. The *dmōes* are of a higher status than the *thêtes*, the hired labourers, precisely because their bond to a *basileus* gives them a recognised and reasonably secure place in the social order.[2] It is to this status that Eumaios aspires; Odysseus, he says

> Would have treated me as very much one of his own and given possession,
> The sort of thing a king of good spirit gives to one of his house,
> A house and a *klēros* and a much courted wife,
> When one has toiled for him much, and the god increases his work,
> As he increases for me this work, where I am faithful.
> Thus the king would have benefited me much, if he had grown old here.
>
> xiv. 62–7

The worst of fates is to be *aklēros*, without land — or by an impossible hyperbole, to be *thes* to an *alkēros*, a hired man to one with no farm (xi. 489–90). Conversely the leading families are *polukleroi* (xiv. 211); they have at their disposition many *klēroi*, and thus have many *dmōes*.

This social structure is enacted and therefore sustained by the organisation of labour and of the exchange of commodities. Commodities may be roughly categorised as vegetable, animal and mineral. Vegetable produce, the staples of existence, are evidently produced by the *klēroi*; each smallholder, I would suppose, lives off the produce of his own land and labour. The house of a *basileus* has a kind of home farm for its own maintenance; such is Dolios' farm in the *Odyssey*. The *basileus* who was *primus inter pares*, the Greek for which is *basileutatos*, had also a *temenos*, a special allotment of agricultural land, the gift (or rather the loan, since he could hold it only as long as he held his special status — xi. 185) of the community as a whole, but worked by his *dmōes* (xvii. 299). The *basileutatos* was expected to feast the other *basileis*, and sometimes the folk at large, and the *temenos* provided the required resources. In general, then, the most basic productivity was handled distributively, on the basis of shares of land, with extra shares for the higher-status houses.

Animal produce, by contrast, belongs to the *basileis* alone. The flocks and herds are kept in the rough land which belongs to no one; here we meet Eumaios, who thinks he has been there much too long. Herding is evidently a life-stage; the *basileus* borrows young males from the families of his *dmōes* and puts them under the direction of some special dependant, perhaps a purchased slave; they tend the flocks until they are old enough to take over *klēroi* of their own. (Odysseus, disguised as a beggar, says he is now too old to keep beasts and obey the orders of the overseer — xvii. 20–1.) The meat comes in to the great house, where it is consumed on festival occasions. Wool similarly comes to the house of the *basileus*; it is made into textiles by young women under the direction of the *basileia*; these are presumably the girls of the *dmōs*-families, not yet old enough to be married. Population is thus kept in balance with the productive system; as Eumaios says, one gets a house a wife and a *klēros* all at the same time, so that families are started only by those who have farms.

Meanwhile the great houses employ labour which is surplus on the farms to produce the specifically lordly kind of wealth: meat and textiles and hides. In the epics we mostly see this wealth disposed within the lordly stratum, in feasting and gift-giving of fellow *basileis* and honoured strangers. Eumaios, however, reminds us that such goods can also circulate between the strata; when Antikleia, the *basileia* of the generation before Penelope, sent him off to the mountain to keep pigs

> With cloak and shirt and garment
> She dressed me very well, and gave sandals for my feet,
> And sent me to the country; she treated me as heartfelt her own.
> But now I miss all that. Here on my own
> The blessed gods increase the work where I am faithful;
> From it I eat and drink and give to the needy.
> But no longer can I hear some healing word
> Of my mistress, or any thing, since evil fell on the house,
> Reckless men. The *dmōes* feel the lack very much
> Of talking face-to-face with the mistress, and getting the news,
> And eating and drinking something, and then taking something
>   back

To the country, the sort of thing that rejoices the heart of *dmōes*.
xv. 369–79

Animal produce thus circulates in the kind of network the economic anthropologists call *redistributive*, whereby commodities are collected at a centre and then dispersed to the periphery. In the process the commodities change their meaning. What is sent up to the great house as a sign of subservience and deference is returned to the subservient as a sign of the master's generosity. The exchange is thus a form of co-operation which reinforces and at the same time seems to justify the unequal relations between the parties.

Mineral commodities are largely metals, along with a few precious materials, such as ivory and amber. Metals are needed for tools and weapons, for ornaments and precious items of display, also for *keimelia*, those objects which circulate only through lordly gift-exchange.[3] These materials are also monopolised by the *basileis* as well as being associated with a special category of skilled workmen, the *dêmioergoi*. Those who work in metals or use metal tools, smiths and carpenters, are *dêmioergoi*, as are seers, physicians and bards. There is a certain magic in all these arts, which are associated with specific gods. *Dêmioergoi* evidently work for the *basileis* but are not their dependants; their special skills allow them to move from community to community, since their skills are welcome everywhere (xvii. 382–6).

A *basileus* may provide his dependants with some agricultural tools (xxiii. 832–5) but mostly metal objects are for his own use and that of his women; the *basileis* display their superior status by the possession of weapons and precious objects. Horses, which in this society are only for display, also belong to this category of commodities.

All this no doubt is an idealised picture; what counts is the idea it embodies. The *Odyssey* provides a picture, lucid to the point of schematism, of a pre-market economy. Goods circulate in restricted networks, and the distribution of land, labour, and commodities are talked of in the language of loyalty and obligation. The economy is what Clifford Geertz calls a 'cultural system', with the characteristic collapse of fact and value whereby those who share a culture are assured that things are as they ought to be. Commodities, along with authority, are a sign of social status; conversely, the status thus signified constitutes a claim to authority and commodities. The *basileus* is entitled to demand more because he is a *basileus*;

conversely his success in enforcing this demand proves that he is indeed and ought to be a *basileus*. At the same time, *noblesse oblige*; in making his claims the *basileus* implicitly promises to acknowledge the counter-claims of those who acknowledge him.

This is not, of course, to suggest that the behaviour of the parties is in any special sense altruistic, or anything less than rational, in a broad sense of rational. They are pursuing their interests. It is only that the overriding concern in this pursuit is the development of relations which will be dependable. The great houses hold the surplus; they are in the best position to defend it. The smallholders make faithful contributions; in return they have a claim on the great house at times of shortage or danger. This is surely rational behaviour under risk. In the absence of secure political institutions, gift-exchange, in which the transaction is in the service of the relation, is rationally preferred to market-exchange, in which the relation is entered into for the sake of the transaction.

The world of the epics is presented as to the last degree insecure, owing to the pervasive *leisteres*, raiders. Raiding seems to be a young man's activity, and as such another employment for surplus labour. A few men fill a boat and go off to see what they can find. Raiding is in contrast to travel *kata prêxin*, with some definite purpose; *leisteres* 'wander wantonly', 'staking their lives, bringing trouble to alien peoples' (iii. 71–4 = ix. 252–5). What is brought home, by those who survive to come home, is usually booty; sometimes, no doubt, *leisteres* made some more peaceful contact in a foreign land, and brought home commodities acquired by gift or barter. It is confusing to call such behaviour 'commerce'.

All this is quite consistent with the archaeological record of Middle Geometric One, 850 to 800 BC. The diffusion of Attic pottery styles shows that Greek communities were in contact with one another from Argos in the south to southern Thessaly in the north, and east to Asia Minor. (Pottery is omitted from Homer, another epic deletion.) Evidently there was a certain amount of going about in boats, either *kata prêxin* or raiding. It is unclear how far such venturing could go — probably as far as Cyprus. Beyond this, in the Levant, there are practically no traces; at last report the Greek finds relevant to the period from Near Eastern sites amounted to exactly four vessels.[4] It is probable that Greek pottery was already appreciated outside of Greece for its superior glaze; we need not think that these items were carried by Greeks.

Then there are the Near Eastern items in Greek tombs. These are very like the items we find in Homer, whose prestige goods — gold jewellery and ivories and fine bronzes — are often ascribed to Phoenician workmen. Some of the archaeological finds may have been made in Greece by travelling Near Eastern workmen, *dêmioergoi*, or by Greeks under their influence. The Near East may also have been a source of perfumes, opium, and such stuff. We may imagine that these items were brought by Phoenicians who appeared in Greek waters rather irregularly and unexpectedly, much as they do in Homer. We need not think that their primary purpose was the importation of luxury goods; these Phoenicians are more likely to have entered Greek waters in quest of precious metals, especially the silver of Attica[5] and the gold of Thasos.[6] Another commodity which could help finance a voyage was human beings, acquired not by purchase but by theft; a woman or child kidnapped by a home-bound crew could be sold in the Near Eastern slave markets.

This kind of trafficking involves commodities and a certain amount of haggling and barter, but it does not establish in any important sense a market relation. The trader is not integrated within the sphere of economic forethought, as one whose wares are relied upon or whose purchases are anticipated as a source of income. He provides unexpected opportunities at certain moments, but is also perceived as an alien, and as a threat.

About 800 BC, at the beginning of the phase we call Middle Geometric Two, the economic situation in Greek lands begins to change in important ways. We have, in the first place, indications of agricultural development with a correlative increase in population. In Attica, where habitation up to this time had been clustered around the acropolis, new peripheral communities were founded — at Eleusis, Palaia Kokkinia near the Piraeus, Anaphlystos, Myrrhinous, and Marathon.[7] All of these places are on or near the coast; it seems that the threat of raiding had decreased sufficiently to make it possible to occupy dispersed agricultural areas near the sea.

Corinth is also developing, with peripheral communities to the north and west of the old village, and evidence of Corinthian control of two sites on the Megarian side of the isthmus, at Crommyon and Perachora.[8] The most spectacular development, however, was on Euboea, where the city of Eretria was founded, some time soon after 800 BC. This evidently involved a shift of population from Lefkandi, the old community up the coast which had been inhabited continuously since the Mycenaean epoch. The motive for the shift must be found in increased use of the sea; Eretria is farther from Euboea's good agricultural land than Lefkandi, but has the advantage of an excellent harbour, sheltered by an offshore island. At the same time Eretria is a somewhat difficult site; the acropolis, which provides the only secure defence, is two kilometres from the sea, and the seashore is marshy. The site only becomes usable when it is occupied all at once, with provision for drainage and for uniting the harbour to the acropolis. We may thus think of Eretria as the first of the Greek 'built' towns — a kind of colony *avant la lettre*.

Middle Geometric Two development thus involves an early stage of the *polis*, which includes within its ideology the notion of the community as an artefact, something designed and founded by a definite collective act. Here again we have a Homeric reflex in the poet's description of Phaeacia, which has been called the first Greek Utopia. King Nausithoos brought his people there to get them away from the oppression of the Cyclopes:

He drove a wall around the city, and constructed houses,
And made temples of the gods, and distributed ploughland.
vi. 8–9

Odysseus is impressed by the ships, harbours and 'assembly-places of the heroes, and the long high walls fitted with stakes' (vii. 44–5). Greek city walls for the period before 750 BC are so far documented only for Old Smyrna, which with its peninsular site could even have provided the physical model for Phaeacia.

In Middle Geometric Two graves we find some evidence of new styles of social differentiation. Well furnished male graves from Attica now begin often to include representations of horses, 'most naturally explained as badges of knightly status'.[9] The earliest representation of a man breaking a horse, reminiscent of the 'horse-taming' Homeric heroes, is on a Euboean fibula; this representation later became typical of Argive geometric pottery. I would tend to believe that 'heroic' values, specifically associated with the horse, were, so far from being immemorial, a new cultural development in the generation before Homer, a cultural response to that phase of social development. But this would take us far from our present topic.

We may also notice evidence of a cultural development very much underplayed in Homer, if not entirely deleted: the elaboration of the ritual sphere. The four richest Attic graves from the Middle Geometric Two period are of women, and it seems to me likely that all four were priestesses. Two are from Eleusis, two from Anaphlystos; the occupation of the peripheral countryside may have been accompanied by an elaboration of peripheral sanctuaries. This is certainly true of Eleusis, which has such an important later history. In many other communities sanctuaries, later important, were founded about this time; we may mention the Argive Heraion and the sanctuaries of Athena Alea at Tegea, of Aphaia on Aegina, and of Hera Akraia at Perachora. The first temple at Samos also dates from this period. At this time also the international sanctuaries begin to be important; Olympia is older, but both Delphi and Delos date their first dedications *c*. 800 BC.[10] These international sanctuaries are a sign of what we might call the Hellenisation of the Greeks; the Hellenes were beginning to acquire a common consciousness as a single people bound together by common cults, meeting peacefully at common sanctuaries. The ritual sphere thus helped to provide an infrastructure promoting peaceful exchange within the Greek world.

To return to long-distance trade: after 800 BC there is a striking increase in Greek material from Near Eastern sites. Middle Geometric Two sherds, mostly of Cycladic origin, have turned up in more than a dozen places on the mainland. In Cyprus, also, such material sharply increases. It is not clear, once again, that all this material came there in Greek hands, but this is at least evidence of an increase in trafficking.

The really striking evidence from the period, however, comes from Veii in Southern Etruria, where excavation of the vast cemetery at Quattro Fontanili has turned up a substantial amount of Middle Geometric Two material, mostly, again, Cycladic or Euboean. This material belongs to the phase called Veii IIB, which is also the phase in which iron weapons begin to appear in the Etruscan tombs. Etruria is well supplied with iron ore; it seems probable that Greeks now began to involve themselves in the search for metals (no doubt in imitation of the Phoenicians) and that the Greeks brought with them the technology for working the ore.[11] This implies a relatively high level of interaction between the Greeks and Etruscans, interaction going beyond sporadic visits or even the longer stay of a vagrant craftsman or two.

The visible cultural influences in the Etruscan material from this period, however, are not Greek but Near Eastern; this is the beginning of the orientalisation phase in Etruria. Greek potsherds in the Near East and Etruria thus represent the two ends of a trade route; the Greeks are beginning to act as middlemen between two large culture-areas, exchanging Etruscan metal for Near Eastern prestige goods along a sea-lane extending some 1,500 miles. The linking of complementary demand in these two large areas provided a reliably profitable opportunity, exploited by those Greeks, mostly Euboean and Cycladic, who were cultural specialists in seafaring within the Greek community. The result, we should notice, is not (fundamentally) trade between the Greeks and their neighbours; the Greeks come in as a third party — although profits of course come back to the Greek heartland, in the form both of raw metal and of prestige goods; Greek agricultural development had created a Greek demand for both.

For the relatively small number of Greeks involved in this sort of long-distance exchange, trade could now become a livelihood, rather than mere sporadic venturing. The trader established himself as a social role, in competition with the heroic raider. The model (once again) was the Phoenicians, who continued as a people to exploit their own opportunities as middlemen.

We also have, however, some evidence as early as Middle Geometric Two for another type of Greek trade, trade in Greek-produced agricultural commodities. I refer to the Corinthian transport-jars found with the earliest Greek material from Otranto, at the southern tip of Apulia.[12] These jars were used to ship liquid produce, usually wine or oil. It has long been known that the Corinthians were traversing the Corinthian gulf as early as 800 BC; the substantial quantity of early Corinthian material from Ithaca was a sufficient indication. These new finds show that this voyaging from the beginning involved commerce.

The exchange of agricultural commodities no doubt originated in inequalities of local production; the Mediterranean, as Braudel points out, has throughout its history been an area subject to localised droughts. When a district, on the other hand, had a good year, it produced a surplus which could be sold where crops had failed. The earliest Greek account of agricultural trade, in Hesiod's *Works and Days*, need imply no more than this. When the good weather comes the farmer takes his boat off the blocks and puts to sea:

Do not put all your livelihood in the hollow ships,
But leave the greater part behind, and load the lesser.

Ibid. 689–90

Hesiod is generally hostile to seafaring, stressing the risks of storm; still, people do do it, since 'wealth is become life to miserable mortals' (686). He says nothing about what the seafaring farmer brings home in exchange for his crop, calling it only *kerdos*, gain. Presumably the starving districts had to part with some of their horded valuables, usually in the form of metals.

Exchange between Corinth and Apulia, however, offered greater possibilities for development. The Greeks early mastered the specialised agriculture of the vine and the olive; Apulia, while no Kansas, was by Greek standards a rich grain-growing area. Exchange could thus be based on specialisation of production. In contrast to the long-distance middleman trade based on Euboea, this Corinthian trade involved Greeks as primary producers and consumers. In contrast to trade responding to local shortage, it established a continuing commercial relation between the communities, and created a market which was for the producer a reliable source of income. The beginnings were modest, but this for the Greeks was the wave of the future, as we shall see.

By 750 BC Euboean middleman trade had taken off, and had become enough of a livelihood to attract a population. Al Mina, on the Syrian coast, had become an *emporion*, evidently for the western trade; its population, while predominantly Semitic, was partly Greek. The literary sources mention Euboean communities westward along the trade route, at Corcyra and Zankle on the straits of Messina; we as yet have no archaeological evidence of these. We are, however, well informed about Pithecousa, at the western end of the route, on the island of Ischia facing Etruria. The population here was predominantly Greek, with a Semitic element.[13] In spite of Homer there is in the archaeology of this early period no sign of hostility between Greek and Phoenecian; the two peoples co-existed peaceably, exploiting common opportunities.

Pithecousa is often called the first of the Greek colonies; it could better be called a pre-colonial settlement. It was something of a boom town, reaching a population of several thousand in the first generation of settlement. The pottery indicates that it attracted a mixed population, with extensive near-eastern connections. The cemetery remains suggest an egalitarian atmosphere proper to the frontier; grave offerings are all pretty much on a level, with little silver and no gold.[14] Remains have been found of iron-working; the ore has been shown to come from Elba, 250 miles to the north. Pithecousa was in fact a mining town, even though it was so far from the mines it exploited. It seems to have had a young population; the graves in the cemetery are 75 per cent children and young people. I find it hard to believe that the early mortality was so high; this would be out of line with other places. It seems to me more probable that few grew old and died in Pithecousa; when a young man made his pile he took his family elsewhere — back to the Greek homeland, or to Cumae across the water on the Italian mainland.

The long trade route made a connection between two large culture areas which had previously been cut off from each other; it was economically 'hot', and provided two generations of Greeks with an opportunity to leave the land and seek their fortunes. We may think of this venturing as a life phase, like raiding, but whereas raiding had inhibited economic development, trade provided a basis for further development. Probably the atmosphere of the two activities was not that different; this early trade was informal, entrepreneurial in a world which provided security neither of contracts nor possession, and bringing an erratic and unpredictable return; it is not for nothing that the young Phaeacian in Homer calls the trader's profits *harpalea*, snatched at. Furthermore trading attracted raiding; where goods were circulated they could be stolen. No doubt many of those involved divided their energies between trade and theft. Nevertheless there is this crucial difference; raiding had merely redistributed existing productivity, whereas the trade route stimulated new productivity, and enabled the Greeks to benefit from the productivity of distant peoples.

It is perhaps not extravagant to think that the trade route fuelled the whole Greek economic takeoff in the mid-eighth century BC. This takeoff was certainly abrupt. One scholar has estimated the increase of population in Attica and Argos (which we may take as typical of the 'developing' Greek communities) at sevenfold between 780 and 720 BC.[15] Even if this estimate is too high the increase must have been considerable; it is signalled not only by the numbers of Attic and Argive graves, but by the foundation of new communities — not only the western colonies (of which more later) but also of peripheral communities within the Greek heartland, communities such as Zagora on Andros and Emporio on Chios. Nearly every Greek site shows a surge of building around 750 BC. Furthermore there is evidence of a considerable increase in personal wealth, at least in the higher strata of society; the evidence here is largely from sanctuary dedications.[16]

The trade route provided families with the prospect of a

livelihood for their extra sons; this in itself helps to explain the soaring population — since, as we know, population is responsive to economic opportunities. At the same time the new wealth provided a foundation for agricultural investment in such improvements as terracing and olive groves; families who received wealth from outside the system were enabled to forgo immediate returns from the land in favour of greater long-range returns. Furthermore the increase in peaceful trafficking, chaotically organised though it was, probably provided a greater level of security overall, and this in turn made long-range investment more worthwhile. An increase in population densities also made possible and necessary a higher level of social organisation, and thus more effective collective protection of the land.

Economic development is, as we know, a synergistic phenomenon; it is not possible to say flatly that trade fuelled agriculture, or agriculture, trade. Nevertheless we have one important piece of evidence that the springs of Greek development were not internal to the Greek economy, but rather external: the parallels between Greek and Phoenician development. Around 750 BC the Phoenicians were also beginning to find a livelihood in the West; new settlements were established at Carthage, at Motya, and in a string of communities along the southern coast of Spain. The Phoenicians, as we have seen, were also trading with Etruria, but their special sphere of exploration was around the fabled Tartessus, on the Spanish Guadalquivir. The Phoenicians, like the Greeks, prospered by linking complementary demands: for western metal in the East and eastern prestige goods in the West.

By the latter part of the eighth century, however, Greek and Phoenician development were beginning to diverge. The early Phoenician settlements were trading posts; Motya is an offshore island, the Spanish sites are perched between the mountains and the sea, and Carthage does not seem to have begun to exploit its potentially rich agricultural hinterland much before the fifth century BC. (This impression is now being confirmed by Joe Greene's survey of the Carthaginian hinterland, a University of Chicago dissertation.) After Pithecousa, however, Greek colonies followed a different pattern: Cumae, Syracuse, Leontinai, Sybaris, Taras, and their successors aimed at control of agricultural land. A Greek colonial city was surrounded by Greek farms; Greek colonisation thus represented an extension of the sphere of the Greeks' superior agricultural technology.

This point can be seen most clearly in districts like that around Metapontum, on what is now the Adriatic coast of Basilicata. The rich land here is a narrow strip between the mountains and the sea. The productivity of this soil turns on the control of water; the land must be drained in the wet season, and irrigated in the dry. Between the collapse of ancient civilisation and the nineteenth-century *bonifica* this soil went out of effective use; travellers in search of the ancient ruins found it grown up in scrub and occupied only by a few cattle farms. The Greeks on their arrival in the early seventh century BC evidently found it in the same condition; the Metapontum survey shows that by the sixth century they had turned it into a landscape of productive small farms[17] — which had had no indigenous predecessors. Similarly the archaeological survey of Gela has established that before Greek occupation of this rich plain the land was virtually unoccupied.

We can thus understand how the Greeks would have thought that while there were (of course) indigenes, the land they were occupying was essentially virgin soil. The prototypical indigenes are Homer's Cyclopes, a race of rough pastoralists without any properly organised communities. The Cyclops has some kind of rough wine — these districts were not without agriculture — but Odysseus' Ismarian wine tastes to him like nectar and ambrosia (ix. 357–9).

Greek colonisation can thus be thought of as reinvestment in agricultural productivity. Families which could afford to send extra sons off the land — to pay them, that is, their share of the inheritance not in land but in movables — could send them, not to seek their fortune off the land, but to develop new land. Reinvestment is as we know the key to economic development, reliable opportunities for profitable reinvestment secure an orderly and continuing process of development. The expansion of Greek agriculture continued more or less steadily for 400 years. In the early fourth century Socrates can still assume that anyone who wants to leave his own city will find some colony ready to receive him (Plato, *Crito* 51d).

These colonies obviously entered into exchange relations with the indigenes, on the basis of local specialisation of production. As Braudel reminds us, the Mediterranean is a world in which the most important differences are often between 'up' and 'down'; a few hundred metres of elevation are often more important than hundreds of kilometres of distance. As the Greeks occupied the shore they acquired the good ploughland and the low hills; the grain, wine and oil there produced could be exchanged for commodities characteristic of the highlands — meat and wool primarily, but also such items as honey and pitch. These commodities could be locally consumed, or re-exported, along with the surplus grain production, to the Greek heartland. From the seventh century the heartland had evidently ceased to be agriculturally self-sufficient. By the sixth century we see that Greek commerce is making contact with peripheral areas which would provide a reliable source of cheap grain: Southern France, Egypt, and especially Southern Russia. The last two are outside the northern and southern limits of the cultivation of the olive; we may imagine that the bulk of these imports were paid for by the export of Greek oil. The result, clearly, was further specialisation of production in the Greek heartland and further dependence on the international market. By the fifth century Athens was importing three-quarters of her staples. Athens was evidently an extreme case, but the ideal of self sufficiency had, for many Greek communities, long been only an ideal. The pattern of trade which we found heralded by the Corinthian transport-jars at Otranto — exchange based on specialised agricultural production — had become the norm.

By 700 BC the boom at Pithecousa was over; the community continued as an obscure island village. About this time Euboean material disappears from Al Mina, and is abruptly replaced by Corinthian; the Corinthians, who in the previous generation had taken over the Euboean community at Corcyra and had founded Syracuse, now came to dominate the western trade. The middleman trade between Etruria and the Near East had evidently lost its great profitability; it continued on a reduced scale, but was increasingly overtaken by trade in agricultural commodities. Increasingly, also, the Greeks themselves became the source of prestige goods in the West; the little ornamented Corinthian perfume jars which are found everywhere in western indigenous graves are, as George Vallet remarks, like 'articles de Paris',[18] goods cheaply produced at the centre which acquire a prestige value when transmitted to the periphery. These items cannot have accounted for the bulk of the exchange, but they are symptomatic of the cultural relations between the parties. The Greeks were able to present themselves to their neighbours as civilised and civilising: everywhere Helenic expansion is accompanied by peripheral Hellenisation.

The seventh century was a period of relatively orderly, 'cool', development. The expansion of agricultural trade is signalled by the wide diffusion of Attic transport-jars,[19] along with Corinthian.[20] The established western colonies expanded through sub-colonies: Cumae founded Neapolis, Zankle founded Himera, Megara Hyblaea founded Selinunte, Syracuse founded Akrai and Helorus, securing a wide semi-circle of Greek settlement. There were new foundations at Gela, Locri, Siris, and Cyrene in Africa, and a new wave of colonial development in the northern Aegean. The seventh century was the golden age of Corinth; the city prospered, first under the first of the great Greek oligarchies, that of the Bacchiadae, then under the first of the tyrannies, that of Cypselus. Economic development was accompanied by political conflict and transformation. By the early sixth century both have been generalised. There was a new wave of colonial development, which brought new population to such established colonies as Cyrene and Metapontum, and an important new foundation at Massalia, at the mouth of the Rhone, and another at Akragas in western Sicily. The Black Sea and the Egyptian connections now become important. This is also the age of the Sages in Greece, of Periander at Samos, Solon at Athens, and Chilon at Sparta. It is an age of political disorder and reform. The story of these political transformations cannot be told here. I do, however, take the view that in the most general terms they can be described as a political response to the social impact of the market, and I conclude with some speculations on that impact.

The market affects different societies differently, depending (among other things) on the definitions and differentiation of the social strata engaged in market activity. Middleman trading is (or can be) the project of a relatively differentiated group, of those who have left the land to pursue other opportunities. Al Mina and Pithecousa were such communities. The proto-typical modern example is Venice. These are communities of traders — as in general the cities of the European Middle Ages developed in the context of a social and jural discontinuity between town and country, a discontinuity marked by the principle that 'town air makes free'. The bourgeoisie developed within the *Burg*, which served as an asylum from the feudal organisation of agricultural land and labour. Archaic Greece was never feudal, but we have seen that the pre-market economy — at least in the Homeric picture of it — was structured by traditional patterns of fealty and deference. Those who left the land left those patterns behind them; they sought fortunes, further, among alien peoples. In the case of early Greek, as of Phoenician, middleman trade, the discontinuity between trader and primary producer, was secured by ethnic difference.

In the trading communities we would expect status to follow wealth — with a certain social preference accorded 'old money'. Wealth was the good generally sought; it would follow that economic success was the approved path to social power and quite naturally translated itself into political authority. Such is Aristotle's picture of Phoenician Carthage: a community where the constitution put the highest offices up for sale (*Politics*, 1273a).

In the Greek *polis*, however, the connections between wealth, status and authority were never so simple; the complexities have to do with the fact that these were urbanised agricultural communities. The traders and the primary producers were the same people; manufacturing (and except in a very few communities such other sources of wealth as mining) remained economically insignificant, so that the control of primary productivity meant the control of agricultural land. Nearly all free families owned some land, and the rich citizens were without exception landowners. The family farm, at all levels of society, was supposed to provide the resources needed to maintain the role of citizen. The ideal, for both the individual households and the community as a whole, remained agricultural self-sufficiency.

This ideal, however, was constantly falsified at both levels. The urbanisation of these communities was the source of their prosperity; the adjustment of agricultural productivity to the demands of the international market literally transformed the landscape. 'Capital accumulation' produced a tax base which enabled the cities to maintain the infrastructure which sustained further profitable reinvestment. The cities needed their rich, and there was never enough land for wealth to be based to any important degree on large landholding. The real money was in trade — not in the actual travelling and negotiating (which was left to lower strata) but in financing and managing the developing international market.

We might have expected the commercial development of the archaic *polis* to have resulted in the commercialisation of agriculture, with the rich acquiring title to the land, and subjecting the poor to the status of employees or tenants — or (since the Greeks did not employ labour, preferring to own it) the replacement of free labour on the land by slave labour. As we know, this happened at a later period in Rome, and produced the social upheaval we associate with the Gracchi. Certainly the new wealth produced a great increase in the numbers of chattel slaves — who were not Greeks, but foreigners from the barbarian fringe, 'guest workers' of the classical type, imported under compulsion. The 'family farms' of the richer families were worked by slave families, and those sectors where the rich themselves organised production, especially mining, were worked by slave gangs. But free agriculture remained the basis of the Greek economy.

The reasons no doubt were partly economic — in a narrow sense. The family farm remained the most effective way of organising Greek agricultural technology; the vine and the olive respond to intense care, and give of their best in the hands of those who know every individual plant and who have every incentive to maximise production. The social charter of this mode of production is Hesiod's *Works and Days*, with its celebration of thrift and agricultural labour as the highest morality.

Economically more important in the broad sense, I suspect, was the maintenance of a free population as a highly qualified labour pool — available not so much for employment as for the various collective projects of the *polis*. When we speak of the *polis* as the urbanisation of the countryside we mean, among other things, the distribution of material resources in such a way as to achieve a general increase in the standard of living, and the extension of education to the populace at large. These free farmers were generally well-nourished and were trained for war; the Greeks were also the first people in history to be generally literate. This free population provided a sophisticated electorate and (perhaps more important) an audience for the poets and for the plastic arts. They were also remarkable soldiers, constantly in demand among their barbarian neighbours as mercenary troops and officers. The small farm was thus the basis of Hellenism, and of that self-validating assumption of superiority to others which transformed the world through Hellenisation.

The primacy of agriculture was maintained on the cultural level through its 'mystification'; agriculture was conceived as a transaction with the gods, those 'givers of good things', and fertility was sustained by ritual. (Hermes is I suppose the god of trade, and Aristotle mentions an altar of Charis near the market, but trade was never taken into the ritual system.) The most important of these rituals was, in a sense, agriculture itself; as Braudel says: 'In the

Mediterranean the land dies unless it is protected by crops.' Warfare, conceived as the defence of territory, was ennobled as the extension of agriculture. The ideal citizen was the smallholding hoplite, who owned his armour as he owned his tools, and was ready to join in the collective defence of the land he and his fellows distributively worked. As the small farmer, further, sustained the *polis*, so the *polis* was conceived as existing to protect the small farmer, whose labour united man and nature in a bond with mythic power.

This ideology in turn shaped norms of social differentiation. Certainly the respected and the powerful were generally also the rich; since Greek taxes were mostly on capital through the *eisphora* — literally 'contribution' — and the *leitourgia* — literally 'public service' — it was understood that private wealth directly funded public life. But the superiority of this stratum was defined not in 'economic' but in 'social' and 'political' terms, for which the general Greek word is *aretê*. The men of *aretê* were distinguished by superior education, more sophisticated experience, military valour, success in rhetorical and athletic competition, ritual functions and privileges, display of expenditure, and generosity to the poor — and, of course, the ability to point to ancestors like themselves. It was understood that wealth was a necessary precondition of *aretê*, but that *aretê* is achieved not in pursuit of gain but of honour, since the quest for honour — *philotimia* — involves an attentiveness to the social audience, a socialisation of egoism, which ensures (or was supposed to ensure) that the great man was great on behalf of the group. In these terms we can understand why the eighth century, the period when the *polis* received its first organisation, was a period characterised by the assertion of heroic values and also by the elaboration of the ritual sphere; both are ways of holding an increasing social differentiation within the frame of collective norms and purposes.

The impact of the market must be seen within this continuing frame of cultural values. We can say, for instance, that the market brought about a breakdown of redistributive institutions. This is really a truism, since the shift from redistribution to market exchange is another name for the arrival of the market. We can talk about this shift in still other terms — for instance, as a shift from status to contract. Surely there was in the seventh century a progressive rationalisation of the relation between the great houses and the smallholders, whereby the smallholders no longer 'honoured with gifts' the upper strata, but paid a definite share of production or even a rent as the condition of tenancy. It also seems very probable that new agricultural land was being opened up on the basis (more or less informal) of what was later called 'empheutic tenure'; the smallholder who improved the land with terracing and fruit-trees acquired tenure and even alienable title. Such seems to have been Hesiod's farm at Askra, in the hills above Thebes (cf. *Works and Days* 341). The result was the liberation of the smallholder, and also his dispossession. The fruits of his labour were his own, but he ceased to be able to make claims on the surplus, and when his labour failed to bear fruit he had to borrow from the rich. In this new system *noblesse n'oblige plus*; the paternalism of the great houses was replaced by money power. Thus originated what was everywhere the great social question of the archaic *polis*: the problem of agricultural debt.

On the other hand it is also true that agricultural debt was conceived in the *polis* as a political problem; the dispossession of the smallholder was not an acceptable result, but called forth a range of political responses. This, as I said, is not the place to tell that story, which is the story of the interplay of oligarchy, tyranny and reform. We may, however, observe that in general redistribution was shifted in the classical city from the private household to the state. Capital accumulated in private hands, and then was taxed to provide public welfare. The rich were also expected to be privately generous, and we have some evidence from Athens for something like the Roman patron-client relationship (cf., for example, Lysias xix. 59); rich men helped out their poor connections with dowries for their daughters, funeral expenses, ransoming of prisoners. The Greek name for such benefaction is *euergesia*. It was not, of course, disinterested, but helped the rich man secure his social position. Whereas, however, in the pre-market economy such gift-giving resulted in claims on productive labour and in the recruitment of followers for private warfare, in the classical state it has been politicised, and provides the rich man with a constituency.

The market, therefore, produced not so much the breakdown of redistributive institutions as their reconstruction on a new basis. By the middle of the sixth century this reconstruction was more or less complete, and the resulting institutions were more or less in place. The adjustment was surely not made without tension; these tensions were politically coded as the tension between the few and the many, between those who had capital liable to tax, and those who wished to tax it. Most of the time, and in most places, however, some kind of balance was achieved. The market economy thus eventuated in communities more stable than before, more committed to the joint security and welfare of the people.

Yet it is generally true that the Greeks looked upon the market as a threat to the political order. The function of the state, to a large extent, was to correct the effects of the market — not by regulation, but by creating a superordinate structure of social relations. Rich and poor were differentiated by the play of economic forces, and then reunited within the common bond of citizenship — which, in the classical city, increasingly replaced the heroic model as the ideal type of manhood. One important symptom of this shift is the proliferation of sumptuary legislation restricting the display of wealth.

The market certainly changed the practical conditions of life, changed the patterns of production consumption, and exchange. More important, however, were changes on the level of consciousness; the market changed the terms of the problem, increasingly caused the social order to be seen as shaped by a tension between politics and economics — viewed ethically as a tension between the quest for honour and the quest for gain. The economy is constantly asserting itself and threatening to escape from the normative frame thrown around it by the polity. The motto of the age may be taken to be the elegiac lines ascribed to both Solon and Theognis:

> Many bad men are rich, and good men poor,
>   But we with them will not exchange
> Wealth for *aretê*, since that is ever stable,
>   While different people at different times have possessions.
>   Solon 6 = Theognis 315–18

In Homer wealth is an unqualified good; embedded in the cultural system it both follows status and confers it. Telemachus says: 'It's not so bad to be *basileus*; his house soon becomes rich and he himself more honoured' (i. 292–3). Conversely the successful raider can say: 'Soon was my household increased, and thereupon I was made feared and respected' (xiv. 223–4). Similarly Hesiod says that '*aretê* and glory attend on wealth' (*Works and Days* 313). By the time we reach the elegiac writers of the sixth century, however, wealth has become a problem. Chilon of Sparta said *chrêmat' anêr*, money makes the man; he obviously did not think this a desirable state of affairs. 'For the mass of people,' said Theognis, 'there is

The Market in Archaic Greece 53

only one *aretê*, to be rich' (Theognis 699–700); the mass of people have obviously gone wrong. So also:

> Just about anyone honours a rich man, dishonours a poor one;
> The same understanding is present in all mankind.
>
> Theognis 621–2

This also evidently is a lament: the glitter of wealth threatens to eclipse all other forms of social appearance, and thus to deprive *aretê* of the social support it needs to survive.

Wealth, further, is ethically dubious; this has to do with the fact that its pursuit has no natural limit. 'There is *koros*, satiety, of everything except wealth' (Theognis 596); 'with wealth the spirit never goes beyond the point of satisfaction' (Theognis 1158). The pursuit of wealth is the appetite that gains increase by what it feeds on, and it literally drives people crazy. The following verses are also attributed to both Solon and Theognis:

> Of wealth there is no limit plainly marked for man;
>   Those of us who now have the richest life
> Seek twice as much; who could satiate them all?
>   You know that profits come to mortals from immortals
> And from profits delusion [*atē*] next appears; Zeus sends it
>   In punishment; different people at different times have it.
>
> Solon 1. 71–6 = Theognis 227–32

The phrase that elsewhere (see citation above) was used of possessions is here used of the delusion or moral blindness which is seen as the inevitable consequence of possessions. It is not failure in the market which poses the greatest threat, but rather success. Satiety (*koros*) and delusion (*atē*) are linked to outrageous violence (*hubris*); those who have too much and reach for more lose all sense of limits, both ethical and practical, all sense of what should be done and of what will work.

> So many more men than hunger has, has surfeit (*koros*)
>   destroyed already —
> Men who were willing to have more than their fated share.
>
> Theognis 605–6
>
> Surfeit (*koros*) breeds insolent outrage (*hubris*), when riches
>   come to a bad man,

And to a man who has not a mind well fitted within him.
>> Theognis 153–4

Many men has surfeit (*koros*) destroyed in their folly;
It is hard to know the mean when wealth surrounds us.
>> Theognis 693–4

The elegiac poets, then, do not speak of the rationality of the market, but of its irrationality; they speak not of liberty and individualism, but of moral danger. There is no question in their world that all men desire wealth, and pursue it, and that poverty deprives a man of *aretê*; failure is an ethical disaster of another kind:

Alas, dread poverty, why do you sit on my shoulders
And make ugly my body and the mind within me?
By force you teach me against my will much that is shameful,
Although I know what is good and noble among men.
>> Theognis 649–52

Poverty is soon recognised even when unfamiliar;
It never comes into the assembly or to litigation.
It always comes out behind, is always scoffed at,
Is always the enemy, however, wherever it is.
>> Theognis 267–70

On the other hand, wealth, while a necessary condition of *aretê*, is far from sufficient:

Many have wealth without intelligence. Others seek
Nobility but are worn down by harsh poverty.
Helplessness stands before both in the path of action:
Some lack money; the others, sense.
>> Theognis 683–6

Wealth is doubly dangerous in the wrong hands, in that it can produce the appearance of excellence:

O wealth, of gods the noblest and most desired of all;
With you even a bad man becomes good.
>> Theognis 1117–18

Some have vices but manage to conceal them
With wealth, as poverty hides the virtues of others.
Theognis 1061–2

True admiration should be reserved for the man who serves social ends — prototypically, the warrior:

To many worthless men the god gives prosperity,
   Which is good, but no better for him, so is nothing,
Nor for his friends. But of *aretê* the fame never dies;
   The spearman saves his land and his city.
Theognis 865–8

It is not that wealth invariably does harm, but it is harmless only to the rare individual who is generally immune to circumstance:

Kyrnos, a good man has a mind that is steady always;
   He endures, if placed in evil things or in good.
If god to a bad man gives livelihood and wealth
   In his folly he is unable to keep from vice.
Theognis 319–22

Wealth, further, is merely a matter of circumstances; while in a way admired — as enviable, powerful — it comes and goes so erratically that its possession casts no credit on the possessor:

Let not the soul-consuming poverty of a man provoke you,
   Nor bring his cursed penury up against him,
For Zeus can tip the scale this way and that:
   At one moment to riches, at another to nothing.
Theognis 155–9

No one, Kyrnos, is the cause of *atê* or profit himself
   But the gods are the givers of both these things.
No human being does his work with knowledge
   Of the end, whether it will be bad or good.
Often when he thought he had done badly he had done well,
   And thinking to do well he did badly,
Nor to any human being comes what he wants:
   He is harshly held in by the limits of his control.
We men have idle notions knowing nothing;

The gods complete their plans in their own way.
Theognis 133-42

One oath you must not swear, that 'this can't happen'.
　The gods begrudge that; they control the end.
Do something then. From evil resulted good
　And from good, evil, and the impoverished man
Quickly became very rich, and he who had much
　Suddenly lost it all in a single night,
And the sensible man went wrong, while the fool's idea
　Worked out, and even the bad man had a share of honour.
Theognis 659-66

The gods who distribute wealth so unpredictably have no regard for justice:

Dear Zeus, you amaze me. You are king over all,
　You have the honour and the great power with it.
Of men you know well the thought and the heart of each;
　Your power over all is highest, king.
How can your mind endure, son of Kronos, that frauds
　Should have the same share as a man who is just
Whether in good sense he rears his mind or in *hubris*
　Of men who put their trust in unjust acts?
There is no distinction made in the fortune of mortals,
　Nor a path for them to walk which would please the
　　immortals.
Theognis 373-82

To say that god gives no direction is to state theologically the condition the sociologists call 'normlessness'. The sense that society is become irrational is, I think, a reflex of the perceived irrationality of the market and its impact; the making of money is not achieved by social norms, yet those who make money are able to claim the kind of social status which the norms are supposed to secure. Theognis makes the connection most explicit in relation to marriage contracts — which are, after all, the most consequential of transactions, since the parties acquire not commodities but kindred, and thus constitute the social fabric.

Although he knows perfectly well she's of bad family

He brings her into his house when the money persuades him;
So good repute takes bad repute, since harsh necessity
Wears him down, and makes his mind to stand it.
                                                Theognis 193–6

In rams and donkeys, Kyrnos, and horses, we seek
   Good stock; one wants a good pedigree
For his mount. In marriage, though, a good man does not mind
   A bad woman with a bad father if he gives plenty of money.
Neither does a woman refuse to be wife to a bad man
   Who is rich; she wants wealth more than goodness.
They honour money. Thus good marries into bad
   And bad into good; riches mix up kindred.
So don't be amazed, Kyrnos, if the city's kin
   Wither. The good are mixed up with the bad.
                                                Theognis 183–92

The Greek market never found its Adam Smith; theirs was an economics not of maximisation but of the mean. The pursuit of profit was always distrusted as dangerous to ethical norms and proper social order. Perhaps this was because the market came to the Greeks so suddenly, and at the centre, rather than moving in slowly from the social periphery; the international market in agricultural produce early 'monetised' — long before the invention of coinage — those commodities which in their production and ritualised consumption served as the most meaningful tokens of the cultural order, and which in pre-market redistributive exchange had circulated to maintain the economy as a cultural system. The shock was too great, and the market became, from the cultural point of view, a repressed fact: obviously crucial to Greek productivity and prosperity, but never ethically reputable. And this ambivalence we still, I think, to some extent inherit from them.

Notes

   1. E. L. Smithson, 'The Tomb of a Rich Athenian Lady c. 850 B.C.', *Hesperia*, 37 (1968), pp. 77–116.
   2. M. I. Finlay, *The World of Odysseus*, 2nd edn (New York, 1978), p. 58.
   3. Ibid., p. 61.
   4. P. Coldstream, *Geometric Greece* (New York, 1977), p. 66.
   5. Ibid., pp. 70–1.

6. A. J. Graham, 'The Foundations of Thasos', *British School at Athens*, 73 (1978), pp. 61–98.
7. Coldstream, *Geometric Greece*, p. 78.
8. Ibid., pp. 85–6.
9. Ibid., p. 77.
10. C. Rolley, 'Les grandes sanctuaires panhelleniques' in R. Hägg (ed.), *The Greek Renaissance of the late 8th Century B.C.*, Swedish Institute at Athens, 30 (Stolkholm & Lund, 1983), pp. 109–14.
11. D. Ridgway, 'The First Western Greeks; Campanian Coasts and Southern Etruria' in C. and S. Hawkes (eds), *Greeks, Celts and Romans* (Totowa, NJ, 1973).
12. D'andria, 'Salento Arcaico. La nuova documentazione archaologica' in G. Congedo (ed.), *Salento Arcaico* (Lecce, 1979).
13. G. Buchner, 'Testemonianze epigraphiche semitiche del VIII secolo a.c. a Pithekoussai', *Pavolo del Passato*, 33 (1978), pp. 23–32.
14. G. Buchner, 'Articolazione sociale, differenze di rituals e composizione dei corredi nella necropoli di Pithecusa' in G. and J. P. Gnoli (eds), *La mort, les morts dans les sociétés anciennes* (Vernant, Cambridge and Paris, 1982).
15. A. Snodgrass, *Archaic Greece: The Age of Experiment* (London, Melbourne, Toronto, 1980), pp. 23–4.
16. Ibid., pp. 53–4.
17. J. C. Carter, 'A Classical Landscape. Rural Archaeology at Metaponto', *Archaeology*, 33 (1980), pp. 23–32.
18. G. Valet, *Rhegion et Zancle* (Paris, 1958).
19. A. W. Johnston and R. E. Jones, 'The "SOS" Amphona', *British School at Athens*, 73 (1978), pp. 103–42.
20. C. G. Koehler, 'Corinthian Developments in the Study of Trade in the Fifth Century', *Hesperia*, 50 (1981), pp. 449–58.

3 EARLY FAIRS AND MARKETS IN ENGLAND AND SCANDINAVIA[1]

Peter Sawyer

Historians and archaeologists have recently devoted much attention to the international trading centres that flourished along the coasts and major rivers of northern Europe in the eighth and ninth centuries.[2] Some, including York, London and Cologne, had been important Roman cities while others, such as *Hamwih* (the predecessor of Southampton), Quentovic, near Boulogne, and Dorestad, on the lower Rhine, were in the vicinity of former Roman forts. Similar centres developed beyond the limits of the Roman Empire around the Baltic in the ninth century or earlier, for example Ribe and Hedeby in south Jutland, Birka in Lake Mälaren, west of modern Stockholm, and Staraja Ladoga on the River Volkhov, just south of Lake Ladoga. Far less attention has been paid to local markets and fairs that were attended not by merchants from distant places but by members of local or neighbouring communities exchanging their surpluses. This contrast is not surprising. There are many references to international markets in such contemporary texts as saints' lives, chronicles and charters, coins were minted in some of them and they are all archaeologically rewarding. Local markets and fairs, on the other hand, are more elusive institutions and have left little trace.

Linguistic evidence suggests that the distinction between local exchanges and long distance commerce was basic in Indo-European society. Emile Benveniste has asserted that 'there are in Indo-European no common words to designate trade and traders, there are only isolated words, peculiar to certain languages, of unclear formation, which have passed from one people to another'. He emphasised that the terms for commerce have no linguistic connection with the words used in those languages for the activity of buying and selling; 'to sell one's surplus, to buy for one's own sustenance is one thing: to buy, sell, for others, another'. Some of the words used in Latin to describe commerce, including the group *merx*, *mercator* and *commercium*, present great etymological difficulties while others, like *caupo* 'innkeeper, trader' and *arrha* 'pledge' appear to be borrowings.[3] Most remarkable of all is the word *negotium*, a negative construction meaning literally 'absence of leisure', which may be compared with English *business*, French *affaires*, German *Geschäft* and Swedish *handel*.[4] The reason for this lack of special terms for commerce is, according to Benveniste, that ' — at least in the beginning — it was an occupation which did not correspond to any of the hallowed, traditional activities'.[5]

As an alien phenomenon, markets for international commerce tended to attract attention. Strangers visiting them needed special protection, and the seventh-century English law dealing with the responsibilities of those who gave shelter to 'a stranger, a trader or any other man who came across the frontier' is followed by other, later laws regulating the activity of such men.[6] Local exchanges attended only by men and women of their neighbourhood were, in contrast, a normal part of social life in early medieval Europe and consequently tend to be unremarked in contemporary texts.

In the modern world such local exchanges appear to be virtually universal and have been the subject of many investigations by anthropologists. It is their observations that have provided the main basis for an elaborate classification of different types of exchange that was advanced by Karl Polanyi and has been explained, defended and refined by his disciples, notably George Dalton.[7] This analysis distinguished three 'modes of transaction': gift-trade, which is based on the principle of reciprocity, administered-trade, with controlled distribution and regulated prices, and thirdly the type of market-trade familiar in capitalist economies. Polanyi claimed that these could be states of development, a primitive economy being one in which market exchange is absent or of minor importance, as for example in the Trobriand Islands, but they could also exist side by side in more complex economies.

This analysis has been supported or, rather, illustrated by a bewildering range of examples drawn from many areas and periods: ancient Babylon, Viking Scandinavia, nineteenth-century America and twentieth-century Polynesia are but a few. It is difficult, if not impossible, for an individual to assess such varied evidence. That drawn from the period and area of which I have some knowledge, western and northern Europe in the early middle ages, encourages the suspicion that this theory has not so much been critically tested as buttressed by carefully selected examples, some of which have not been properly understood. That suspicion is reinforced by specialised studies of evidence that has been cited in support of Polanyi's interpretation. For example, Polanyi argued that in archaic societies one of the factors preserving social status was the existence of different types of money with different, exclusive functions.[8] Prestige goods, including precious metals, could only be obtained by exchanging their like. His claim that 'poor man's money' was 'an instrument for maintaining upper-class privileges' has been elaborated by Mary Douglas who cited the copper rod currency of the Cross River region of Nigeria as the best example of a special-purpose currency.[9] She argued that these copper rods were indivisible and could only be used to buy prestige goods and status symbols such as guns, slaves and cattle. This had the effect of preserving, or rationing, status. The copper rods, it was claimed, could not be used for such ordinary purchases as chicken, baskets, pots or grindstones, and the lower orders of society were therefore unable to acquire rods in their everyday transactions, and were thus kept in their place. John Latham has, however, convincingly demonstrated that this interpretation is based on a misunderstanding.[10] The copper rods could be subdivided into wires for petty purchases, the wires could be accumulated to buy rods and the rods could be exchanged for gold. He draws the reasonable conclusion that 'as the rod was supposed to be the best example of a primitive rationing system, although it was in fact a general purpose currency, the entire question of primitive rationing systems needs reconsidering'.

Polanyi's analysis is not now widely accepted by economic historians or anthropologists,[11] but it has been enthusiastically adopted by some archaeologists who think it provides a basis for reconstructing social, economic and even political phenomena in periods for which only material evidence survives.[12] There has even been an attempt to interpret the development of early medieval Europe in this way.[13] The resulting review of the archaeological evidence is a useful progress report but the classification of the towns, markets and fairs of post-Roman Europe according to anthropological models contributes little or nothing to our understanding of a period for which we have the welcome control of written evidence.

In many parts of Europe local exchanges were greatly affected by the organising power of Rome. A comparison of these areas with others, such as Ireland, Scandinavia or Eastern Europe, that never formed part of the Roman Empire, would be a rewarding, if ambitious, exercise. This chapter has a more limited aim, to discuss the evidence for early fairs and markets in England and Scandinavia. Britain was less Romanised than the provinces across the Channel and as power passed in the fifth century to native rulers and later, in a large part of the island, to English invaders, traces of Roman influence grew fainter. They did not, however, completely disappear. Scandinavia, which was only indirectly influenced by Rome, offers an interesting contrast. It was converted to Christianity much later and some traces of pre-Christian arrangements can be detected with the help of archaeology and place-names to supplement the meagre written evidence.

In the eighth century the only places in England at which toll can be shown to have been paid to royal agents were coastal markets called *wic* and one inland salt-producing centre now called Droitwich but that was formerly known as *Saltwic*. The evidence is provided by charters granting exemption from toll. In 734, for example, Æthelbald of Mercia granted the bishop of Rochester 'the entrance, that is the toll of one ship, whether one of his own or of any other man, hitherto belonging to me or my predecessors by royal right in the *portus* of London'. The bishop of Rochester thought it worth having this concession confirmed a century later.[14] Other charters issued between 733 and 764 grant remissions of toll at London and at the Kentish ports of Fordwich and Sarre.[15] At the end of the ninth century Mercian rulers certainly levied toll at Droitwich and they may have been doing so in the early eighth century, although the only direct evidence for this is an Evesham charter of doubtful authenticity.[16] We have no early evidence for the other main inland centres of salt production, the Cheshire Wiches, but Domesday Book describes an elaborate tariff of tolls at them that is more likely to be an ancient than a recent arrangement.[17] It is indeed arguable that these names in *wic*, and the custom of collecting toll at them, both derive from Roman arrangements that survived the collapse of imperial authority in the fifth century.[18]

In the ninth century English rulers were extending their claim to levy toll elsewhere. The earliest example concerns Worcester. The rulers of Mercia granted a charter to the bishop of Worcester between 889 and 899, sometime after the city had been fortified. They granted the bishop half the 'rights in the market or in the street, both within the fortification and outside', but they retained in their own hands the 'waggon-shilling and load-penny' which 'are to go to the king's hand as it always did at *Saltwic*'.[19] The clear implication is that the toll on waggons and on horse- or man-loads being claimed at Worcester was a novel extension of rights that Mercian rulers had long enjoyed at Droitwich.

English rulers fortified many other places in the ninth and early tenth centuries. The result was a network of strongholds called *burhs* or *ports* that were under the control of royal agents, port-reeves. In the early tenth century there was an attempt to limit buying and selling to these places. The laws of Edward the Elder include the rule that 'no-one shall buy except in a *port*, but he shall have the witness of the port-reeves or of other men of credit who can be trusted'.[20] This clause was repeated by Edward's successor Athelstan with the exemption of small transactions involving goods worth less than 20 pence.[21] The explicit reason for this rule was to ensure against theft and cattle-rustling, but the king must also have hoped to profit from tolls and other incidental payments.

Domesday Book shows that the Norman conquerors soon began to claim tolls at local exchanges that had formerly been toll-free.

> In Saltfleet Haven, Mare and Swine a new toll has been established . . . and the Wapentake of Louthest says, and the whole South Riding also, that this toll did not exist in the time of King Edward . . . Archil of Withern testifies that he saw Ansger receive the toll in respect of 24 ships from Hastings. In Saltfleet Hugh the sergeant takes the custom of ships which come there, which custom did not exist there in the time of King Edward, and these men began this as a new practice . . . In Barton on Humber and South Ferriby, Gilbert of Ghent's men take another toll than they took in the time of King Edward in respect of bread, fish, hides and very many other things for which nothing was ever given in the time of King Edward.[22]

South Ferriby was on the south shore of the River Humber at one of its main crossings, and the new tolls there could possibly have been levied on ferry traffic, but the next entry, 'In Caistor the king's men do the same', cannot be explained in this way for Caistor was a royal manor about 15 miles inland.

A century later English kings had brought such seigneurial claims to levy toll under their control and by the thirteenth century the doctrine was firmly established that no market or fair could be held without royal licence. It was because of this rule that many landlords obtained royal charters granting the right to hold markets and fairs; well over 1,500 such charters were issued between 1199 and 1350.[23] It is, however, clear that some of these charters granted markets that already existed. Wolverhampton, for example, gained its charter in 1258 but there is good evidence for a market there by

1204.[24] Many similar examples could be given. Other markets and fairs never obtained a charter but were accepted by the king and his agents as 'prescriptive'. So, for example, in *Quo Warranto* proceedings the prior of Dunstable successfully pleaded that Dunstable Fair had been held on the feast of St Peter *ad Vincula* (1 August) from before the time of memory.[25] In Yorkshire fairs and markets were claimed by prescriptive right at Beverley, Ripon, Selby and Thirsk, as was the fair of York.[26] Charters are, therefore, a misleading guide to the number of markets or fairs at any time in the twelfth and thirteenth centuries, and to their antiquity.

The earliest evidence for many markets is provided by Domesday Book, compiled in 1086. It records 60 markets but the list is certainly incomplete.[27] None is mentioned in 14 counties and the one yearly fair for which there is independent, and earlier, evidence, at Stow in Lincolnshire, is omitted.[28] All eleventh-century boroughs probably had markets but Domesday Book only notes 19 of them. Several are only mentioned incidentally, the York *macellum* is only revealed by the statement that the count of Mortain had *ii banci in macello*.[29] It is clear that the compilers of Domesday Book made no systematic attempt to record markets or fairs. In many, perhaps most, places any revenues from them must have been included under some other head, such as the farm of the borough or the render from an estate.

We are fortunate to have an eleventh-century description of the Law of St Cuthbert, declaring that all those attending the September feast of that most powerful saint were under his protection for seven days before and after the festival, coming from and returning to their homes.[30] It must have been a major regional event, attracting people from the whole of Northumbria. Another fair of St Cuthbert was held at Embsay in Yorkshire. The right to hold it was apparently granted by Henry II but a century later it was argued that there used to be nothing but a certain gathering of men called a wake (*quedam congregatio hominum que vocatur wach*).[31] Other *congregationes* have been discussed by L. F. Salzman.[32] In 1306 the farmers of measures and tolls at Cockermouth in Cumberland complained of a Sunday *congregatio gentium* at Crosthwaite church, about twelve miles away, 'who buy and sell corn, flour, peas, beans, flax, yarn, flesh and fish'. In the *Quo Warranto* proceedings it had been claimed that this was not a market because the owner took no stallage or toll. At the other end of the country, when complaint was made that a new market at Ramsbury had been created to the damage of Malmesbury, the bishop of Salisbury replied 'that he has no market at Ramsbury, nor does he at present claim to have any, but he says that when the men of the district come together on Sundays and feast days they buy flesh, fish and other foodstuffs, but they do not sell anything else there', and the bishop denied taking toll.

Similar *congregationes* were held much later. In the seventeenth century one is described at Coaley in Gloucestershire. The church there was dedicated to St Bartholomew:

> On whose feast day yet continueth such concourse and resort of people That it hath the name of Cowley Faire day, whereon most kindes of country wares are brought and sold in boothes and standings purposely set up. But by noe grant or Charter from the Crowne or otherwise then the intertainment of the said John Browninge [the rector] and his Ancestors and some other of the inhabitants, both on that day and on the Sunday after called Cowley Feast or Wake day.[33]

Churches that attracted regular gatherings of people on Sundays and festivals provided ideal opportunities for buying and selling, and the last provision in the Statute of Winchester of 1285 was the prohibition that 'henceforth neither fairs nor markets be held in churchyards'.[34] Many markets for which there is early, that is eleventh-century, evidence were associated with important churches. The Oxfordshire Domesday only mentions one, at Bampton, a tenth-century minster.[35] In Bedfordshire Domesday reports three markets, two of which, Luton and Leighton Buzzard, were on royal estates that boasted major churches.[36] In Lincolnshire Domesday notes seven markets.[37] One of them, at Bolingbroke, is called new, but five of the others had significant religious associations. Partney was an abbey in the time of Bede, an abbot of Louth became archbishop of Canterbury in 792, Barton on Humber has a pre-Conquest church built over an earlier cemetery that suggests the site had some religious importance at an early date, the name of Kirton implies that its church was locally significant and at Threckingham Domesday reports two churches.

Attention has been drawn to the association between many medieval markets and hundredal manors, that is estates that once served as centres for the collection of royal dues.[38] The explanation for this may, however, owe less to the direct role of the king and his agents than to the fact that many of these places also had early and important churches. Wolverhampton, where a market is first evidenced in the thirteenth century, had a collegiate church in the tenth,[39] Bakewell, which was similarly granted a market charter in the thirteenth century, has a rich collection of eighth-century carved stones that suggest that it was an early religious centre.[40] The ecclesiastical significance of many other markets is even clearer. In Huntingdonshire there were markets at Ramsey as well as at St Neots and St Ives, and there were prescriptive markets or fairs in Yorkshire at Beverley, Ripon and York.

Sunday trading appears to have been normal in pre-Conquest England. Athelstan unsuccessfully attempted to prohibit it, as did Ethelred a century later.[41] But Sunday trading remained common in the twelfth century and was only abandoned in the thirteenth century, largely thanks to the efforts of preachers like Eustace of Flay who visited England in 1201 to preach against the abuse.[42]

The silence of early sources about local markets means that the evidence of place-names and coins, although slight, is especially valuable. As the word *port* only acquired the meaning 'market' in the tenth century, it cannot help locate early example.[43] The word *ceaping* was used earlier with the same meaning but it only occurs in one Domesday place-name.[44] Another rare place-name element is *byge*, from Old English *bycgan* 'to buy'. Unfortunately it is not possible to distinguish formally between place-names formed with that word and those incorporating *byge* in the sense of 'a corner' or 'a bend in a river'. The only name in which topography supports the sense of 'a buying place' is Beeston in Cheshire, 'the buying stone'. It lies on the Peckforton Hills, a prominent range of hills that divide the county in two, and is on the line of an ancient boundary that gave its name to the nearby place Tarvin, from Welsh *terfyn*, which in turn derives from Latin *terminus*.[45] Boundaries were appropriate locations for some early markets because people could gather from both sides without having to travel through strange territory. With these rare exceptions, there seem to be no specialised place-name elements to designate markets in early England. Many appear to have been called simply *stow* 'a place of assembly'. This was commonly used for religious centres but several early markets and fairs were held at places with that name, for example at Stow in Lincolnshire.[46]

The evidence of coin finds is more revealing. Eighth-century silver coins called *sceattas* are relatively rare but significant concentrations have been discovered at coastal *wics* and at major churches. The most recent list records well over 70 from both *Hamwih* and York and at least 40 from London. Reculver has yielded 51 and Whitby 29.[47] Such large numbers are unusual, Ipswich, Dover and Jarrow, each with three, are more characteristic. It has been argued that these coins have little value as indicators of commercial activity but the large numbers found at known trading centres suggest that they were used in trade. Some of the small concentrations may indeed indicate the sites of markets that may not be recorded until centuries later. The five *sceattas* found at Dunstable help bridge the gap between Roman *Durocobrivae* and the market mentioned there in the early twelfth century.[48] Some of the coins found at churches may, of course, have been dropped by worshippers or priests, and some may be from graves, but we should not exclude the possibility that some were used for much the same purposes as those found at York. In this connection it is worth drawing attention to the voluminous copper coinage of ninth-century Northumbria.[49] These coins, called *stycas* by numismatists, are often found in excavations of Northumbrian sites, and were also hoarded in large numbers, but they are rarely found outside Northumbria. This implies that, on the eve of the Viking attacks, Northumbria had a more sophisticated system of small change than has commonly been recognised.

The English evidence suggests that long before the Norman Conquest buying and selling took place wherever there were regular assemblies, *congregationes*, for whatever purpose. Churches provided good opportunities, for they attracted people every Sunday and especially on festivals. There were other places at which regular gatherings occurred, such as royal vills and the meeting places of shire and hundred courts, but the opportunities for buying and selling were much improved when, as happened at many royal vills, a church was established. The right of kings to toll, originally limited to the coastal *wics* and the inland salt producing centres was, in the ninth and tenth centuries, extended to other places, later called *ports*. Some were old places of assembly for secular or religious purposes, or both, but kings now claimed rights over them, a claim that was greatly strengthened by the building of fortifications that were maintained and manned by royal authority. As new churches were established they too naturally attracted markets and apparently late foundations, like Wolverhampton, figure in the list of early markets alongside such ancient churches as Oundle and Partney. Some of the new markets of the eleventh and twelfth centuries may indeed have been old *congregationes*. Cookham in Berkshire, for example, had a new market according to Domesday Book, but it was an important minster in the eighth century.[50] Stratford upon Avon, founded as a 'new' town in the late twelfth century may have owed part of its rapid success to the existence there of an earlier *congregatio*, associated with the ninth-century minster placed conveniently close to an important crossing of the River Avon.[51]

There are therefore grounds for suspecting that the novelty of some markets lay not in the buying and selling but in the claims of lords to collect toll and stallage. After the Conquest kings and their tenants claimed such rights in old *congregationes*, as the Lincolnshire Domesday shows, but in time the royal prerogative was asserted, and by the thirteenth century all markets and fairs required royal licence. Local exchanges between producers must always have been important and we may be confident that there were assemblies for worship and entertainment as well as for buying and selling long before the English were converted, even before the Romans came. We can do little more than speculate about the places in which this happened, but it seems likely that at least some of the earliest, and most important, churches were founded at old cult centres.

That certainly happened in Scandinavia. The names of several medieval towns, some of which became episcopal sees, incorporate words that denote pagan places of worship. The cathedral city of Lund, for example, is named after a *lund*, meaning a small wood or grove, especially one set apart as a holy place.[52] Several others are named after a *vi* 'temple' or, rather, 'place for worship'[53] — pagan Scandinavians do not seem normally to have had special temple buildings until, possibly, the eve of their conversion when they may have reacted to the challenge of the Christian churches by building similar structures, for example at Uppsala.[54] Visby, in the island of Gotland, appears originally to have been called *Vi* and later, after the development of the settlement, the name was changed to 'the *by*, that is settlement, perhaps even town, of *Vi*'.[55] The recent discovery in one of its early churches, St Hans, of a pagan picture stone that was later used successively as a Christian monument with a runic inscription, and in a coffin, is perhaps a pointer to the continuity of religious functions in that place. In Denmark two episcopal cities are similarly named after a *vi*; Viborg 'hill(s) by a *vi*'[56] and Odense which first appears in 988 in the Latinised form

Othenesuuigensem and means 'Odin's *vi*'.[57] In the twelfth century the Swedish archbishopric was established at Uppsala, the site of a pagan cult centre described by Adam of Bremen. It was also the location of a great winter fair called *Distingen*, 'the *ting*, or assembly, of the *Diser*, female goddesses'. This was never 'converted' to a Christian festival but was held when the first new moon after mid-winter was full.[58] Its date could therefore be worked out by people throughout Scandinavia, including the far north whence came trappers and traders with their precious furs and skins. All other Swedish fairs were associated with Christian festivals when they are first mentioned, but some, perhaps most, are likely to have had pagan roots like *Distingen*.

Some other medieval fairs were associated with apparent centres of pagan cults or observances. The best documented example was held at the spring at Svinnegarn, near Enköping in Uppland. Before the Reformation votive offerings were made at that spring, and to the church built nearby, by people of both high and low social rank. Until modern times it continued to attract thousands of people, some travelling a hundred kilometres or more, every Trinity Sunday.[59] The first reference to a fair there is in 1488 when an attempt was made to suppress it, but without success.[60] In 1813 the local landowner reported that a fair was held there every year with booths specially set up, and he complained about the accompanying drunkenness and noise.[61]

There was undoubtedly a close connection between church festivals and fairs, many of which were officially recognised and either held by prescriptive right or licensed by charter. In the cathedral city of Skara, for example, there were three, on Maundy Thursday, the nativity of the Virgin (8 September) and also when the annual synod (*prästmötet*) was held in July. As early as 1280 the bishop of Skara defined the penalties incurred for breach of the special peace protecting these *samfunthum* or *congregationes*.[62] Not all fairs associated with church festivals were considered legal. Svinnegarn was not the only *olaghe marchnade* that was ordered to close in 1488, others were at the Cistercian nunnery of Skokloster and at a church called *Ness*.[63]

Medieval coins found in Swedish churches lend support to the idea that these buildings played a significant role in rural buying and selling. Excluding hoards that were deliberately concealed, larger concentrations of medieval coins have been found in the excavation of churches than in farms, castles or even town sites. In some

70 *Early Fairs and Markets in England and Scandinavia*

Figure 3.1 Coin Finds, Alvastra Monastery

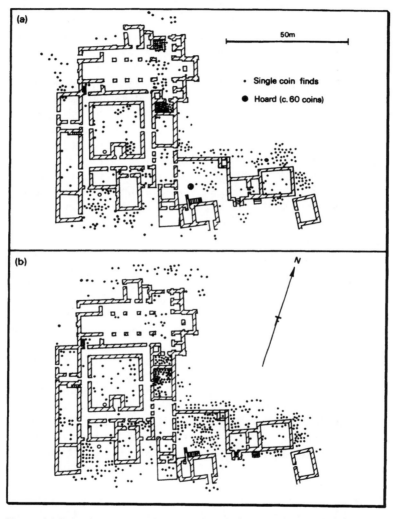

Notes: (a) Coins from the twelfth, thirteenth and fourteenth centuries found in Alvastra Monastery. The big dot represents a hoard of *c.*60 coins struck *c.*1290–1318. (b) Coins from *c.*1400–1520 found in Alvastra Monastery.
Source: Diagrams from Malmer, 'Monetary Circulation in South-Eastern Sweden' (cited note 64), pp. 151, 153.

churches very large numbers of coins have been found. The Cistercian monastery of Alvastra, in Östergötland, is the extreme case with 1380 coins of the sixteenth century or earlier scattered in the church itself, in the abbey buildings, especially the chapter house, and in the abbey grounds.[64] The distribution is illustrated in the accompanying figures. Large numbers of medieval coins have also been found in other monasteries, for example Vreta and Varnhem (both Cistercian) and in Birgitta's foundation, Vadstena, as well as in the cathedral church of Linköping. Smaller concentrations have been found in less important churches. The only region for which a systematic survey of these finds has been published, Östergötland, has 20 churches other than those already mentioned in which medieval coins have been found, and three of them have each yielded over 100 coins.[65] Some may have come from disturbed graves but that can hardly explain all these finds and the most natural explanation is that the church buildings, including monasteries, were used for buying and selling as well as for worship. These places not only offered the best opportunities for regular meeting, they also provided the sheltered space that was badly needed for much of the year.

There is little direct evidence of Sunday trading in Scandinavia. Swedish market charters, beginning with that for Jönköping in 1288, are concerned only with weekday markets,[66] but the law of Gotland provided for the sale on Sundays of cheese, butter, fish, fowls and meat but not flour, seeds or other goods.[67] More revealing is the complaint made in 1531 by Gustav Vasa that the frequency of illegal markets was increasing so much that there would soon be one held at every church mass (*att Marcknader hållas j hwar kyrkiomesso*).[68] We may suspect that unlicensed markets were commonly held on Sundays in association with church services long before the sixteenth century. In many parts of Scandinavia, especially those with sparse populations, seasonal fairs were more important than weekly markets. Many, like *Distingen*, were held in the winter when communications were easiest over frozen ground or, best of all, on frozen lakes and rivers.

From the fifteenth century, if not before, urban councils and national rulers attempted to stop or control rural trading. One method was to create new towns with licensed markets. Alingsås, for example, some 45 kilometres inland from Gothenburg and its predecessor Nya Lödöse, was granted a charter in 1619 but there had been a market there earlier. In 1593 it was suppressed in

72 Early Fairs and Markets in England and Scandinavia

response to complaints by the burgesses of Nya Lödöse that Danish traders were going direct to Alingsås market and bypassing their town. We do not know how old that market was, but we have no reason to assume that it was a new development of the sixteenth century.[69] Rural markets clearly served a useful purpose and attempts simply to abolish them or to transfer them elsewhere met with resistance. A good example is the failure of the plan of 1640 to replace and combine four rural fairs that were widely scattered to the west of Lake Vänern by a new town at Åmål.[70] As late as 1775 there were at least 150 such rural fairs throughout Sweden.[71]

Historical evidence for Scandinavian fairs and markets is necessarily late, but archaeological investigations are gradually enlarging our knowledge of pre-Christian as well as of Christian fairs and markets. Excavations in towns sometimes reveal that they had surprisingly early origins. So, for example, the Norwegian town of Skien in southern Telemark, about 22 kilometres from the coast, was granted a charter in 1358, but excavations have revealed good evidence for the existence of a seasonal market there, attended by craftsmen, before the year 1000.[72] Traces of similar early trading centres that did not develop into towns have been found in many parts of Scandinavia. Löddeköpinge in Skåne, has been interpreted as a seasonal market,[73] but that apparently depends largely on the name; there is otherwise little to distinguish it from an ordinary village. A more convincing case can be based on discoveries made at Ystad, also in Skåne, which have led the excavator, Märta Strömberg, to describe the site as a market for the nearby communities in the seventh and eighth centuries, if not earlier.[74] Paviken on Gotland was a more elaborate trading centre that flourished in the ninth and tenth centuries, importing goods from many parts of the Baltic.[75] A similar, and contemporary, site has been found at Skuldevig, just inside the entrance of Roskilde Fjord in Denmark.[76] All these places had ready access to the sea and could be visited by people coming considerable distances by boat. In the later middle ages farmers from the Danish islands visited Lübeck, just as Norwegian farmers sold their produce in Denmark.[77] Archaeological evidence suggests that their predecessors did much the same in the Viking period and earlier.

Travel by land was more difficult than by water but it was not impossible and some inland trading centres had extensive contacts. The apparently isolated valley of Setesdal in south Norway, for example, received imports from all directions in the Viking period and it seems likely that there were seasonal fairs then as there were in the nineteenth century when men travelled from the coast to exchange salt, cloth, leather and fish for hides and skins.[78]

By the beginning of the ninth century a few of these Scandinavian trading places had developed into major centres of long distance trade. They were apparently under some form of royal control or influence. The ninth-century *Vita Anskarii* shows that a Danish king had control over Ribe and Hedeby and that a Swedish ruler had some responsibility for Birka.[79] The request made in 829 by a Swedish king that Frankish missionaries should be sent to Birka seems to have been made in the hope of reassuring Christian merchants from Western Europe that they would be safe there.[80] There is no suggestion that any general conversion was expected or even desired, but the missionaries did build a church in Birka. We are not told what effect this had on Birka's commerce, but after describing the construction of a church at Hedeby, the *Vita Anskarii* explicitly says there was great joy there because

> people of this race [that is, Saxons] as well as merchants from this district [the diocese of Hamburg-Bremen, where the *Vita* was written] and from Dorestad made for the place readily and without any fear — something which was not possible previously — and at that time there was an abundant supply of goods of every kind.[81]

In both Scandinavia and England we can therefore recognise traces of *congregationes*, more or less frequent, for religious, social or political purposes which were also opportunities to buy and sell. There was a natural tendency for rulers to claim authority over the more successful places and to provide protection in return for a share of the profits of trade. Scandinavia can, indeed, offer a very early parallel to the efforts of English rulers to extend their regalian rights. According to the Frankish Royal Annals, in 808 the Danish king Godfred removed merchants from *Reric*, in Slav territory, to his own lands because the *vectigalia* were of great benefit to his kingdom.[82] That technical term may owe more to the interpretation of the Frankish writer than to a conscious adoption by the Danish ruler of imperial prerogatives but, taken together with the evidence of the *Vita Anskarii* it does suggest that some Scandinavian kings had begun to acquire rights that were very similar to, and may even have been based on, those enjoyed by rulers in Christian Europe.

Nevertheless, in Scandinavia as in England, many *congregationes gentium*, especially those that were of no more than local importance, remained independent. Some may have played a part in wider economic exchanges by supplying food and raw materials needed by the *negotiatores* who visited such major centres as London, York, Birka or Hedeby, but regular gatherings of people to buy and sell local produce were not a by-product of international trade, they were rather a natural response to local needs that were social and religious as well as economic.

Notes

1. The English evidence is discussed more fully by the writer in 'Fairs and Markets in Early Medieval England' in Niels Skyum-Nielsen and Niels Lund (eds), *Danish Medieval History. New Currents* (Museum Tusculanum Press, Copenhagen, 1981), pp. 153–68, of which the present chapter is a development.
2. H. Jankuhn, 'Frühe Städte im Norde- und Ostseeraum (700–1000 n. chr.)', in *Topografia Urbana e Vita Cittadina nll'alto medioevo in Occidente* (Settimane di studio del Centro Italiano di Studi sull'alto medioevo, 21; Spoleto, 1974), pp. 153–201.
3. Emile Benveniste, *Indo-European Language and Society* (Faber and Faber, London, 1973), pp. 113–20.
4. Emile Benveniste, 'Sur l'histoire du mot *negotium*', *Annali della Scuola Normale Superiore di Pisa*, 2nd ser., vol. 20 (1951), pp. 21–5.
5. Benveniste, *Language and Society*, p. 118.
6. P. H. Sawyer, 'Kings and Merchants' in P. H. Sawyer and I. N. Wood (eds), *Early Medieval Kingship* (School of History, Leeds University, Leeds, 1977), pp. 150–1.
7. Karl Polanyi, *The Great Transformation* (New York, 1944); *Trade and Market in the Early Empires*, Karl Polanyi (ed.), C. M. Arensberg and H. W. Pearson (Glencoe, 1957); *Primitive, Archaic and Modern Economies. Essays of Karl Polanyi*, G. Dalton (ed.) (New York, 1968).
8. Karl Polanyi with Abraham Rotstein, *Dahomey and the Slave Trade. An Analysis of An Archaic Economy* (University of Washington Press, Seattle and London, 1966), pp. 173–5.
9. Mary Douglas, 'Primitive Rationing. A Study in Controlled Exchange' in Raymond Firth (ed.), *Themes in Economic Anthropology* (Tavistock Press, London, 1967), pp. 119–47.
10. A. J. H. Latham, 'Currency, Credit and Capitalism on the Cross River in the Pre-Colonial Era', *Journal of African History*, vol. 12 (1971), pp. 599–605.
11. George Dalton *et al.*, 'Theoretical Issues in Economic Anthropology', *Current Anthropology*, vol. 10 (1969), pp. 63–102; Robert McC. Adams, 'Anthropological Perspectives on Ancient Trade', *Current Anthropology*, vol. 15 (1974), pp. 239–58.
12. For example, Colin Renfrew, 'Trade as Action at a Distance: Questions of Integration and Communication' in Jeremy A. Sabloff and C. C. Lamberg-Karlovsky (eds), *Ancient Civilization and Trade* (University of Mexico Press, Albuquerque, 1975), pp. 3–59; William L. Rathje and Jeremy A. Sabloff, 'Ancient Maya Commercial Systems: a Research Design for the Island of Cozumel, Mexico', *World Archaeology*, vol. 5, no. 2 (1973), 221–31.

13. Richard Hodges, *Dark Age Economics. The Origins of Towns and Trade A.D. 600–1000* (Duckworth, London, 1982).
14. P. H. Sawyer, *Anglo-Saxon Charters. An Annotated List and Bibliography* (Royal Hist. Soc., London, 1968), no. 88; translated in Dorothy Whitelock, *English Historical Documents c. 500–1042*, 2nd edn (Methuen, London, 1979), no. 66.
15. Sawyer, *Charters*, nos. 29, 86, 87, 91, 98, 143, 1612, 1788.
16. Sawyer, *Charters*, no. 97. For Droitwich see also Sawyer, 'Kings and Merchants', pp. 147–8, and Della Hooke, 'The Droitwich Salt Industry: An Examination of the West Midland Charter Evidence' in David Brown, James Campbell and Sonia Chadwick Hawkes (eds), *Anglo-Saxon Studies in Archaeology and History*, no. 2 (British Archaeological Reports British Ser. 92, Oxford, 1981), pp. 123–69.
17. *Domesday Book*, vol. 1, fo. 268.
18. Sawyer, 'Kings and Merchants', pp. 143–4, 152.
19. Sawyer, *Charters*, no. 223; Whitelock, *Documents*, no. 99; F. E. Harmer, '*Chipping* and *Market*: A Lexicographical Investigation' in Cyril Fox and Bruce Dickins (eds), *Early Cultures of North-West Europe: H. M. Chadwick Memorial Essays* (Cambridge, 1950), p. 339, note 4.
20. I Edward, clause 1 in F. Liebermann, *Die Gesetze der Angelsachsen*, vol. 1 (Halle, 1903), pp. 138–9, and F. L. Attenborough, *The Laws of the Earliest English Kings* (Cambridge, 1922), p. 114.
21. II Athelstan, clause 12 in Liebermann, *Gesetze*, pp. 156–6, and Attenborough, *Laws*, p. 134.
22. *Domesday Book*, vol. 1, fo. 375b.
23. R. H. Britnell, cited by D. M. Palliser and A. C. Pinnock, 'The Markets of Medieval Staffordshire', *North Staffordshire Journal of Field Studies*, vol. 11 (1971), p. 62.
24. Palliser and Pinnock, 'Markets of Staffordshire', p. 51 and note 8.
25. *Placita de Quo Warranto* (Record Commission, London, 1818), p. 73.
26. Ibid., pp. 217–8, 221.
27. H. C. Darby, *Domesday England* (Cambridge, 1977), pp. 369–70.
28. Sawyer, *Charters*, no. 1478; Harmer, '*Chipping* and *Market*', pp. 358–60.
29. *Domesday Book*, vol. 1, fo. 298.
30. E. Craster, 'The Peace of St Cuthbert', *Journal of Ecclesiastical History*, vol. 8 (1957), pp. 93–5.
31. I. Kershaw, *Bolton Priory: The Economy of a Northern Monastery, 1286–1325*, (Oxford, 1973), pp. 7, 29, *Placita de Quo Warranto*, p. 212.
32. 'The Legal Status of Markets', *Cambridge Historical Journal*, vol. 2 (1928), pp. 205–12.
33. John Smith, *A Description of the Hundred of Berkeley*, Sir John Maclean (ed.) (Gloucester, 1885), p. 151.
34. William Stubbs, *Select Charters*, 9th edn (Oxford, 1913), p. 466.
35. *Domesday Book*, vol. 1, fo. 154b; W. B. Sanders (ed.), *Facsimiles of Anglo-Saxon Manuscripts* (3 vols., Ordnance Survey, Southampton, 1878–84), vol. 2, Exeter, no. xvi.
36. *Domesday Book*, vol. 1, fo. 209.
37. Ibid., fos. 338b, 345, 351, 354b, 355, 356.
38. R. H. Britnell, 'English Markets and Royal Administration before 1200', *Economic History Review*, 2nd ser., vol. 31 (1978), pp. 183–6.
39. Sawyer, *Charters*, no. 1380.
40. F. C. Plumtre, 'The Parish Church of Bakewell, in Derbyshire', *Archaeological Journal*, vol. 4 (1847), pp. 37–58; T. E. Routh, 'A Corpus of the pre-Conquest Carved Stones of Derbyshire', *Journal of the Derbyshire Archaeological and Natural History Society*, new ser., vol. 11 (1937), pp. 6–19.
41. II Athelstan, clause 24, IV Athelstan, cl. 2, VI Athelstan, cl. 10 in Lieber-

mann, *Gesetze*, pp. 164, 171, 182, and Attenborough, *Laws*, pp. 140, 146, 166; V Ethelred, cl. 13, VI Ethelred, cl. 22, 44, VIII Ethelred, cl. 17 in Liebermann, *Gesetze*, pp. 240, 252, 258, 265, and A. J. Robertson, *The Laws of the Kings of England from Edmund to Henry I* (Cambridge, 1925), pp. 82, 96, 105, 122.

42. J. L. Cate, 'The English Mission of Eustace of Flay (1200–1201)', *Études d'histoire dediées à la mémoire de Henri Pirenne par ses anciens élèves* (Bruxelles, 1937), pp. 67–89; L. F. Salzmann, *English Trade in the Middle Ages* (Oxford, 1931), pp. 124–5.

43. Sawyer, 'Fairs and Markets', pp. 158–9.

44. E. Ekwall, *The Place-Names of Lancashire* (Chetham Society, new ser., vol. 81, 1922), p. 143.

45. J. McN. Dodgson, *The Place-Names of Cheshire*, vol. 3 (English Place-Name Society, vol. 40, Cambridge, 1971), pp. 281, 302–3.

46. A. H. Smith, *The Place-Name Elements* (2 vols., English Place-Name Society, vol. 25–6, Cambridge, 1970), vol. 2, pp. 158–61.

47. S. E. Rigold and D. M. Metcalf, 'A Check-list of English Finds of Sceattas', *British Numismatic Journal*, vol. 47 (1977), pp. 31–52.

48. Ibid., pp. 39, 40, 48, under Dunstable, Houghton Regis and Totternhoe; G. H. Fowler, *Digest of the Charters Preserved in the Cartulary of the Priory of Dunstable* (Bedfordshire Record Society, vol. 10, 1926), p. 240.

49. C. S. S. Lyon, 'A Reappraisal of the Sceatta and Styca Coinage of Northumbria', *British Numismatic Journal*, vol. 38 (1955–7), pp. 227–42; H. E. Pagan, 'The Bolton Percy Hoard of 1967', *British Numismatic Journal*, vol. 43 (1973), pp. 1–45.

50. Sawyer, *Charters*, no. 1258.

51. E. M. Carus-Wilson, 'The First Half-Century of the Borough of Stratford-upon-Avon', *Economic History Review*, 2nd ser., vol. 18 (1965), pp. 46–63; Sawyer, *Charters*, no. 1278.

52. Smith, *Place-Name Elements*, vol. 2, pp. 27–8.

53. *Kulturhistorisk Leksikon for nordisk middlelalder* (22 vols., København, 1956–78), vol. 19, cols. 684–90.

54. Olaf Olsen, Hørg, Hov og Kirke (København, 1966), pp. 116–25.

55. Ingemar Olsson, *Ortnamn på Gotland* (Stockholm, 1984), pp. 19–20.

56. Bent Jørgensen, *Dansk Stednavneleksikon: Jylland – nordlige del* (Copenhagen, 1982), p. 142.

57. Kr. Hald, 'The Cult of Odin in Danish Place-names' in Arthur Brown and Peter Foote (eds), *Early English and Norse Studies presented to Hugh Smith* (Methuen, London, 1963), pp. 99–109.

58. *Kulturhistorisk Leksikon*, vol. 3, cols. 112–15.

59. Nils Ahnlund, 'Svinnegarns Källa', *Rig*, vol. 5 (1922), pp. 59–76.

60. G. Carlsson (ed.), *Stockholms stads tänkeböcker*, vol. 2 for 1483–1492 (Stockholm, 1921–44), p. 281.

61. Ahnlund, 'Svinnegarn', pp. 73–4.

62. *Diplomatarium Suecanum*, vol. 1, J. G. Liljegren (ed.) (Stockholm, 1829), no. 709.

63. See note 60.

64. Brita Malmer, 'Monetary Circulation in South-Eastern Sweden c. 1350–1500 in the Light of Three Major Church-Finds', *Nordisk Numismatisk Årsskrift* (1981), pp. 147–59.

65. Brita Malmer and Ian Wiséhn, *Myntfynd från Östergötland* (Kungl. Myntkabinettet, Stockholm, 1982).

66. *Kulturhistorisk Leksikon*, vol. 18, col. 480.

67. Åke Holmbäck and Elias Wessén, *Svenska Landskapslagar tolkade och förklarade*, vol. 4 (Stockholm, 1979), p. 209.

68. *Konung Gustaf den förstes registratur*, vol. 7 (Stockholm, 1877), pp. 547–9.

69. Birgit and Peter Sawyer, *Innan Alingsås blev stad* (Viktoriabokförlag, Alingsås, 1985), p. 123.
70. A. A. von Stiernman, *Samling utaf Kongl. Bref, Stadgar och Förordningar etc. angående Sweriges Rikes Commerce, Politie och Oeconomie*, vol. 2 (Stockholm, 1750), pp. 292-3.
71. Nils Staf, 'Marknader och marknadsterminer i Sverige' in A. Schück (ed.), *Handel och Samfärdsel* (Nordisk Kultur, vol. 16B, Stockholm, 1933), pp. 191-9.
72. Siri Myrvoll Lossius, *Skien i Middelalderen. En antikvarisk registrering* (Riksantikvaren, Oslo 1979). Information on more recent finds from the excavator, Siri Myrvoll.
73. Tom Ohlsson, 'The Löddeköpinge investigation I and II', *Meddelanden från Lunds universitets historiska museum*, new ser., 1 (1976), pp. 59-161, and 3 (1980), pp. 68-111.
74. 'En kustby i Ystad — före stadens tillkomst', *Ystadiana* (1978), pp. 7-101.
75. Per Lundström, *De kommo vida . . . Vikingars Hamn vid Paviken på Gotland* (Stockholm, 1981).
76. Ole Crumlin-Pedersen, *Søvejen til Roskilde* (Vikingeskibshallen, Roskilde, 1978), pp. 67-9.
77. Ibid., pp. 62-3; Curt Weibull, 'Lübecks sjöfart och handel på de nordiska rikena 1368 och 1398-1400', *Scandia*, vol. 32 (1966), pp. 1-120.
78. Jan H. Larsen, 'Vikingtids handelsplass i Valle, Setesdal', *Universitetets Oldsaksamlings Skrifter*, ny rekke, nr. 3 (Oslo, 1980), pp. 143-8.
79. P. H. Sawyer, *Kings and Vikings* (Methuen, London, 1982), p. 54.
80. Ibid., p. 135.
81. Ibid., p. 137.
82. *Annales regni Francorum 741-829*, F. Kurze (ed.) (Monumenta Germaniae historica, Scriptores rerum Germanicarum in usum scholarum, Hanover, 1895), p. 126.

4 MARKETS AND FREEDOM IN THE MIDDLE AGES

A. R. Bridbury

When we select an institution for historical investigation, we inevitably take it out of context. Indeed the very idea of an institution as a separate organism isolates a group of activities from the social process to which it belongs and does violence to its nature. There are, of course, immense advantages to be gained by studying any organism without the distraction of seeing it as part of something more complex. But anything abstracted from the totality of events is bound to be distorted, if not falsified, by such a procedure. This applies with particular emphasis to markets, because regular and mutually beneficial exchanges between consenting parties cannot possibly take place unless an irreducible minimum of appropriate political and social conditions permit the making of such exchanges. And it is by no means self-evident that medieval authorities saw their responsibilities in terms of encouraging such exchanges, particularly if it meant doing so to the detriment of their other obligations and interests.

This was partly a question of practical politics. Medieval politicians had the problem familiar to politicians in all ages of having to yield to pressures they could not resist without giving more offence than they cared to provoke. The statue book is full of concessions made to this interest or that which, taken together, add up to a farrago of contradictory policies as inextricable as those of any government's today. But this is not the only reason, or indeed the most significant reason, why medieval political authorities did so much less than we might think they ought to have done to promote exchanges of goods and services. They failed to do more because they did not take the same view as we do of the importance, not to say the sanctity, of markets and of the value of promoting market facilities.

Where they differ from ours it is tempting to conclude that medieval values were either higher or lower than ours, so that when it is not being commended for its exalted ideals, medieval society is commonly disparaged for its failure to live up to ours. But medieval society had its own values, and for this it is not answerable before the bar of any historical court of moral judgement. Social commentators may be forgiven, perhaps, for perceiving the world's history in terms of an evolutionary development in which past events are valued according to the contribution they can be said to have made to the achievement of what is thought to be best about present society. But any survey of past ages which gives prominence to those aspects of the past which can be made to wear an appearance of modernity and which, as a result, treats everything else as quaint or reactionary, is bound to hold up a distorting mirror to history. This does not mean that we ought never to go to the historical record, such as it is, in order to find out how something which interests us has evolved over time. When we ask about the development of Parliament or the evolution of steelmaking, we need make no anachronistic assumptions about the importance of Parliament to political society or the significance of steelmaking to the economy in earlier times. We distort history only when we assume that the things that interest or concern us had, or ought to have had, as much significance for our forebears; and we falsify history when we then proceed to judge men and societies by standards they never dreamt of observing and would have repudiated utterly had they been presented with the opportunity of making a choice between their standards and our own.

The values of past ages cannot be judged in this way. They are sacrosanct and beyond dispute because life at any time is its own justification. Life may be said to look to the future, at any particular moment, rather than remain imprisoned in the present, in the sense that the biological and evolutionary system is arranged so that each generation is responsible for the creation of its successor. But it does not look to the future in the sense that it finds its spiritual justification in the contribution it can make to the formation of that particular pattern of social organisation and that particular system of values which any one group of historians at any one phase of history happens to approve of and support. The conceit of supposing that the past culminates in the present afflicts economic historians even more than others, because as a result of twentieth-century material success, they can patronise the past, not only with hindsight and that confidence in their own moral standards which are the common prerogative of all historians but also with that sense of superiority with which the rich invariably contemplate the life of the poor.

This problem is presented to us in an acutely aggravated form by the question of markets and their relationship to freedom in the

Middle Ages. Markets occupied an altogether different position in the hierarchy of medieval social values from the exalted one to which we assign them today; and freedom meant something entirely alien to our ways of thinking. Indeed we can tell that there was something very different about medieval attitudes to markets by looking at their attitude to freedom. Acton's preoccupation with history as the story of how men struggled towards political liberty would have meant nothing to the reflective minds of the Middle Ages; and the idea that certain institutional arrangements, introduced then, may have laid the foundations for what we call our liberties, would have filled them with dismay. When medieval people spoke of freedom, particularly in connection with trade, they meant what we should mean by privilege. They meant a right, incorporated into a charter or engrossed in a licence, which emancipated a named person or institution from an obligation; or entitled such a person or institution to enjoy certain lucrative perquisites or advantages to the exclusion of everyone else. The freest man, according to medieval ways of reckoning such things, was the most privileged, according to modern Western ways of thinking.

When we look at the Middle Ages we must be prepared to see a world in which the words used are familiar but the ideas expressed are foreign to our experience and often uncongenial to us. We can see this fundamental difference of outlook in questions of what we call welfare. On the face of it, medieval governments were intensely concerned about the welfare of the commonwealth. No one can turn the pages of the statute book, or examine the petitions presented in Parliament and answered in the king's name, without being impressed by the constantly reiterated expressions of solicitude for those in want, by the endless and apparently anxious search for equity in the relationships of man with man, and by the unwavering determination of those in authority at every level to do whatever possible to provide conditions in which life could prosper for members of every social class and group. If we were to take such expressions of concern at face value we might be tempted to compare them with those made today and conclude that there was not much to choose between the social ideals of then and now.

But we should be quite wrong to do so. The Middle Ages were wholeheartedly committed to the belief that the classes in society should be preserved in their due separation. Indeed they went further than that. They were determined to preserve the commonwealth intact; and by the commonwealth the Middle Ages meant, not the sum total of all who lived in a certain area, nor even the sum total of all who dwelt within certain lordships and acknowledged, however indirectly, an allegiance to a particular sovereign prince or king. They meant the federation of those whom lordship itself linked with the king, wherever that lordship happened to be, at home or abroad. National frontiers, as we understand them, meant nothing to members of the commonwealth. Those who belonged were thoroughly cosmopolitan in lifestyle, in culture, in language, in family ties, and in personal loyalty and political allegiance. Xenophobia was strictly for the lower classes. To medieval ways of thinking, membership of the commonwealth depended, not upon having a soul to save or a home and livelihood where the king's writ ran but upon having a material and social stake in society. At bottom, the commonwealth consisted of those who possessed property and exerted influence. It consisted of what we should now call the establishment. And establishment attitudes to problems of welfare were, to say the least, pragmatic. Attitudes to the poor were, in fact, as ambivalent as they were to women. Poverty was not the intrinsically manageable problem it is now thought to be. Poverty was blessed; but it was also a huge, permanent and potentially overwhelming political problem. It was sensible, therefore, for the sake of peace here and salvation hereafter, to make some attempt, however perfunctory, to relieve an infinitesimal fraction of the poverty that seethed and pullulated all around, and prudent to remember that, fundamentally, poverty was, from a political point of view, a matter of law and order, and should always be treated as such. Like women, whom the Middle Ages saw as a diabolical blend of Eve the Temptress and Mary the Mother of God, the poor were a necessary evil, a perennial threat, and a fateful embodiment of prophetic truths.

It is entirely in keeping with this attitude to welfare that medieval society should not have condemned out of hand the use of money to solve all kinds of social problems and expedite all sorts of issues of policy which we have withdrawn from the market-place. In a society whose overriding purpose seems to have been to promote the interests of members of the establishment, patronage inevitably dominated the political scene. Patronage was largely a matter of mutual aid. But money had its part to play. Indeed the landed estates which supplied the material basis for personal influence and were the material reward for success in the power-game, had the important obligation of supporting the family and a miscellany of other dependants. The revenues of these estates were employed, accordingly, in a variety of ways which may strike us as, by turns, whimsical and culpable. For money ransomed prisoners of war, purged sins, and redeemed innumerable transgressions of the criminal law which we should not consider to have been properly punished without the public humiliation of the transgressor. Everything could be bought; or to put the matter more exactly, everything had a price and some part of that price could be paid in money. Justice could be bought: that is to say, either by purchase or other forms of suborning, courts of law could be made to work in the interests of those who had every reason to expect that their influence and authority entitled them to satisfaction when they submitted their disputes to the formal arbitrament of the law. By the same token, Church livings could be bought; even remission of taxation could be bought. Above all, licences and charters of various descriptions could be bought, authorising their possessors either to ignore bans and restrictions, or to impose them upon others, so as to limit access to lucrative sources of income and profitable occupations. And the work of those who superintended or merely assisted in the running of the administrative machinery that controlled and regulated the flow of demand and supply in this quarter of the service sector of the economy, that too could be bought; so that those who paid could dispatch their affairs, whilst those who could not, found themselves, like the suitor in Spencer's Mother Hubberd's Tale, condemned

> To fawn, to crouch, to wait, to ride, to run,
> To spend, to give, to want, to be undone.

It is indeed some measure of the strangeness, to modern ways of thinking, of medieval standards of behaviour and social custom, that whereas patronage was tolerated, if not sanctioned, in the Middle Ages, usury was universally deprecated and formally anathematised. The subsequent history of these two social institutions illustrates the capricious fate of moral imperatives; for the moral stature of usury has risen over the centuries as that of patronage has sunk. Banking now stands high in social esteem and the exercise of preference has been discredited, but like usury in the Middle Ages, not extirpated. If some medieval bankers managed to live down their disreputable and clandestine activities, that was usually because fortunes made by way of foreclosure soon matured into genteel acceptability as rapacious usurers concealed the shabby origins of their wealth in the county families they founded.

Loans which made money for the lender may have been condemned by canon and statute law. But at a period when reserves were pitifully small in relation to the risks undertaken, even by those who were engaged in pursuing the homeliest and most necessary occupations, large numbers of people who were neither so poor that no one in his right mind would lend them a penny except out of compassion, nor so rich that creditors fell over one another in their eagerness to be the one to do them a favour, found themselves in the hands of the moneylender. Indispensable though their services may have been, those who made some part of their living by lending were as morally opprobrious to the Middle Ages as landlords are today.

Did this mean that the Middle Ages ran short of loanable funds for investment purposes, and that many people starved or endured greater privation than necessary, because many of those who were affluent enough to be able to lend, felt they ought not to lend for gain and saw no point in taking a risk without making a profit? No doubt there were some who took this view and deprived the economy of investment capital thereby. But the dilemma of the usurer raises wider issues than that of usury, because it raises the perennial problem, for governments as well as for individuals, of reconciling theory with practice, of taking the hopelessly quixotic witness of the world's prophets and making political or personal sense of it. The world's work must be done despite the shrill vociferations of its ideologues. Whenever their extravagant demands and apocalyptic hopes have been seriously heeded, the world about them has either dissolved into an anarchy of unappeasably conflicting idolatries, or rigidified into some sort of social crustacean.

Medieval merchants were peculiarly vulnerable to attack, because the climate of opinion, in the Middle Ages, was not favourable to those who made profits or accumulated wealth from trade. The acquisitive appetites, however, continued to be active enough, in those centuries, to earn their rating as a popular theme of pulpit communication. And the evidence certainly shows that medieval people needed no tutelage in the handling of economic affairs. The king's preoccupation with commerce as a source of revenue, or as a weapon of economic warfare, does not mean that medieval kings were 'innocents abroad' where money-making was concerned. Politics are about sharing, not creating, wealth, so that records of political activities are bound to give a misleading impression of royal attitudes to commerce. In fact when medieval kings saw a good thing, such as the potentialities of the tin-mining industry, they responded unhesitatingly to its needs. In effect they suspended the feudal system for the sake of tin miners so as to attract labour to the mining areas, promote output, and thus swell the harvest of taxes that they cropped from this source. And others acted in like manner when occasion offered, Churchmen with no less enthusiasm and alacrity than the laity, founding towns as speculations in real estate, promoting colonisation by conceding preferential terms for initial periods of tenure, procuring charters for markets, and so forth. Even when we find that, beyond a certain point, medieval people seem to have lost interest in the kind of sedulous devotion to hard work that was later to be propagated as a sacramental duty, they may well have done so, not because they lacked tenacity or even because they felt some compunction about profit-making, but because they saw very clearly that, in an economic environment in which marriage and patronage were far more likely, at every level of society, to further their ambitions than the most pertinacious application to their callings, they would be much better employed in devoting themselves to those commercially sound, but in the narrower sense, uncommercial activities in which the comparative return to effort was greater.

Nevertheless merchants found themselves in a dilemma in the Middle Ages which was none of their making. What they did was useful and even necessary; and sooner or later everyone in the community discovered for himself that this was so. But their occupation was suspect and its rewards were disreputable. This may not have worried some men. But is it not possible that social disapprobation acted as a brake upon enterprise and effectually constrained merchants who might otherwise have thrown themselves uninhibitedly into their work, with incalculable consequences for market forms and marketing techniques?

This may seem to be a curious construction to put upon the meaning of the concept of freedom in the context of markets; but social constraints, though intangible, are often decisive. And the moral dilemma of the merchant was shared in the Middle Ages by many others. It was shared, for example, by Churchmen. Success had transformed the Church from a struggling, penniless band of outcasts into a dominant authority of inconceivable affluence and incomparable power. Its organization and leadership called for administrative and political talent of the highest quality. Those to whom the running of this extraordinary institution was entrusted were under some sort of compulsion to conduct the business side of things as well as they could. When they did so, they conducted the business of the Church in ways of which we heartily approve because they are the ways in which we believe that business must be done if it is to be done as well as possible. But doing the work in this fashion meant transgressing many of the canons by which priests of the Church and dignitaries of the ecclesiastical establishment were supposed to conduct themselves. Doing it in any other way meant clearer consciences for them, perhaps, but loss and vexation for the immortal institution of which they were only briefly honoured trustees.

Nowhere in medieval history can we see the relentless pressure of this dilemma more vividly depicted than in the history of the Church. Throughout its medieval history, the conduct of those who governed the Church and carried out its spiritual obligations, provoked successive reform movements whose inspiration was the wrathful indignation expressed by contemporary critics with what was done in the name of the Church by its leaders. These reform movements are undoubtedly some measure of the compromises that temptations of flesh and spirit betrayed such leaders into making. But recurrent efforts to restore the church to a pristine purity of conduct and purpose which, even in the segregation and placidity of the monastic round, it invariably failed to sustain, indicate that what was being pursued was not so much an ideal as a chimera. Consequently these reform movements are more significant than they would have been even if they had really stood for nothing more than the periodic revolt of public opinion against the excesses of self-indulgent or self-seeking careerists. They are in fact some measure of the compromises that unworkable ideologies forced upon a succession of more or less able men who neither rose very high above nor sank very far beneath the common level of humanity in matters of morality and responsibility, and who were saddled with the problem of reconciling the realities of business and politics with the uncompromising doctrines of which they were at once the custodians and the appointed exponents.

Did considerations such as these deter men of the highest moral integrity from accepting posts of responsibility in the Church, so that as a result of the radiant spirituality of its message, the Church was condemned to dependence upon men of inferior moral stature for its leadership?

Commerce and politics, however, were not the only indispensable social activities for which the Church had no decent and honourable place in its scheme of things. Marriage was another; and the history of medieval attitudes to marriage may provide us with a clue to the way in which ordinary men and women came to terms with the forbidding austerities of doctrines which seemed to condemn everything that made life possible as well as pleasurable or even tolerable. In an ecclesiastical system served by a priesthood dedicated by the most solemn vows to invincible ignorance of the married state, and neurotically obsessed by the idea of chastity to the point of believing and inculcating the belief that propagating the species was irrevocably tainted by concupiscence, marriage was inevitably judged to be a second-best state for spiritually second-rate people. This belief haunted some married people just as the spiritually-defiling activities associated with commerce haunted some merchants. Those who renounced marriage, or commerce, for a life consecrated to prayer and self-denial, were rapturously applauded. Those who did not but felt that they should have done so, led profoundly troubled lives, knowing that they were jeopardising their souls by succumbing to temptations which better men had been able to resist. Those who repented of their lives in this way often revealed their afflicted consciences in their wills. But theirs was not the normal reaction. The majority of married people, like the majority of merchants, made dispositions of their effects which, without casuistry or hypocrisy, betrayed no hint of remorse for their status in society and expressed no desire to make reparation for their choice. And they were able to live and die with pride in the dignity of the social positions they occupied because pragmatic Churchmen knew that social necessity had a stronger claim than abstract doctrine. 'In my father's house are many mansions' may not have been a notably popular text for medieval theologians; but it was, perforce, a commonplace theme of medieval ecclesiastical policy.

The problem of accommodating ideals to the realities of daily life creates difficulties for any society which lays down strict rules about human behaviour based on a flagrant misreading of human nature. We know these difficulties today as well as they knew them in the Middle Ages. They are the difficulties, for example, that we all have with competitive theory. Competition requires that governments should hold the ring not the whip hand; that consumers should be collectively sovereign but individually devoid of bargaining power in the market; that factors of production should be valued at prices which reflect their scarcity and opportunity costs; that foreign trade should be altogether unimpeded; that all prices, including interest and exchange rates, should be allowed to fluctuate freely so as to clear the market. But conditions such as these carry ingenuousness to the far limit of political recklessness and absurdity. Strictly adhered to, competitive conditions will inevitably, in the course of time and change, sacrifice all coherent groups and interests, all associations of workers and employers, all party machines with their commitment to particular regions, particular industries, or particular classes, and will do so, perhaps, at the dictation of consumers in remote markets who are no less indifferent to, than they are oblivious of, the social and political consequences elsewhere of their vagaries of taste and changes of need. A government which was heedless of these consequences could not hope to last. Competition in the market-place can be a recipe for disaster in the polling booths, if not at the barricades. Hence in the last analysis all governments are mercantilist and protectionist, however rugged the creed of individualism they may preach, because governments cannot afford to offend their supporters even when the interests of their supporters run counter to the interests of the community at large.

At the political level, the modern problem is somewhat different from the medieval one. Modern governments with their commitment to economic growth, find, nevertheless, that they cannot hope to survive unless they make concessions to political realities which may render nugatory their best efforts to achieve what they acknowledge to be one of their highest purposes. Medieval governments had the same problem in reverse. They had to find a place for market operations which gave far more latitude to those who worked in the market-place, and to those who used the services offered there, than a strict interpretation of what the Church said about such things would have allowed or a strict adherence to those social ideals which required everyone to know his place and keep to it, would have conceded.

At the personal level, the problem is always the same. Those who touch pitch, said Innocent III, must defile themselves. But how is pitch to be handled if everyone who could handle it is so fastidious, so spiritually self-absorbed, so careless of the social consequences of not handling it, so deficient, in fact, in the ordinary social virtues, that no one with the necessary skill or flair is to be found who is prepared to tackle the degrading work of coping with the practicalities of organising and running society, because work of that kind contaminates the soul? Moreover, those who find themselves, for whatever reason, pitchforked into such morally risky occupations, inevitably fall prey to censure and misrepresentation, however honourably they endeavour to conduct themselves, because the rules are not devised with these occupations in mind. Consequently it is easy to find fault with those who are successful in such occupations because those who are successful are bound to have broken the rules.

Some of the best minds of the Middle Ages struggled with this problem. But not all of those with extensive experience of practical affairs shared Innocent III's dark thoughts about it. According to his first biographer, Anselm saw no difficulty, for any man whose conduct was wholly governed by what he knew to be right, in reconciling the demands of the spirit with the demands of the world. Perhaps there was no problem for him. But even Anselm had to be forced to accept promotion; and when asked to explain how a man dedicated to the life of the spirit could be expected to cope with the business affairs which promotion brought with it, took refuge in the sort of foolish allegory that achieves its effect by assuming away the problem to be solved.[1]

For many people, however, in the Middle Ages as at other times, the problems of conduct raised by the official canon were problems created by the canon rather than by their conduct. Authorised social values are always a poor fit because society is infinitely more complex than its prophets and analysts allow for. Such values invariably need modifying and supplementing therefore, informally if not otherwise, so as to allow for the kind of problems that it never occurred to those who formulated the rules to take account of. And those who live by other rules than those laid down in the official canon, compensate themselves for the sense of alienation they might otherwise feel, and screen themselves from the pain and humiliation to which they might otherwise be exposed, by forming themselves into unacknowledged coteries, closed societies perhaps, silent passive-resistance movements, within which they can keep one another in countenance by providing comfort and recognition for all who think or behave as they do. Consequently society is divisible not only by class but also by groupings which cut across the lines of class and turn society, from that point of view, into a federation of what are tantamount to freemasonries whose bond, in every case, is common problems and experiences; and whose conventions of behaviour are those that are accepted and respected by everyone who values his association with others of his kind.

The Jews were a special case in the Middle Ages; but they were also an extreme example of this kind of functional bond. They were able to specialise very profitably in usury, by forming an irredentist group in society, since their values made them utterly indifferent to local standards of conduct, and local beliefs and inhibitions, wherever they found themselves in Christian Europe. Eventually, this indifference and their incorrigibly alien behaviour and outlook made them intolerable nearly everywhere within that region. But other groups, which had evolved out of shared Christian traditions and common racial origins, were able to thrive in conditions which, in the end, defeated the Jews, who had formed ganglions of unassimilable irritation in a social system which was simply incapable of accommodating their flagrantly antagonistic values.

Those who married, in a society which, at the highest level of spirituality, spoke slightingly of marriage, formed the largest movement of passive resistance of all, and were able to offer support and reassurance, more perhaps by example than by any other means, to everyone who, by marrying, found himself at odds with the central orthodoxy of a Church which made contemptuous provision for those who were too frail in body and mind to abjure marriage in favour of a more exalted and ennobling condition. Those who enabled society to accomplish a simulacrum of its political purposes instead of running into the sands, as it assuredly would have done if they had heeded Anselm's advice, were able to turn to others of their kind for consolation and strength when they were publicly traduced for their failure to adhere to the abstract stipulations of the currently fashionable writers of didactic treatises and manipulators of scriptural theorems. And those who transacted the commercial business of society could protect themselves from the dangerously isolated and vulnerable position in which their work often placed them, by forming those associations with which we are all so familiar, and which, from this point of view, were not so much conspiracies against the public as refuges from an uncomprehending and hostile world.

Unless we postulate the existence of a whole series of sub-groups in society we shall find it very hard to explain how men and women, who lived in a social system which explicitly discountenanced so many of the necessary and wholesome activities of mankind, were able to defy the system, not furtively and shamefully, but with confidence and dignity. Indeed it would be straining credulity to the limit to claim for the Middle Ages that human behaviour was so profoundly affected by the formal doctrines of the Church that markets and the men who served them were radically altered in character as a result of the pervasive influence of the refined spirituality of those centuries. On the contrary, the most striking features of the economic institutions of medieval life is how like they were to those that we find both earlier and also later in European history. There seems to have been a sort of timelessness about the basic conditions of life over a very long period of history, a fundamental sterility, or perhaps, an immovable torpor, which seems to have set firm limits to what economic development could achieve and militates against the notion that medieval spirituality emasculated the economic potential of the times.

Thus the horse was the fastest means of communication, as the ox was the most powerful source of traction, in Julius Caesar's time as it was in Napoleon's. Before the canal age, conditions on roads and rivers had remained virtually unchanged since men had first colonised the region. Only the building of bridges had marked a significant advance; and that advance had been made earlier rather than late in historical times. By the Middle Ages we hear much about the inadequacy of bridges; hardly at all about the want of bridges. Coast trade is a closed book to historians. Foreign trade is not. But we learn nothing from the records of foreign trade which might lead us to suppose that there were any revolutionary improvements in shipbuilding or manning levels; merely the adaptations required as trade patterns shifted marginally.

The striking fact about communications systems in these centuries is that they do not develop. And their failure to develop is symptomatic of a deeper changelessness. Transport costs enter into all costs. Societies which cannot reduce transport costs are condemned to a regimen of narrow markets and restricted growth.

We see this narrowness and the restrictions, so far as medieval conditions are concerned, in the organisation and structure of medieval business. Both in technology and organisation, the making of commodities based on the commonest materials, such as wool, leather, iron and wood, was carried on then, and until comparatively recent times, in ways which would have been familiar to craftsmen and business men of the classical age. Farming techniques are notoriously slower to change than business techniques; consequently once the iron plough had displaced the wooden, we should hardly be surprised to learn that the farmer's round and the farmer's tools knew scarcely any improvement until market changes in the seventeenth century enabled the more enterprising farmers to suppress the fallow and embark upon a course of continuous and often rapid development.

The astonishing immutability of the established usages of economic life was reflected, as it was bound to be, in the social structure. Whether we examine Domesday Book or the sumptuary legislation of the mid-fourteenth century; whether we look ahead to the survey that Thomas Wilson drew up in 1600, or further forward still, to the calculations made by Gregory King in 1695, when times really were beginning to stir; we cannot help being struck more forcibly by the similarities than by the differences to be found in the social structure revealed in these very diverse compilations.[2]

Naturally there are difficulties about comparing surveys made for very different purposes and separated by a gap of centuries from one another. Nevertheless the broad conclusions to be drawn from such a comparison can scarcely be in doubt. At all these periods the social hierarchy was dominated by a landed aristocracy supported by a squirearchy. Merchants occupied only a minor and subsidiary place in this company. One reason for this was that the merchant disappeared in the gentleman as soon as wealth permitted men of business to acquire gentility. But the principal reason was that the profits of trade made few great fortunes in these centuries, and that manufacturing made fewer still. Manufacturers formed no separate class in a world in which even the biggest of them merely exercised financial dominion over a series of small-scale enterprises organised on the basis of the putting-out of work. Putting-out meant low entry costs for industry, and low entry costs meant low profit margins.

Below these ranks, and sometimes in parallel with the wealthier merchants, came the lesser landed families, followed by several classes of tenant-farmers, some more independent and perhaps more affluent than the rest. In feudal times these classes included villeins and cottars with unique features about their terms of tenure which we do not find later. When we examine these terms, however, we find that they were so very varied in practice that it is often impossible to distinguish them from terms of tenure by lease or by copy of the manorial court roll; and that even when these terms really meant that villeins and cottars were actually being called upon to serve their lords as labourers, we find that they were not usually being depended on for skilled regular work on their landlords' farms, but merely for supplementary assistance.[3]

How much of this supplementary assistance they provided in their own persons we cannot tell. But below the level of the landed peasantry spreads the incalculable mass of the landless. The landless have virtually no history because historical records are almost exclusively preoccupied with the affairs of those with property. Even poll-taxes pass them by in silence because the landless are too poor to pay taxes. They emerge in later centuries because they arouse the curiosity of statisticians or the concern of poor-law administrators. But they are new only to history when they emerge in this way; they are not new as a social phenomenon. We can get some measure of their social significance in the Middle Ages at one moment only. It is at the moment when the Black Death devastated the English countryside. We can calculate the mounting toll of deaths by counting the succession of new tenants as they register their occupation of suddenly vacated holdings. Vacancies were nearly all filled, however; and vacancies went on being filled, without great difficulty, for a generation after the first visitation of the Black Death, despite subsequent visitations of comparable virulence. That they were filled is surely a tribute to the size of the reserve army of the landless, thanks to whom landlords were able to maintain their estates and their profits more or less intact until, and indeed in many cases, for some time after, the Peasants' Revolt. It was to this abject class of destitutes, moreover, that villeins and cottars presumably turned for help when they were called upon to fulfil their more laborious tenurial obligations, deputing them to do, for a pittance, the farm work they were reluctant to do in person.[4]

If the medieval countryside had indeed been choked with people as the Black Death evidence suggests that it was, then it would be wrong to think of the social structure as an edifice reared upon foundations of lesser smallholders. In a community with so many landless families, there was, presumably, throughout England, an even more extended social hierarchy in the village than the one that Dr Razi has revealed at Halesowen.[5] Villeins with full virgate-sized holdings formed a peasant aristocracy which looked down its nose at rung after rung of social inferiors, terminating at the bottom, not with cottagers, but with an even less-favoured group which doubtless even the cottagers could despise. Poverty in such circumstances was severe and incorrigible, being reflected in terms of tenure for land which left even the most favourably-placed villeins with much less of the net product of their farms than the size of their holdings might lead one to suppose that they enjoyed.

In England, before the Black Death, landlordism was not the cause of peasant poverty. Nor can landlordism take the blame for the narrowness of the markets patronised by the overwhelming mass of the people. Landlordism was the inevitable result of the conditions that prevailed at the time. Land reform is the cry of political activists throughout history. But land reform is always foredoomed because wherever the call is for changes in the laws of tenure, for the cancellation of indebtedness and for the redistribution of the land, reformers inevitably find, whenever they have dispossessed the landlord, that the sub-marginal peasant remains.

Seen in this light, feudalism was not, as it is so often made out to have been, a repressive system imposed upon the social structure, creating an environment in which everything conspired to obstruct development and paralyse enterprise. It was simply one of the forms that landlordism, particularly military landlordism, took when pressure on the land created scarcities that the social structure was bound to reflect. Consequently when certain prominent features of feudalism decayed, as they did in the fifteenth century, when pressure relaxed as a result of the Black Death, they did so because landlordism was temporarily on the defensive. By the end of that century, however, the Black Death had begun to lose its virulence. Thereafter feudalism was partially restored; and landlordism came back in strength; thus demonstrating that feudalism as a system of oppression was either unnecessary or unenforceable: unnecessary when land shortage dominated social relationships, and unenforceable when it did not. Serfdom, defined as a specific condition rather than used as a synonym for a state of general dependence or subjugation, only succeeded in shackling people when they had been immobilised for other reasons. And in the sixteenth century, landlords found other ways, or other names for traditional ways, in which to assert a power which they owed to circumstances and not to themselves.

The limitations upon development that we see illustrated in these various ways imposed severe restrictions upon the range and scope of markets. Patterns of expenditure are determined by the distribution of income; and markets can do very little to work those miracles of liberation, with which they are credited by certain modern social thinkers, when prevailing conditions narrowly circumscribe variations in the distribution of income. These conditions, with one or two notable but temporary intermissions, endured for a very long time. For how long it is impossible to say. Historians make it harder than it need be for us to appreciate the timelessness of this phase of human experience because, if they are to hold children from play and old men from the chimney corner, they must depict the past as a drama, with movement, crisis and denouement. It is no accident that the word crisis, once the prerogative of the newspaper-headline writer, should have been borrowed by the historian who now features it quite regularly as the integrating theme of his narrative. The headline writer uses the word in order to arrest the reader's attention. At the heart of every successful news story lies a drama. Much the same is true of memorable stories about the past. But the urge to tell the story of the past so as to give evolutionary significance to everything that happens can easily tempt the historian into concealing the fact that many things can change without anything developing.

Strictly speaking, therefore, there can be no economic history of this long period, only an economic analysis of its prevailing features and a diary of events. The rise and fall of empires, the irrevocable disruption, through schism, of the institutions of ecclesiasticism, even the advent of radically new fashions in thought, seem to have made little impression on a succession of social systems in which farms, variously known as villas, colonates and manors, were fundamentally indistinguishable from one another in structure and operation. And the testimony of historians to the contrary, is bound to leave the reader nervously exhausted by a succession of inconclusive dramatic climaxes when he finds, after centuries of evolution, that society, at bottom, looks very much the same at the end as it had done at the beginning; when he finds, for example, that the peasants of Hardy's Wessex lived lives which differed only superficially from the lives lived by their forebears in Alfred's Wessex.

Society is always local in such circumstances. At best it may be federal. Consequently loyalties are usually circumscribed by family and lordship rather than enlarged by remoter allegiances to church and state. Politically, therefore, Europe in these centuries consisted of a congeries of tribal or near-tribal groups organised into a dissolving succession of wider, mainly dynastic, federations, and interspersed by city-states. Conquest sometimes extended the area of political control. But empires rarely survived their creators. Rome was the exception in this, not the rule. It was lucky in its timing as Napoleon was in his. It expanded into a political void, as Napoleon did. And it was lucky in having internal lines of communication. Its empire was organised round the perimeter of an inland sea. With the fall of the western Roman empire, the secret of empire-building in western Europe passed from the territorial successors of Rome to the Christian church, which maintained its universal dominion by taking the city-state as its model and spiritualising it into the diocese.

Naturally there were exceptional periods when social relationships were disrupted. Usually such periods are associated with population movements such as the Barbarian invasions or the Black Death. Subsequently traditional relationships reassert themselves; and when we can once more examine and analyse society we find that the realities of social life have not changed, however different the names of things may be.

The markets that characterised this long phase of human development were of two main types. One was local in range and narrow in provenance. The other was cosmopolitan and sophisticated. Inevitably these two main types of market interacted. In particular, they interacted when the products of local farming or industry entered into international trade. And the best-attested case of this is the medieval English wool trade.

The average medieval sheep yielded about $1\frac{1}{2}$ lbs of wool. This meant that it took 243 sheep to fill a sack of wool weighing 364 lbs. At the height of the wool export trade some 30,000 sacks went abroad annually. This required the wool of over seven and a quarter million sheep. Only the very largest landed estates kept flocks which produced as much as 50 sacks of wool. Canterbury Cathedral Priory, one of the biggest of them, with about 14,000 sheep in the early fourteenth century, could and did. But there were very few estates in Canterbury's league. This meant that the export trade had to call on the resources of smaller farmers. To possess 200 sheep marked you out as a man of substance in most medieval social circles. But the wool of 200 sheep would not fill a sack. The export trade obviously had to reach deep into the farming community for its huge requirements. And the export trade was only one part of the wool trade. Everyone wore woollen clothing even though many wore only second-hand clothing. Clearly local farmers of humble status were making their tiny contributions, perhaps no more than a few pounds-weight at a time, through their local markets, to the huge tribute of wool that went abroad to pay for the food, drink, clothing, ornaments and the like, that diverted the tedium of life for the landed classes, or went elsewhere within the country to be made up into cloth for domestic consumption.[6]

Historians are always tempted to welcome any commercial influence that reaches into the recesses of the marketing system as an earnest of better things to come. But any exchange is not necessarily better than none. The landed classes whose needs were the main impetus behind foreign trade, and hence behind the most powerful of the forces linking local trade with regional and even national trade, generated these forces by spending the rents that deprived those who paid them of the means with which to bid for goods and services in local markets. Dispossessing the landowning classes, if such an idea had occurred to anyone in ancient and medieval times, would not have proved to be the panacea that generations of more recent reformers have seen it to be, because the fundamental problem of mass poverty caused by high rents must be traced to the insatiable propensity of populations of every species to fill any area favourable to its occupation.

Trade raises productivity by way of specialisation and thus undoubtedly creates more wealth than it destroys. But in these periods transport costs severely limited the gains from trade. Moreover in conditions of labour abundance any gains from the specialisation of labour enriched neither the labourers nor their employers, nor even perhaps their employers' suppliers, all of whom competed for work on the keenest terms. Somewhere along the chain of supply certain international merchants competed on less onerous terms and took a greater share of the gains than they might otherwise have done, and certainly a greater share than ever fell to the regrators, forestallers and engrossers of notorious repute in internal markets. But there was enough competition even in the handling trade to ensure that a very great deal, if not most, of the gains of trade were garnered by those who entered the market as final consumers. In short, the spending of their incomes from rent did more for those who enjoyed the right to receive rents than for anyone else.

Thus for all the glamour of its achievements, long-distance trade, like so much else that was done for the landed classes, could do no more for the substantive development of successive economic systems than the building industry, whose most glamorous products also dominate our recollections of the outstanding achievements of past societies. Cathedrals were technologically the most sophisticated products of medieval industrial enterprise. Yet the skills developed by those who worked in the industry, the employment provided, even the product itself were, like the skills, employment and products of international trade, without beneficial ramifications for economies which were choked with labour, and in which, therefore, rent charges dominated income distribution.

It is for this reason, perhaps, that wherever we look in the historical record we find societies, otherwise primitive and even stagnant economically, which nevertheless supported a trading and even an industrial system as advanced as any to be found in the most progressive regions of Europe on the eve of the Industrial Revolution. Elaborate specialisation of function in producing hand-mirrors and similar baubles was, so far as we can tell, commonplace in Roman Italy. Trade routes which traversed ocean and desert, negotiated high mountain passes and marched across endless plains, were to be found in virtually all such societies. And we know from the detailed evidence that survives from the Middle Ages that such routes were used by merchants of many races and creeds; that freights were financed and insured by bankers whose methods of business would have excited the admiration of their nineteenth-century counterparts; and that goods were carried by ships and in caravans which ran scheduled services and achieved punctual delivery times at a multiplicity of markets and fairs throughout Europe and the Middle and Far East. But the extraordinary achievements of such international marketing ventures did nothing to rescue them from ultimate sterility.[7]

Wherever we find such hurryings and scurryings on behalf of the landed classes, we also find that urban development follows. Historical interest in markets had recently been supplemented by the study of towns. But the towns that grew out of a rack-rented countryside owed their development, if not their origins, to the same forces that created and promoted spectacular trade routes and the intricately specialised products that travelled along them. Some of these towns succeeded in swelling to monstrous dimensions; and historians are naturally tempted to see in them, as in other evidence of economic maturity, intimations of future achievement, engines of economic growth, milestones along the hard road down which economic progress had to be made. But the interest of all these developments for historians is to be found, surely, in precisely the opposite sense: in their sterile precocity, their absolute failure to carry any lesson or influence beyond the enclave to which they owed their existence, and also in their extraordinary capacity to reassert themselves whenever conditions favoured them. The reason why so much of the economic history of these ages gives the reader a sense of *déjà vu* is just because successive societies, however unrelated culturally or in other ways, seem to have been able to reproduce the skills of the long-distant merchant and the expertise of the specialist manufacturer, without borrowing or inheritance; and to have been able to build and run the huge towns from which such men so often operated with equal success wherever we find them.

The purchasing power that made possible these prodigies of commercial organisation did not depend exclusively upon the wealth of the landed classes. It also depended upon governments, because governments enter the commercial system as buyers in every age. And the bigger the political units controlled by governments, the wider the catchment area for taxation and the richer the government buyer. It is easy to understand why the Roman empire could build on such a prodigious scale. There was plenty of money from extensive imperial resources for investment in public grandeur. In the Middle Ages only the Church comprehended a realm of imperial dimensions. And it is easy to understand why the Church was able to out-build everyone else. Compulsory tribute flowed in from all parts of the Western world; and compulsory tribute was lavishly supplemented by voluntary contributions. Secular kingdoms, in the Middle Ages, could not spend on this scale. The incorrigible fragmentation of political society that was characteristic of the time meant that there were many governments rather than just a few, so that none controlled large resources. This curtailed foreign policy; for in the Middle Ages government stood, more than for anything else, for the pursuit of objectives abroad. At a time when the regions of Europe were all locked in a timeless vicious circle of low productivity, narrow markets, high rents and endless servitude, what else was there for governments to do? Domestic policy meant dispensing patronage to allies and friends and keeping the mass of the peasantry docile by treating welfare mainly as a problem of law and order. Everyone who could, gave alms. But sensible men knew the problem was not a simple one of maldistribution of resources, and gave alms, as we have seen, partly as an insurance against insurrection, and partly as a pledge of redemption in the world to come.

Curtailing foreign policy meant curtailing war. Despite its reputation, therefore, the Middle Ages was a period during which war was far less disruptive of peaceful pursuits than it could have been, at contemporary levels of technology, in different political circumstances. Countries had to be big before wars could be seriously destructive. Where countries were small, governments quickly ran out of money and hence out of men. When small countries, such as England and France were in the fourteenth century, attempted to fight a big war, they promptly went bankrupt, and having bankrupted everyone who might be able to lend them the money required for the prosecution of a big war, found themselves compelled to fight more modest wars thereafter. Exceptional wealth, as in the Italian city-states, was undoubtedly a substitute for size: wealthy communities could hire mercenaries in a world in which men were cheap. But this was unusual. During the Middle Ages, therefore, there were many small wars rather than few big ones. Long periods of peace were unknown because such periods required the undisputed ascendancy over wide regions of a single political power, such as Rome. Until trouble began to brew beyond the imperial frontiers, Rome maintained an order which was only broken when members of the ruling class, having destroyed all possible external opposition, fell out with one another. The multiplication of centres of political power, in the Middle Ages, set the stage for centuries of frequent wars but limited warfare.

Armies could still do a good deal of damage, however, notwithstanding the medieval limitations upon their size and strength. But damage, from an economic point of view, ought to be measured, not in terms of lives lost or capital destroyed, but in terms of the recuperative power of the social and economic system. Technology has been neutral, in this respect, more often than we always appreciate, because improvements in the means of destruction at the disposal of combatants, which have an immediate impact, are often accompanied by improvements in the means available to those who have to make good the damage done once the war is over, which may be just as important but not so obvious. In the Middle Ages, however, technology was neutral because improvements made in the techniques of fighting were not such as to make wars more destructive than they had been in earlier times. Other considerations were more important. The high level of self-sufficiency that spelt poverty for the mass of the people had the dubious advantage that it limited the dislocation that war could cause. And the low level of capital formation characteristic of such societies meant that there was very little to destroy. Scarcity, in such matters, makes everything there is correspondingly more precious. But there was nothing that men could not quickly replace. Manpower was the easiest of all to replace: there was no shortage of men. Homes, and therefore whole villages, could be rebuilt virtually overnight.[8] Oxen for ploughs, and seed-corn, were more difficult. But the records certainly convey the impression that recovery was never long delayed. When Edward III decided to keep the Scotch border quiet by devastating the countryside round about, he found that he could only do so by returning again and again to the area so as to keep recovery in check. The campaigns of 1334/5 and 1336, had to be followed up, therefore, by those of 1346 and 1356.[9] When the French attacked the leading towns on the south coast of England, in the fourteenth century, they were unable to check recovery in this way. Southampton, for example, was so seriously damaged by a Franco-Genoese fleet in October 1338 that the Italians, whose trade was vital to the port, took themselves off to Bristol until repairs, or the pacification of Italian fears, brought them back by the summer of 1341. With their return Southampton's trade, so far as we can measure it in the export figures, returned to normal.[10]

Effective contemporary propaganda, particularly in the form of French accounts of the devastation wrought by English armies in later fourteenth-century France, doubtless encourages us to believe that war could inflict permanent, or at any rate, serious material damage upon society. But if the evidence seems to show that it was unlikely to have been able to do so, because medieval warfare was generally small-scale and inconclusive, what the evidence cannot so easily show is the destruction of confidence that warfare can bring about. Confidence is harder to repair than homes. Those who spread fear and demoralisation, and thus increase the element of risk in holding markets and venturing capital in commercial enterprises, do far more damage than those who merely swoop and destroy without leaving their pray with lingering suspicions that they are able to return at will and do as much again. William the Conqueror's 'Harrying of the North' was clearly much more successful as a triumph of personality than as a punishment for insurgency.[11] And in medieval conditions it may very well have been the case that local violence, and even perhaps neighbourhood disturbances, particularly when these were the result of organised feuding, could prove to be more damaging to economic life than formal warfare, in which armies so often consisted of little more than the combined retinues of their aristocratic leaders, and military operations were so often confined to casual skirmishing and raiding, that we are hardly justified in raising the manoeuvrings that took place to the dignity of campaigns.

Organised feuding was certainly a central fact of what we should nowadays deprecate as the hooliganism of the landed classes. When asked, by a nineteenth-century English traveller, how they spent their money, a Druze emir replied: 'we spend it on injuring one another'.[12] His reply would have appealed to representative members of the landed classes throughout medieval Europe. Nevertheless the disruptive effects of warfare, and of the anarchy created by warfare in its more informal manifestations as brigandage, piracy and feuding, were severely limited. Nothing illustrates this fact more vividly than the pattern of medieval political geography. According to that pattern England was the most progressive region in Europe, if we measure such things in terms of modern standards of nationhood; and the city-states were the most reactionary or even anachronistic elements in the political scene. Nowhere else in Europe did geography confer such advantages upon government as it did in England, where the land was flat, the area was small and compact, and the frontiers were sharply defined by the sea, if not always protected by it from the depredations of powerful neighbours. Offa's Dyke, completed at a time when England was far from unification, shows how important well-defined frontiers were thought to be, even then, by demonstrating what laborious efforts were made to secure them against the pinpricks of a weak neighbour.

These geographical advantages made it possible for the kings of England to wield immense power. Their control of the political and fiscal system was impressively effective and matured extraordinarily early. Abroad, medieval England had the reputation of dealing harshly with its kings. Perhaps Englishmen had to take their kings seriously because they were so much more powerful than rulers were elsewhere. Certainly English kings held by an unsecured tenancy. Between Hastings and Bosworth there were 19 of them, of whom no fewer than eight were either murdered or died, some in mysterious circumstances, as did William II, others just in time to avoid another sort of end, as did John. But they locked the social system together by providing the social hierarchy with a pinnacle and regulated the flow of patronage by redistributing the counters when they fell out of play. Nor was there anything factitious about their grip on English political life. The effective size of a political system can be measured by the degree of disintegration that sets in during periods of stress. When civil war broke out in England, the central institutions held firm. In France the story was very different. France was not merely England's nearest European neighbour; it was also, of all European countries, the one which was closest to England in political development. Yet in France civil war tore the country apart. Ireland, Scotland and Wales were always problem areas for England, but these were peripheral regions. Resistance to central authority in France often originated in the French heartlands.

Now this precocity in matters political might be thought to favour precocity in commercial and industrial affairs. Getting the political conditions right may not be a sufficient condition for economic advance; but, according to modern views on development, it is certainly a necessary one. England, to all appearances, fulfilled this condition in the Middle Ages. Did this in fact give England the edge over its rivals? To this question we are bound to give the answer that it did not. England may have been advanced politically, in the Middle Ages, according to modern ideas of political progress; but the most sophisticated commercial systems and the most highly developed industrial organisations were to be found where the political system accorded with classical notions of polity, namely in the city-states of northern Italy, the Low Countries and Germany, where the largest aggregations of mercantile wealth known to the Middle Ages were to be found. Quite obviously political fragmentation did not inhibit the growth of international banking; nor did it hinder the development of immensely successful industrial enterprises, particularly in clothmaking, based on extensive division of labour, long credits, distant markets and international raw material supplies.

What makes this evidence all the more relevant to the question at issue is the fact that, although the medieval world may have reproduced the city-state that was so familiar to classical times, it utterly failed to reproduce the comprehensive imperial control that gave the Roman city-state its incomparable distinction. In fact these medieval city-states, far from working together, or even tolerating one another, were constantly at one another's throats. Nor was that all. So far as a medieval city-state was concerned, all trade beyond its frontiers was foreign trade; and foreign trade, in the Middle Ages, was trade carried on virtually beyond the power of political authority. There was, it is true, an international law, rudimentary and undeveloped though it may have been. And there were treaties between powers. But, at bottom, retaliation was the only effective weapon to hand.

Nevertheless, as we can tell from many sources, difficult liquids like wine, bulky and delicate cargoes like wool, precious spices and textiles, metals, dyes, foodstuffs and an infinitely varied miscellany of other things, travelled regularly and extensively, by land and sea, throughout the Middle Ages, in war and peace, during periods when piracy and brigandage are said to have been rife and in quieter times. We can gauge how regular such travel could be by examining England's unique archive of foreign trade statistics. Such travel was not without risk, and hence cost; and such costs compounded all the other uncertainties of foreign trade: uncertainties about the reliability of ships and carts, about markets, about the condition of goods upon arrival at their destinations, about credit, about the foreign exchanges, about taxation, about commission agents, about the safety of goods which might be seized by foreign governments in retaliation for harm done to their citizens abroad, or in payment of debts incurred by fellow-merchants who shared nothing but a common nationality with those who were embroiled as a result of wrongs for which they bore no personal responsibility.

None of this appears to have inhibited the development of foreign trade in the Middle Ages, which changed direction and went through a variety of evolutionary phases that seem to indicate that the luxury markets with which the city-states were exclusively concerned were virtually unaffected by risk and uncertainty. Despite their extraordinarily elaborate specialisation, and hence dependence upon others, medieval city-states were able to cope with interruptions of flows of trade which ought to have played havoc with profits calculated on the basis of assumptions about prices to be paid for supplies and prices to be obtained for products, some of which had travelled from, or were about to travel to, the far limits of the known world. And yet exposed as they were, a great many of the leading merchants of the more famous city-states made more money out of commerce and industry than the members of any other communities of merchants to be found in medieval Europe.

The lessons to be learnt from the history of medieval foreign trade, about the influence of social and political factors upon economic relationships, are not without relevance to a study of domestic markets within a particular region. Even in England, beneath the carapace of national unity, feudal society reflected a social pattern which bore some resemblance to what prevailed internationally. Even in England, during the Middle Ages, each market, the preserve and prerogative of a manorial lord, stood to the rest as the potentates of rival feudal kingdoms did in the wider sphere of international society.

Medieval markets were not always a matter of commercial activities which took place at certain times and places. They often consisted of current ideas about prices brought into equilibrium, or something like equilibrium, as a result of bidding and a response to bidding, which was unaided by the physical presence of participants at a known place and at an ascertainable time. Such markets were beyond manorial, and even beyond royal, control. The labour market was the outstanding example of this. Most markets, however, or more exactly, the markets we know most about, were to be found at established or appointed places and functioned at known times on recognised days. They were usually held on land. But a good deal of trade was done on board ships tied up at wharves at river-ports or sea-ports, or even anchored offshore or in mid-river. The famous galleys of Venice and Florence, for example, provided innumerable ports of call on their way north to the Low Countries, or on their way home, with all the colour and excitement of a floating bazaar.[13] Nor did markets always depend upon particular locations in quite this sense. Pedlars did a good deal of trade as they journeyed through the countryside and were so important even in London that fish salesmen were given a special dispensation to sell at will in the streets and lanes.[14] One man's trade done by chance encounter does not make a market. But in an economic system in which there was every material inducement to substitute labour for capital in marketing, the pedlar was likely to have been an important element in distribution. We may surely assume, though we can never hope to prove, that pedlars went everywhere, plied a regular trade, maintained stable rounds, and even, perhaps, competed with one another for custom. Their work created an unusual sort of market by sophisticated modern Western standards, but it is difficult to see what marketing functions pedlars failed to perform.[15]

Much industrial work was sold speculatively in markets, either by craftsmen or their employers. Some, perhaps much, was sold by shopkeepers, stallholders and the like who had had no part in the manufacturing processes involved. But a good deal of industrial work was sold elsewhere than in markets by craftsmen who made to order. Again, a market for what they had to sell existed in the sense that known craftsmen were to be found, or craftsmen were to be found in known places, whose products could be had on terms whose limits were set by the easy availability of alternative supplies. Such products were not homogeneous; indeed the strength as well as the weakness of having something made to order was that in commissioning something that answered to your own particular needs you might very well find yourself lumbered with something that turned out to be not in the least what you had bargained for. But those who deal on these terms usually manage to make allowance for differences which were intended and disparities which were unforeseen, and of pricing things accordingly by reference to what is available elsewhere. Tailors, for example, were to be found everywhere in the Middle Ages: the Poll Taxes are full of them; and elsewhere, so far as medieval tailors were concerned, meant presumably what was available, ready-made or secondhand, in established markets. In such cases price formation depended upon a continuum of opportunities. In the last analysis, neither pedlar nor craftsman could impose upon his customer in normal circumstances because, by taking a little more trouble and incurring a little more expense, his customer could find something which was more nearly what he wanted in another place.

The market for labour was very much a market in this sense. Men were undoubtedly hired at fairs, as we can tell from the labour legislation.[16] But the impression one gets from the records is that relatively few were hired in this way. Manorial accounts do not tell us how hired labour was come by. But hired labour was very important in manorial farming; and since we do not hear of farm managers being paid their expenses for going to hiring fairs, the likelihood is that hired men were generally members of local families hired, so to speak, at the farm gate. And yet it would be quite wrong to say that there was no market for labour; for the manorial accounts show how quickly wage-rates responded to a general rise in prices and even to a general fall. Men voted with their feet. The labour market did not consist of a series of isolated pockets. We can tell that it did not from the problems created by the earliest exercise in the politics and economics of incomes policy.

When the Black Death seemed to threaten the labour supply, the king and his Parliament declared that no one should pay or demand wages which were higher than those current before the Black Death. An unsupported declaration of policy was likely to be fruitless, so courts of law were instituted to enforce the king's and Parliament's will. But more was required. This first exercise in incomes policy presently created the need for the first Settlement Law.[17] Members of Parliament, many of them no less important locally as landlords and farmers than they were influential as politicians, were forced to recognise that anyone who refused to pay more than statutory wages was bound to lose his labour because men who were offered such wages simply went elsewhere; and went, not just to neighbouring farmers, but away from the villages to which they belonged, to other districts where, presumably, they got work and pay with no questions asked. In this way wage-rates adjusted themselves in terms of supply and demand until they achieved some sort of equilibrium, and did so without benefit of formal marketing arrangements; and governments, in that characteristic way that governments in all ages seem to have, did their best to obstruct the path to equilibrium.

Other services, apart from labouring work on the farms, were also bought and sold without benefit of formal marketing. The range of such services, in an economic system in which labour was the cheapest factor of production, was immense. Most were provided, as many are today, by practitioners skilled, not only in their chosen callings, but also in the fine art of knowing what the market will bear. These have no special interest. But there is another group of services, some of which are no longer provided, others no longer paid for, as they used to be. This group includes all those services that expedited the processes of law and administration and provided loans for those who needed more money than they had got. The absence of formality in the arrangements made for the purchase of such services; the lack of uniformity in the services provided; and the clandestinity inseparable from the workings of markets which were either unlawful, like the market for loans, or were dependent upon conditions in which bids could be made, as they are at auctions, without arousing the competitive interest of potential rivals; all this means that we cannot possibly hope to find out how supply and demand were brought into equilibrium. Doubtless in such imperfect markets only a very rough and ready equilibrium was possible, with the equivalent of stocks being left unsold and consumers being left unprovided for, simply because the machinery of exchange functioned so badly. But markets are not important only when they work perfectly; nor are the important markets only the ones about which we are best informed.

All markets, whether domestic or foreign, depend for their survival upon the observance of certain norms of behaviour. Markets cannot function without a measure of confidence that merchants and merchandise will have safe passage wherever they happen to go; that contracts will be honoured, or if not honoured, then either enforced or compensated for; that dealings will be expressed in terms of a currency which, if not uniform and stable, will at any rate have the merit of being readily negotiable; and that weights and measures, if not standardised, will at any rate be familiar and acceptable to all the parties concerned. Fraud and collusion, if not kept within tolerable bounds, bring their own retribution in the end, because markets which became notorious for their cheats will not survive. Nor will they survive unless those who are enfranchised to make some concessions to those whom they would rather exclude absolutely from the benefits of access to opportunities for profitable dealing, however unpalatable such concessions may be.

All these norms of behaviour were observed, by those engaged in foreign trade during the Middle Ages, not so much because governments imposed internationally agreed rules upon all who frequented the markets within their jurisdiction, but because of self-regulating mechanisms compounded of a balance of terror and a lively sense of mutual advantage felt by all members of the international mercantile community. Governments complicated and disrupted international mercantile relationships more than they promoted them, because foreign policy interests invariably took priority over other considerations.

Domestically much the same was true. Medieval markets operating within range of the authority of the kings of England were anything but free. Our earliest laws show English kings trying to force merchants to buy and sell before witnesses in authorised places.[18] Obviously there were many who preferred not to do so, and others with political influence who stood to gain by forcing them to inconvenience themselves, and hence their customers, by complying. Somewhat later, kings assumed the right to license markets; and licenses entailed the payment of a fee. Thereafter kings acted as willing instruments of the franchise holders' interests. They legislated against forestallers, regrators and engrossers, all of whom carried on their business outside the licensed markets rather than within them, and therefore to the franchise holders' loss. They legislated in favour of standardised weights and measures, though never with much success, to judge by the constant renewal the legislation required. But the enforcement of standards gave franchise holders a colourable excuse for imposing fines upon those who failed to conform. They sanctioned the foundation of innumerable craft associations in the towns, where so many of the country's markets were to be found; and these craft associations promptly set about raising prices in the market-place by restricting recruitment, by limiting hours of work and by imposing quality controls which, in so far as they had any effect, reduced the supply of goods coming on to the market. And in the interests of law and order, they legislated to restrict the profits of bakers by requiring them, under supervision, to vary the weight but not the price of their bread so as to take account of variations in the supply of corn; and they legislated to restrict the profits of wine and ale sellers by having prices regulated locally, presumably on the grounds that disaffection was to be expected at all social levels if Englishmen were unable to get drunk without being fleeced.

But governments were by no means the only, or even perhaps, the main source of impediment to the operation of what we should recognise as a free-market system. Markets were profitable in the Middle Ages, not in the sense that anyone clever enough to attract trade to a particular centre could expect to make money out of those who came to spend and out of those who paid for stands or shops or for the services provided by inns or hostelries, but in the sense that trade and tradesmen were themselves fair game, legitimate victims of whatever depredations a franchise holder cared to visit on them. The countryside was a network of obstacles that trade had to surmount. There were tolls on goods entering and leaving markets; brokage was levied on sales; fines were imposed for breaches of regulations which had nothing to do with the maintenance of good order in markets; fees were exacted from those who used or were compelled to use communal services such as weigh-beams; and separate charges were made for the registration of bonds of obligation. Nor were these the only surcharges that franchise holders could impose on trade. Markets were, in the first instance, the property of those who were lords of the land upon which they stood. And such lords were at liberty to levy toll upon goods as they passed along roads and over bridges, along rivers and under bridges, within the boundaries of their lands.

Those who held market franchises had even more extensive powers. Indeed they enjoyed powers which were extra-territorial in the sense that they could enforce, or attempt to enforce, certain of their rights, over land that was not their own. This came about as a result of the nature of royal grants of markets. As a matter of abstract policy, that is to say, of policy with the politics left out, the king never knowingly granted a charter for a market which was to be sited in such close proximity to an existing market as to threaten its trade. Sometimes such eventualities could not be avoided. Towns might grow up side by side, as Wilton and Salisbury did. When that happened, each town depended upon having a market in order to survive. In such cases each market was assigned to a different day. This was a strategy with wider implications. In any particular region, the careful planning of markets for successive days, proved to be a boon to trade, and was recognised as such by everyone concerned, because it drew merchants to an area they might not have been so keen to visit had there been a clash of days or perhaps fewer markets within easy visiting distance. But many of these privileges and enforceable rights were likely to be extra-territorial in the sense that the catchment area for a particular market might very well extend beyond the territorial limit of its lord's lands. When neighbouring market lords fell foul of one another because one of them had allowed his market to trespass on days reserved for his rival's market, then the extra-territorial authority of market lords was plain for all to see: for the injured party had the right to seek the protection of the law in stopping what the offender was doing on his own land.

Some of these extra-territorial rights were very extensive and grievously harmful, because they enabled certain powerful franchise holders to shut down all rival markets within a stated distance for the duration of their own markets and fairs.[19]

The right to issue charters became important to the kings of England in the late twelfth and early thirteenth centuries, when a particularly sharp bout of inflation cut the real value of their revenues and drove them to search for sources of income which might help to restore their fortunes. The flood of charters that we find at that time, so often attributed to the growing prosperity of the age, may be interpreted equally well as the inevitable reaction of impecunious kings to an opportunity they had not previously needed to exploit. The flood created problems as well as opportunities for lords of markets. A chartered market was properly a market set up where it did not threaten an established market. But what was a threat? A flood of charters meant a flood of privileges; and privileges clashed. This created an anarchy of mutually incompatible claims and counter-claims. All manner of groups and many influential persons claimed exemption from dues charged by neighbours, rivals and the like. The situation was inextricably confused by the agreements entered into by particular places or persons. This in turn provoked litigation. A case law complicated the issues by urging the convention that earlier charters took precedence over later ones. And over the whole question, non-compliance, uncovenanted fees, power politics and patronage, exerted their familiar, and to us, insalubrious influence.

Exemption could be challenged on an infinite number of grounds. It could be challenged because it applied only to goods bought for personal use, not for trade; because it applied in markets but not in fairs; because it did not include trade in one particular commodity, which was always the commodity in question; because it extended only to the tenants of certain important personages; because it no longer had any validity since the place to which it had applied was no longer in the direct possession of the person who had obtained the exemption; because it was chronologically later than another charter conferring exemption on another group; because the privilege at issue had lapsed owing to the escheat of the land to the king; because it had lapsed through non-user; or because it applied to semi-finished but not to finished goods.

In such a labyrinth no one could be quite sure of where he stood. And what was worse, the local collector was king. What could a merchant do whose credentials were unexpectedly challenged? He could protest. But who would listen to him? A well-known merchant plying an established trade along familiar routes might be able to gather witnesses and prevail against wrongful demands for fees. But what if he could not? Wasn't a small toll better than confiscation? He had a choice, perhaps. If he were arriving rather than leaving, he could turn round and go home. But wasn't a small toll better than the loss of a day's, possibly a week's trading? Pay now and claim later must have been the motto of many merchants; and was it not, perhaps, their confidence that merchants preferred to pay that many toll-keepers exploited? Moreover, claims meant litigation; and litigation was no less of a gamble then than now; and whatever the decisions made they were no more likely to be observed afterwards than the rules they vindicated had been before.

There was another and perhaps even more powerful consideration. Markets were symbols of seigneurial power as well as sources of profit. It is arguable that they were more important as symbols than as profit-making organisms; for medieval markets were obviously much more than places for social foregathering and mutually beneficial exchange. They were places where privileges could be exercised and where privileges could be seen to be exercised. How important the exercise of these seigneurial powers was thought to be we can readily appreciate by following the fierce squabbles over trifling sums of money that some of the most powerful and influential landowners in the country engaged in. We can scarcely doubt from this evidence that prestige, not material interest, dominated their motives. Examples are legion and can be drawn from many spheres of life. Professor Southern in his survey of the medieval church, provides a very characteristic one from the papal archives of 1144. From this source we learn of a quarrel about a parish church in the diocese of Lichfield, worth perhaps £10 per year, which had been taken, by the exalted litigants involved, from Normandy to Rome, and from Rome to England, and which was then to be settled by representatives of an earl, an archdeacon, a Cathedral Chapter and two or three vicars or ex-vicars from both sides of the Channel, under the auspices of two English bishops acting with the Pope's authority.[20]

We make these struggles over status and power look ridiculous by concentrating upon the financial significance of what was at stake. But issues which were pursued with what looks like indefatigable litigiousness had other implications than financial ones. There was, as there always is in such cases, the question of precedents. A legal precedent, once established, though not irreversible, was a point gained. There was also the question of social strategy. The property you fail to seize or defend will fall into the hands of someone you would much rather deny it to. This was partly a matter of prestige, and partly, again, a matter of scoring off others. We know these motives well in the sphere of international affairs. Why should we fail to recognise them in more homely settings? When America plunged into Pacific politics by acquiring the Philippines and Britain fought, only recently, to retain the Falklands, contemporaries witnessed pure examples of the genre. If we were to cost these excursions, we should arrive at results which were as ridiculous from the point of view of the material gains made by America and Britain as were those of the medieval litigants who pursued what they conceived to be their rights and interests beyond what we should regard as the limit of reasonable contention. But money was not the issue then any more than it is now. And if there is a difference between then and now, in such matters, then the difference is surely not to our credit; for there is always more point in squabbling over the spoils when there is little or no hope of increasing the size of the spoils-heap than there is when the effort put into squabbling could so easily produce a bigger heap. Consequently society was far more reasonably occupied in the Middle Ages in pursuing status rather than wealth than it is today when continuous economic growth produces greater wealth for comparatively little effort and improvements in status come only after strenuous exertion.

The impulse to maintain seigneurial rights at all costs and against all comers had to be disciplined and controlled, however, by the recognition that anyone who charged more than the market would bear stood to lose everything to the neighbouring rival who was content to charge somewhat less. We can read this recognition into virtually every complaint, and they are legion, that a franchise-holder's market rights are being infringed and his market's business is being diminished by a neighbour who is flouting chartered privileges and attracting merchants who used to frequent his market. The terms and the language of complaint may be medieval; but the tone of injured innocence stiffened by a suitable sense of outrage is one we all know well. It is competition that is being complained of; and competition, then as now, is always unfair, if not unlawful, when it threatens established interests.

Nor was this the only way in which we can see that medieval society was in large measure self-regulating. Successive English kings were gravely concerned about problems of law and order and created, in the course of the medieval centuries, an impressively complex apparatus of courts sustained by a variety of enforcement agencies which were themselves fortified by the lucrative practice of informing: in effect the putting-out system applied to social discipline. They even made provision for those who required special facilities for the quick and cheap resolution of mercantile disputes. We should be seriously mistaken, however, if we were to take these provisions at face value. The legal system consisted, after all, of a very small professional judiciary backed up by an amateur magistracy which ran a variety of local courts without anything like an adequate substitute for a police force.

There were obviously severe limitations to what could be accomplished by such a system; and indeed we should do the system a serious injustice if we were to assume that it failed in its purposes because it failed to accomplish what we should expect of it today. The law fulfils a social not an abstract function. It was important to medieval society as a means whereby men could adjust their relationships with one another without immediate resort to violence. At every social level the law courts provided a political arena and machinery for the arbitration of political, social and personal differences. Enforcement agencies filtered social discipline and political pressure through the system, sometimes by threatening court proceedings, and sometimes by making presentments. Procedural rituals in court offered opportunities for private negotiation between parties, and indeterminate court actions often signified settlements made out of court. Settlements may not always have been according to law. But they were triumphs of a sort if, through the mechanisms of the law, violence had been earthed instead of erupting into injury, damage, or seizure of property.

For the rest, the law was a form of outdoor relief for the landed classes who claimed most of the financial benefits of the system; and a gamble, a sort of informal lottery, for those for whom laws were mostly another kind of taxation. So far as most ordinary people were concerned, one either bought the right to ignore the law, or ignored it in the hope that one would never be caught, or if caught, merely cautioned or fined. It was the illegal parking syndrome. There were the unlucky ones, it is true, who were incarcerated in loathsome gaols or even hanged. But so far as markets are concerned, the system worked domestically as it did internationally, in the sense that intercourse between communities triumphed over a multiplicity of tiresome and frustrating obstacles.

It did not do so without cost. Crime had this in common with market franchises that it made conditions for trade more difficult than they would otherwise have been. There were limits, however, to what society would tolerate. The importance of franchises as a deterrent to trade was enormously diminished by widespread disregard of privileges, by failure to pay charges, by neglect of opportunities to impose them, and by skilful participation in the exemption game, in which all players were entitled to claim and counter-claim against franchise holders who clearly understood that competition between them could easily ruin the man who most stubbornly held out for what he conceived to be his rights. Crime was also contained within what medieval society could accept as reasonable bounds by social forces whose workings we can only follow when they surface in legal proceedings. Evidently these forces were tolerably successful; for most crime, as we see it in the records, was local and confined to familiars rather than general and anarchic. And we can measure their success, in other ways, by examining the expectations that lay behind certain established and well-known patterns of medieval behaviour.

The entire manorial system, for example, was organised upon the basis of everyone involved confidently expecting that money, goods and travellers, committed to regular journeys along familiar routes at ascertainable times of the year, would arrive unharmed and unmolested at their destinations. Manorial lords toured their estates for many reasons, not the least of which was that it was cheaper to move the household than the crops. But the chief product of the manor was, generally speaking, money not farm produce; and, as a rule, money could not be spent where it was earned. Consequently the roads were regularly used by manorial bailiffs or their deputies carrying money back to headquarters. It is certainly true that big consignments were escorted by armed men, as they are today. But the ordinary carriage of manorial rents and dues was not. If men had been hired for this purpose the costs would have been entered as a charge against income and itemised in the accounts. The fact that we rarely find such entries suggests that no special precautions were deemed to be necessary when fairly large sums of money were conveyed from manors to their manorial lords.

Markets and fairs were even more vulnerable than manorial cash to the attention of casual or organised brigandage. They were held at well-known places and at well-advertised times. Some of the biggest fairs were held in tiny places which, like St Ives in Huntingdonshire, were absurdly unsuitable from the point of view of security.[21] When they were in session they looked something like modern agricultural shows. But unlike modern shows, they lasted for weeks. Where everyone stayed is a mystery. Where valuable stocks were kept is another. The roads leading to such centres were probably crowded for days, before and after, with carts and animals loaded with precious, or at any rate, desirable things. The predictability of everything compounded the threat of pilferage or theft. Obviously marauding gangs and enterprising lone highwaymen were not the constant anxiety and imminent danger that we might have supposed they would be; for the big markets and fairs met and dispersed, year after year, and the violence that gets reported in connection with such occasions is generally the violence generated by heated argument over deals which have gone wrong rather than the violence of robbery.

Despite the wars, the civil unrest and the felonies, for which medieval England is still notorious in the historical literature, the evidence is overwhelming that the countryside was essentially tranquil. The toll books of the borough of Southampton, miraculous survivors of what may once have been a large class of records, show Southampton carters maintaining their uninterrupted itineraries throughout the fifteenth century, returning regularly for fresh loads, and taking them without escort to towns and villages all over the south of England.[22] The letters written by merchants and country gentlemen, some of them living, as the Pastons did, in what are supposed to have been very disturbed parts of England, bear out the message of the Southampton tolls. And when we consider the topography of the average English medieval town, what must strike us as forcibly as anything about it is that its defences, useful perhaps as a deterrent to wandering sheep, or as a formal warning to a trespassing vagrant, were hopelessly inadequate against anything or anybody more determined than that.

If, however, the countryside was as peaceful as it seems to have been, we are left with the problem of explaining how it was kept so. Certainly law enforcement is not the answer; for enforcement agencies lacked either the power or the will to do what had to be done in order to keep the peace. Indeed the habit of excusing anyone who was rich or influential enough to be worth favouring, from having to obey the law or accept the consequences of violating it, was one of the chief weaknesses of the system. It was mischievous according to the ethical standard that forbids a locksmith to sell a security system to one customer and the key to anyone with money enough to buy it. But in medieval circumstances it was one of the conditions upon which political stability depended. We must, of course, allow for the fact that life may not have been as peaceful in the Middle Ages as it would have had to be if it were to be judged peaceful by modern standards. And no amount of searching of the records can retrieve from past centuries contemporary notions of what constituted normal or tolerable behaviour, because what is taken for granted is never consciously expressed. Nevertheless whatever current medieval notions on the subject may have been, medieval society seems to have been able to maintain a remarkably elaborate network of communications; and did so presumably by exerting domestic and neighbourhood pressure upon deviants as well as by relying, more than we should today perhaps, upon self-defence and retaliation, resorting to the uncertain arbitrament of the law only in extreme or exceptional circumstances.

In these various ways, trade doubtless looked after itself within the country as it was forced to do, but with much less chance of success, internationally, where sanctions were fewer and weaker and conditions were therefore correspondingly harsher.

What then should we conclude about markets and freedom as a result of this somewhat prolix investigation of the social and economic environment in which markets operated in the course of the Middle Ages? Obviously it was not an environment in which markets themselves could function freely. A thousand obstacles, many formidable, others tenuous, impeded their activities at every turn. Nor was it an environment in which markets could have facilitated freedom of exchange even if they had been able to function with much greater freedom than they ever enjoyed. The social and economic structure of society determined income distribution, and income distribution, not market facilities, settled questions of purchasing power and patterns of consumption. Nor again was it an environment in which the activities of markets could have promoted political freedom, as we understand the term, however perfect markets may have been from the point of view of efficiency, and however favourable to exchange in terms of income distribution. And if it was not conducive to the growth of political freedom, the explanation is not to be found in some failure of the marketing system, but in our failure to understand that medieval people saw neither the individual nor political society in terms of the categories formulated by Locke.

Nor is there any reason why they should have seen either the individual or political society in Locke's terms. Increasing the efficacy of market mechanisms, and then proving the value of freedom of association by demonstrating how incomparably successful it is at making everyone better off, will not necessarily promote the cause of political freedom. To suppose that it will, or even could, is to substitute a materialist interpretation of history for a somewhat more agnostic and eclectic view which cannot rise to magniloquence but merely observes that if materialistic considerations had been paramount in human history then human history would have taken a vastly different course from the one that we can actually trace in the records. Wealth undoubtedly liberates. But wealth, like reason itself, supplies us with means, not ends. The market is not a politically creative leaven. Like education, it reflects social aspirations: it is never a prime mover in change. And medieval people would have been as unmoved by the suggestion that they ought to support political freedom because it pays, as most people are today.

Notes

1. R. Southern (ed.) *The Life of St Anselm* (Oxford, 1962), pp. 74–7.
2. *Statutes of the Realm*, 37 Edw. III c. 8 (1363) for the sumptuary legislation; Joan Thirsk and J. P. Cooper (eds), *Seventeenth-Century Economic Documents* (Oxford, 1972), VIII, for Wilson and King.
3. E. A. Kosminsky, *Studies in the Agrarian History of England* (Blackwell, 1956); M. Fostan, 'The Famulus', *Economic History Review Supplements*, 2, n.d.
4. A. R. Bridbury, 'The Black Death', *Economic History Review* 2nd ser., 24 (1973).
5. Z. Razi, *Life, Marriage and Death in a Medieval Parish* (Cambridge, 1980).
6. A. R. Bridbury, 'Before the Black Death', *Economic History Review*, 2nd ser., vol. 30 (1977).
7. K. N. Chaudhuri, *Trade and Civilisation in the Indian Ocean* (Cambridge, 1985).
8. W. Denton, *England in the Fifteenth Century* (1888); W. Greenwell (ed.), *Boldon Buke*, Surtees Society, vol. 25 (1852) for the services of the villeins of Aucklandshire.
9. G. W. S. Barrow, 'The Aftermath of War', *Transactions of the Royal Historical Society*, vol. 28 (1978), pp. 124–5.
10. C. Platt, *Medieval Southampton* (1973), p. 111; E. M. Carus-Wilson and O. Coleman, *England's Export Trade 1275–1547* (Oxford, 1963).
11. W. E. Wightman, 'The Significance of "Waste" in the Yorkshire Domesday', *Northern History*, vol. 10 (1975).
12. R. Owen, *The Middle East in the World Economy 1800–1914* (London, 1981), p. 19.
13. M. E. Mallett, *The Florentine Galleys in the Fifteenth Century* (Oxford, 1967).
14. H. T. Riley (ed.), *Memorials of London* (1868), p. 268.
15. M. Spufford, *The Great Reclothing of Rural England* (1984) has recently attempted to sketch the later history of these 'petty traffickers'.
16. *Statutes of the Realm*, 25 Edw. III 2 c. i (1351). The statute actually required workers to foregather in the market towns, there to be hired publicly. But the contracts were to be for the entire year, so that it is likely that the words used were intended to apply to contracts made at the annual fairs rather than in the weekly markets.
17. *Statutes* 12 Ric II c. 3 (1388).
18. I. Edward c. i, F. L. Attenborough (ed.), *Laws of the Earliest English Kings* (1963), p. 115.
19. E. Lipson, *The Economic History of England*, vol. 1 (7th edn) (1937), pp. 241–2.

20. R. W. Southern, *Western Society and the Church in the Middle Ages* (Penguin Books, 1970), pp. 115-16.
21. D. Usher, *Two Studies of Medieval Life* (Cambridge, 1953), draws an interesting portrait of medieval St Ives.
22. O. Coleman (ed.), *The Brokage Book of Southampton* (Southampton Record Society, 1960, 1961).

5 EARLY MODERN ENGLISH MARKETS[1]

Eric Kerridge

Markets are the sum total of the voluntary, spontaneous, recurrent, and mutually profitable exchanges of property at agreed prices between imperfect and infinitely diverse men seeking to supply one another's actual and anticipated demands. Markets grow and develop as their participants try to increase their supplies by concentrating on what they have the greatest comparative advantage in producing and supplying, so widening and deepening the technical, geographical and social divisions of labour. Freedom of property is essential to markets. All property whatsoever is private to individuals or to their families, corporations and other voluntary associations. Property is whatsoever is lawfully acquired and protected, and consists of specific goods, chattels and estates. Freedom of property once assured, the extent to which markets will develop depends on the innate abilities of their participants and above all on the industry, ingenuity, inventiveness, intelligence and enterprise of the gifted few. At the same time, however, 'the market possesses a wisdom that does not exist, even remotely, in any discrete individual' (Read).[2]

Each particular commodity may be said to have its own market, constituting part of the market in general. By the early modern period particular markets had been created in a great variety of commodities, including land, labour, and money, and all welded into general markets as all other commodities were traded against the most widely acceptable of them, namely, coins of precious or semiprecious metal or credit in the ability to command them.

Looked at in another way, a market is an area in which like things sell at like prices at like times, subject only to differences in transport charges and terms of payment and delivery. There had long been small local market areas with their focal points in retail, pitched markets in market towns and with participants living within daily visiting distance. And a few commodities were dealt in over larger areas at fairs devoted to one or another of them. In addition, early modern England had already developed regional markets with their centres in towns like London, Bristol, Norwich and Exeter. (Incidentally, a similar regional market was forming around Paris.)

These regional markets swallowed up the local ones within their precincts. People still bought and sold in much the same places, but prices were now made in the regional centre and the old market places were now the scenes of wholesale as well as of retail trade. Whereas badgers and similar dealers had formerly conducted arbitrage between local market areas, they now did so between regional ones. But even in the early sixteenth century England was unique in that she was fashioning a metropolitan market system, with the trade of the entire nation centred on London, all prices being made there, and the regional markets being swallowed up in their turn. Metropolitan merchants gave the initial impulse to this new development by 'country buying', that is, going out and buying up existing provincial stocks. Once formed, the chief characteristics of the metropolitan market were: the regular, contracted consignment of wares by producers, factors and other suppliers in the hinterland to metropolitan factors or merchants; the distribution throughout the hinterland by metropolitan merchants of a great part of the wares they received; the conduct of trade by credit, with banking services provided by factors and others; transport by professional common carriers and drovers; wholesaling in unpitched, sample markets in inns, warehouses, corn exchanges and the like; retailing in sale shops; central provision of such specialised services as banking, insurance, estate agency, publishing and posts; and the extension of the geographical division of labour throughout the nation. This last feature of the metropolitan market was the one that signalled most clearly the great growth in wealth of its participants. Various parts of the kingdom followed more closely than before their lines of comparative advantage, some in wheat, some in barley, malt and bottled ale, some in butter, some in cheese, some in store sheep or cattle, some in fat stock, some in coal, some in ironmongery or cutlery, others in this or that type of textile, and so on and so forth, and all exchanging products one with another. The old pitched markets often continued, for the sake of local consumers, but the badgers and drovers now largely became factors for metropolitan merchants. The old fairs went on, but were now frequented by the agents and factors of these merchants. Cross-country trade and transport increased, but only as part of the metropolitan market and in conformity with its prices and practices. Everyone in the British Isles was drawn into the one metropolitan market.

And then, from the metropolis itself, grew an extended or extra-metropolitan market in the export of accumulated surpluses; in other words, the metropolitan market was extended beyond these islands. This was a new and expanding sector of overseas trade; it was the beginning of world markets as distinct from the endless succession of arbitrage operations between separate and discrete markets that had previously been the business of foreign trade.[3]

In examining the formation of metropolitan markets in particular commodities, we do less than justice to our argument if we delineate them to include only those towns that sent these wares to London. Little or no corn went from London to Bristol, but sellers at Warminster could choose to send to either city, so prices must have been uniform, give or take the usual allowances; and Bristol sent corn to South Wales, so people there had to pay prices formed in London, as did dwellers in the Lake District. The market was nationwide. Such a metropolitan market in corn and malt had been established by the middle of the seventeenth century,[4] and so had ones in lean and fat stock,[5] cheese and butter,[6] wool, textiles and hosiery,[7] ironmongery,[8] coal,[9] land,[10] money and credit,[11] and much else. The strongest and earliest extra-metropolitan markets were in woollen textiles, but eventually others followed in corn, corn products and so on.[12]

Concurrently, England enjoyed one of its greatest ever waves of economic progress: agriculture was revolutionised; textile manufactures expanded enormously and were technically transformed; an 'early industrial revolution' occurred in the extractive and processing industries; the first ever metropolitan banking system was set up throughout the market; overseas trade grew and English shipping, insurance and banking started to spread across the seas and oceans.[13]

Free people make free markets, where transactions are made without force, restraint or monopoly, and therefore at fair and just prices. In such a free market, without any intervention, the prices are natural ones. In practice, however, even in a free and fair market, some prices were occasionally artificial. A price was nevertheless just if, for the sake of general convenience, it was fixed at a point within the range of natural prices, as when competing dealers in a commodity meet and agree a price for the day. Also, if in time of famine and merely to prevent starvation, it was just to set a maximum price on corn. Thus the just price might occasionally be artificial, but it was always the prevailing, and usually the natural, market price.[14]

Since all the prices in a market are interrelated, one false price will send a wave of falsification throughout the whole market, making all the prices more or less unfair. If the prices of food and fuel, for example, be unfairly high, almost all prices will in turn be unjust, and although there will still be market forces, there will be no free market and no free market forces. Whether a market is free or unfree will depend, then, in practical terms, on whether the degree of falsification is considerable or not. Since no perfect market can ever exist, the crucial question is whether or not early modern English markets were substantially free and fair. But the answer cannot be found in the market places; it must be sought elsewhere, in the law courts.

Freedom of property was the sheet-anchor of English society. Justice consisted in rendering to every man what was his own. The principles of the law of property were simple and straightforward: every freeborn Englishman (unless a felon) had the right to live, and therefore to get a living, by his own efforts, as he wished and as best he could, in any lawful occupation, and likewise the right to the fruits of his own labour and the right to do what he wanted with his own. Subject only to the laws against crime and to dire public necessities occasioned by such things as war and fire, to do what he willed with his own was the undoubted right of the freeborn Englishman. (Admittedly, at first, not quite all Englishmen were freeborn, but the tiny minority of bondsmen had entirely vanished by 1617.) The common law was, and is, that men may not be 'hindred in their lawfull trade . . . and the law in this point is grounded on the law of God'. It followed from Scripture, 'A mans trade is accounted his life . . . and therefore he ought not to be deprived or dispossessed of it, no more than of his life.'[15]

The law was not man-made, at least not deliberately contrived or framed by men. The common law was grounded on the law of God and the law of Nature. By natural law was understood legitimate natural instinct, such as the love of life, self-preservation, and family affection. Natural law was eternal, universal, and hence divine. English law 'arose from the ordinary, peaceable habits of the English folk' (Cooper), but was none the less God-given, for their common sense of right and wrong came from God. Whatever was against the law of God was against the common law, which enforced all that was enforceable of the Ten Commandments. 'So is the law of England the very consequence of the very Decalogue itself' (Keble). No one could be ignorant of the law; it was simple, known, certain, universal and predictable. All men were subject to the law and all equal before it. All accepted it; all helped to clarify it by observance and breach; and all had the duty of aiding its enforcement, by hue and cry, and on oath in the courts.[16]

English law was not judge-made. Judges made no law; they merely discovered what the law was and how it applied in particular cases. Even the king, of himself, could not make law, for he, too, was subject to it. He could not, by himself, change the law, for he was sworn to uphold it. He might waive a statutory penalty due to himself, but the law still stood. The truth is, 'The law is the highest inheritance the king has; for by the law he himself and all his subjects are ruled; and if the law were not, neither king nor inheritance would be.' From general principles, particular applications had, of course, to be deduced, for circumstances made cases, and cases, in a manner of speaking, made the law. Reason came into this. Coke put it this way:

> The common law itselfe is nothing else but reason, which is to be understood of an artificial perfection of reason, gotten by long study, observation, and experience, and not of every mans naturall reason . . . If all the reason that is dispersed into so many severall heads were united into one, yet could he not make such a law as the law of England is, because by many succession[s] of ages it hath beene fined and refined by an infinite number of grave and learned men, and by long experience growne to such a perfection . . . as . . . no man (out of his owne private reason) ought to be wiser than the law, which is the perfection of reason . . . Our days upon earth are but a shadow in respect of the old ancient days and times past, wherein the laws have been, by the wisdom of the most excellent men, in many successions of ages, by long and continued experience (the trial of light and truth), fined and refined, which no one man (being of so short a time), albeit he had all the wisdom of all the men in the world, in any one age could have effected or attained unto.

The common law was the combined wisdom of all men in all ages. It was 'tried reason, the quintessence of reason'.[17]

As England was formed into one single, centralised kingdom, much law became common to the entire realm; it became common law. As the king's judges presided over courts throughout the kingdom, they recognised provincial and customary laws that were common to all the realm, and so made the law common, without in any way making the law itself. Any custom that was common to the whole realm was common law. The rule was, 'A custome cannot be alleged generally within the kingdom, for that is the common law.'[18]

Customs, then, came to be one set of laws by which men lived, and the common laws another. Statutes enacted in Parliament framed 'by the authority of that highest court', and so 'the highest and most binding laws', made up a third set. But these three sets were parts of a whole. In the words agreed by the whole bench of judges,

> The law consists of three parts: firstly, common law; secondly, statute law, which corrects, abridges and explains the common law; the third, custom, which takes away the common law: but the common law corrects, allows and disallows both statute law and custom, for if there be repugnancy in statute or unreasonableness in custom, the common law disallows and rejects it.

How the common law corrected, allowed and disallowed manorial customs has been shown elsewhere.[19] The custom of merchants (or law merchant), being general, was *ipso facto* common law. As Hobart, C J, said in 1622,

> The custome of merchants is part of the common law of this kingdome, of which the judges ought to take notice: and if any doubt arise to them about there custome, they may send for the merchants, to know there custome.

So Coke was only following Hobart when he declared in 1628 that the law merchant '(as hath beene said), is part of the lawes of this realme'.[20] How statutes abridged common law is explained by Coke and Holt; it was done through private Acts, by which, for instance, bastards were legitimised or marriages dissolved. Parliament could not do away with bastardy in general or legalise adultery, but it could act in particular and private cases, for it was the highest court of law.[21] Amongst statutes of a more public character, declaratory ones merely declared, explained and publicised the existing law; but introductory statutes ushered in new law, often correcting common law. Just how statutes could make new law and correct common law is explained by Chief Baron Fleming in 1606: the common laws, he says, 'cannot be changed without Parliament, and although that their form and course may be changed and interrupted, yet they can never be changed in substance'. The corrections were concerned mostly with legal procedures and technicalities, but some softened the severity of punishments for certain kinds of offences, and the remainder cleared up dubious points of common law and then became the common law.[22] But the substance of common law was immutable.

The common law, however, not only corrected, it allowed and disallowed statute law. As Coke said in Dr Bonham's case, where the Act would have made a man judge in his own cause,

> It appears in our books that in many cases the common law will control Acts of Parliament, and sometimes adjudge them to be utterly void: for when an Act of Parliament is against common right and reason, or repugnant, or impossible to be performed, the common law will control it, and judge such Act to be void.

This remained the accepted position throughout our period.[23] Whatever statute was made in Parliament could only be enforced in the courts, and, as soon as it was in the courts, itself faced judgement on the equity of the statute. Being written, it had to be construed. Now, 'the best expositor of all Acts of Parliament are the acts of Parliament themselves, by construction and conferring all the parts of them together'; but, also, 'the surest construction of a statute is by the rule and reason of the common law'.[24] In other words, the statute was first examined by means of its own internal evidence in order to find out what it meant, and then this meaning had to be made reasonable to (that is, consistent with) the common law. Sometimes judgement on the equity of a statute resulted in its provisions being extended to things not named in it. In 1605 a judgement on the equity of the statute of 27 Edward III caput 4 extended liability for subsidy and alnage to kerseys and other woollens not enumerated in the statute itself. A good example of a statute impossible to be performed is the Bubble Act of 1720. In all the remainder of the century only one case, in 1723, was ever brought under this Act, for the simple reason it was then found to be an unintelligible 'string of *non-sequiturs*'. An Act of 1534, by which the government was to fix corn prices, was unenforceable. The Acts of 1597 and 1601, prohibiting the use of tenters in clothmaking, were dead letters from the outset. Still other statutes were found, at least in part, to be against law. Some penal statutes, purporting to regulate private business transactions, were not executed because the courts found them 'inconvenient', that is, inconvenient to the common law, irreconcilable with it. In this connection, two points have to be noted: 'First, whatsoever is against the rule of law is inconvenient; secondly, that an argument *Ab inconvenienti* is strong to prove it is against the law.' And, as Coke observed, 'Acts of Parliament that are made against the freedome of trade, merchandizing, handicrafts and mysteries, never live long.' The clearest instance of repugnancy in a statute, other than in Bonham's case, is provided by the one of 1 Edward VI caput 14. It was avoided in a judgement on the equity of the statute some 30 years after enactment because it would have made the queen do service to one of her own subjects. In brief, the courts avoided many Acts of Parliament merely by refraining from executing them in whole or in part, and such ineffective Acts were then ripe for amendment, discontinuance or repeal.[25]

That the courts should avoid inconvenient Acts was entirely fitting. Parliament-men had but short lives and Parliaments even shorter ones. The cursory, hasty, ill-considered, and often tentative judgements of a relatively few men of limited knowledge and understanding ought not to have prevailed over the quintessence of reason and the wisdom of the ages. As Misselden said, 'The Parliament having made a statute with intent to the publique good, yet the same, by reason of something not foreseene at the making of the law, may prove very prejudiciall in the execution.' But there was more to it than that. How far superior was the common law to statute is apparent from the universally accepted doctrine concerning *malum in se*, which was *ipso facto* a breach of the common law, and *malum prohibitum*, which was a breach of statute law. The king had no power to dispense with the common law, whereas it was freely conceded he might dispense with a penalty due to him for the infraction of a penal statute. No act by the king, not even in Parliament, could make lawful what was *malum in se*. 'That offence which is contrary to the ancient and fundamental laws is *malum in se*', and it was these God-given laws that lay at the base of the whole legal system.[26]

In practice, statutes inconvenient or repugnant to the common law were few and far between. Everyone took the righteousness of the common law for granted. It came as second nature to Englishmen to revere the common law, and to threaten it was almost the last thing anybody thought of doing. The courts always assumed that Parliament never intended anything against the substance of the common law, and construed its Acts accordingly. Anyway, Parliament and the common law were largely united in the same persons. Most members of Parliament had been brought up in the common law and its principles. About half the members had drunk from the springs of the common law in the Inns of Court. Many justices of peace had been to one of the Inns, and all referred directly or indirectly to law manuals imbued with the same spirit. Moreover, judges themselves often helped to frame the statutes. Above all, everyone had been brought up a Christian. Had the substance of the common law ever been purportedly changed by Act of Parliament, the rule of law would have been overthrown and replaced by the dictates of mere men. But no one ever envisaged this happening in England, and as Sir Walter Raleigh put it, 'A wise man ought not to desire to inhabit that country where men have more authority then lawes.' In short, in those days England knew the rule of law, and the linchpin of this rule was the common law of the realm.[27] How well the rule of law served the common people we shall now see.

Nowadays, the chief way various kinds of 'politicians' domineer the greater part of the Western world is by controlling the currency, which they can expand, contract and spend at will. Although a free society may, rarely, be preserved when the currency is of paper, and even though money properly so called in the form of coins of precious or semiprecious metal, cannot itself ensure its own protection, yet such money is the strongest buttress of free markets. What is essential for the freedom of trade is that the supply of currency be in the hands of the people at large and not in those of men who seek to impose their rule on others. In early modern England the people themselves controlled the supply of money. How they did, is best explained by Dudley North:

> Have you corn, and do you want meal? Carry the corn to the mill, and grind it. Yes, but I want meal, because others will not carry their corn, and I have none; then buy corn of them and carry it to the mill yourself. This is exactly the case of money.

When people wanted more money, they sent precious metals to the Mint to be coined, or sold gold and silver articles to goldsmiths, who might have them coined. Conversely, unless they were themselves goldsmiths, who could melt down coins for plate, those who had coins to spare bought gold and silver wares. 'Thus the buckets work alternately; when money is scarce, bullion is coined; when bullion is scarce, money is melted . . . This ebbing and flowing of money supplies and accommodates itself, without any aid of politicians.'[28]

Freedom of trade and enterprise resulted not from any ideology; they came from the common law and the common sense of right and wrong. 'Freedom of trade was the ancient wisdom of the law.'[29]

But for the common law, selfish men would have restrained trade in domestic markets by the allied means of forestalling, engrossing and regrating. A regrator is one who buys in a pitched market in order to sell the same again in the same market at an enhanced price. A forestaller is one who buys goods when they are already on their way to a market place, with the aim of forcing up the price. As a corollary, 'It is against the common law of England to sell corne in sheafes before it is threshed and measured . . . for that by such sale the market in effect is forestalled.' The same applies to the purchase of standing corn. An engrosser, strictly speaking, is one who buys in gross within the realm in order to sell the same again here and in gross. However, the term 'engrossing' is often used, in a wider sense, to include also forestalling and regrating. All engrossing, in this sense, is *malum in se*,

> for by this means the price of victuals and other merchandize shall be enhaunced, to the grievance of the subject, for the more hands they passe through, the dearer they grow, for everyone thirsteth after gaine . . . And if these things were lawfull, a rich man might engrosse into his handes all a commodity, and sell the same again at what price he will.[30]

Those caught committing these offences were heavily fined.[31] With the advent of 'country buying', however, the judges had to elaborate further:

> He is no forestaller that comes and buyes at my howse, but that buyes it comeing to the marquett . . . A forestaller is an oppressor of the people . . . But who is a forestaller? Not he that comes to my house and buys my commodities . . . Freedom of trade is the life of trade; trade the life of this island. And if we encourage not the merchant, to give him reasonable gain, he will sit down and take ten in the hundred [32]

No agreement to restrain trade could be condoned by the courts. No guild ordinance restraining the trade of members was enforceable in law. A Merchant Tailors' order, that half one type of work should go to fellow members, was held against law, 'because it was against the liberty of the subject'.[33] The law's attitude is expounded in the case of the Tailors of Ipswich in 1615:

> At the common law no man could be prohibited from working in any lawful trade, for the law abhors idleness, the mother of all evil . . . and especially in young men, who ought in their youth (which is their seed time) to learn lawful sciences and trades which are profitable to the commonwealth and whereof they might reap the fruit in their old age, for idle in youth, poor in age; and therefore the law abhors all monopolies which prohibit any man from working in any lawful trade . . . A dyer was bound that he should not use the dyers craft for two years, and there Hull holds that the bond was against the common law, and by God if the plaintiff was here he should go to prison till he paid a fine to the king; so, for the same reason, if an husbandman is bound that he shall not sow his land, the bond is against the common law; and if he who takes upon him to work is unskilful, his ignorance is a sufficient punishment to him . . . and if anyone takes him to work, and [he] spoils it, an action on the case lies against him . . . Also the common law doth not prohibit any person from using several arts or mysteries at his pleasure . . . The said ordinance can't prohibit him from exercising his trade till he has presented himself before them, or till they allow him to be a workman; for these are against the liberty and freedom of the subject, and are a means of extortion in drawing money from them, either by delay or by some other subtle device, or of oppression of young tradesmen by the old and rich of the same trade, not permitting them to work in their trade freely; and all this is against the common law and the commonwealth.[34]

Seven-year apprenticeships in skilled trades for suitable infants between 14 and 21 years of age received the support of both common and statute law, which 'was not enacted only to the intent that workmen should be skilful, but also that youth should not be nourished in idleness, but brought up and educated in lawful sciences and trades'. Neither apprenticeship nor examination by masterpiece was intended to restrain trade, and the courts construed statutes strictly to ensure no restraint resulted from them.[35] Textile guilds occasionally limited the number of looms a master might keep working, but only to help young masters during bad times for trade,[36] and it was only at such times that guilds and corporations discouraged new entrants. Any attempt by them to restrict trade was unlawful and liable to be contested in the courts.[37] A guild's right to search and seal goods was intended not to restrict trade but to increase it, by controlling quality and putting on recognisable hallmarks.[38] Regulated companies, organised along the lines of craft guilds, provided protection and government to merchants adventuring capital in foreign trade. Members traded on their own accounts and competed one with another, but often with quotas arranged to safeguard young merchants. Where prices were raised artificially, it was only to pay for the financial exactions made by the Crown in return for commercial concessions. We cannot deny any guild or company anywhere ever engaged with impunity in restrictive practices, for it would have done so by means subtle enough to have escaped detection by an outsider; but such restraint was as illegal as it was infrequent, and has seldom or never been recorded.[39] Neither at home nor abroad was any guild or company itself a monopoly and any ordinance made 'to restrain trade and traffic was void'; but 'ordinances for the good order and government of trades and mysteries' were good in law.[40]

Labour clubs or unions were nothing new. The legitimate and freely formed friendly societies of journeymen sometimes harboured conspiracies in restraint of trade, with their inevitable intimidation and violence to property and persons. By common law, declared also in many Acts of Parliament, restraints of trade to raise the price of labour were always unlawful, and conspiracies in restraint of trade criminal. Faced with violent and sometimes armed strikers and perpetrators of criminal damage, the civil authorities did their duty, visiting condign punishment on the criminals and calling on support from the armed forces when necessary. Every feature of modern labour unions was already present in our period, save only for the privileges even now still allowed to them; but usually servants were content to prosper within the rule of the law.[41]

Statutory wage regulation made a modest contribution to the general contentment of working men. The rates assessed by justices of the peace were for the most part nominally maxima, but more or less conformed to the going rates agreed either privately or by free collective bargaining or by arbitration. Thus the wages regulated the assessments, not the assessments the wages. The great advantage of statutory regulation was that in case of dispute between master and servant the assessed rate could be unquestioningly applied.[42]

In fine, given the rule of law and free wage bargaining, labour markets were free and competitive.

Foreign trade was largely free from restraint, in normal times and circumstances, in most kingdoms and states. In England its freedom was firmly established by making customs duties on imports and exports the mainstay of royal tax revenues. The king had the right to impose new duties, but could raise them to a protective height only by foregoing irreplaceable income. Even in the early seventeenth century, when such measures were first proposed, and in the eighteenth, when some customs inward were actually raised and outward ones lowered, the Crown's ulterior motives were always either revenue or defence or retaliation with a view to repelling foreign attacks on the freedom of trade. Import prohibitions were rarely declared and still more rarely enforced. They were illegal except in war or by Act of Parliament and were regarded ordinarily as a despising of God's blessings. But first Spain, then France, tried to subject The Netherlands and England by war and by excluding our exports. The longest trade war was between France and England. France had formerly enjoyed freedom of foreign trade, but from 1644 onwards the governments there raised import duties on English and Dutch goods to prohibitive levels, tending to impoverish all three peoples. England, however, always sought, and finally in some measure achieved, freedom of trade.[43]

At the outset of our period, special licences were required to export foodstuffs in time of dearth. This policy sprang from fear of local famines, but its efficacy was already questioned in 1550, when one man observed,

> I have seen many experiences of such ordinances; and ever the end is dearth and lack of the thing that we seek to make good cheap. Nature will have her course . . . and never shall you drive her to consent that a pennyworth of new shall be sold for a farthing . . . For who will keep a cow who may not sell the milk for as much as the merchant and he can agree upon?

By stages, from 1559 to 1571, a new system was introduced by which export was allowed below a stipulated price level. This succeeded beyond all expectations, for

> the country people . . . when licence was once granted to transport grain, began to ply their husbandry more diligently than before, yea and above that which the laws afterwards made required, by breaking up grounds which had lain untilled beyond all memory of man.

After 1590 food surpluses became normal and in 1624 and later export thresholds were set far above average price levels, virtually freeing exports, while in 1670 the thresholds themselves were abolished.[44] By now corn was superabundant. In 1621 the prohibition of corn imports was mooted; in 1663 duties were laid on them, from 1670 on a sliding scale geared to domestic prices; in 1671 corn export bounties were considered, and in 1673 instituted.[45] The overriding consideration was still the dread of famine, though the danger apprehended was now from too much reliance on imports from other parts of our own climatic zone.

The same haunting fear lay behind the remarkably few governmental interventions in domestic commerce. Originally, the regulations were mostly designed to legalise engrossing for the purpose of arbitrage between regional food markets. Then, in 1552, the food trade was thrown open, subject only to the licensing of dealers by justices of the peace. With the growth of metropolitan markets, licences had to be issued wholesale and in 1627 were done away with, except for times of dearth, which were rare after 1656.[46] When dearth did come, trade was controlled, the fixed prices being deemed the just ones, and everything possible being done to ensure no part of the kingdom went without. Such extreme measures were needed during the wartime crisis of 1646–51,[47] but otherwise the rise of metropolitan markets had already made them obsolete and harmful, threatening to cause famine, as in 1631. Now maxima only reduced supplies; districts that fed themselves by trading coal and other wares against foodstuffs, found the food wagons no longer came; and attempts to prevent hoarding only created panics and disrupted the market. Such measures were therefore discontinued.[48]

Navigation Acts and similar statutes were not in breach of the freedom of trade. They helped to ensure England had a shipbuilding industry, a fishing fleet, a merchant marine and a royal navy strong enough to prevent invasion and protect trade. England had a comparative disadvantage in the rigging out and manning of ships. Yet in order to stay free, Britannia, then as now, had to rule the waves. Without the navigation laws, there might have been no freedom of trade and no England to exercise it.[49]

Many Acts of Parliament seem at first sight to consist of regulations imposed on industry by government; reality was otherwise. The Crown wanted exports of textiles and other manufactures to grow, for the sake of the kingdom in general and its own revenue in particular. It had, too, a duty to ensure true weights and measures and to prevent commercial frauds. The wholesale merchants needed uniformity in qualities and dimensions, and sought agreements on these matters with the manufacturers. Almost all industrial statutes were initiated and promoted by guilds or companies, and their municipalities, in what were in the nature of private-members' bills to which the Crown was pleased to assent. The resulting statutes were not part of government policy, but of the self-regulation of industry and trade.[50]

Depopulation of the countryside by arbitrary enclosure, the putting down of ploughs, the conversion of tillage to permanent grass and the destruction of houses of husbandry, was universally detested as a badge of atheism, and was a felony at common law.[51] When occurring in the Isle of Wight, it was thought also to weaken the defence of Portsmouth and Southampton. But enclosure itself could result in benefit to the commonwealth, and, besides, more and more landowners wanted to have their own parks. On Crown initiative, and with the general support of Lords and Commons, a succession of statutes placated the public, but also converted common-law felonies into statutory offences punishable only by standardised monetary penalties, and, furthermore, extended statutory protection to licensed parks, provided the dispossessed had been offered land in compensation. Statutory protection was needed because imparking was the most hated kind of enclosure, and if protesters pulled down the palings and threw the parks open, local juries took a lenient view. Before long the spread of convertible husbandry made much of this legislation obsolete. Statutes in 1552 and 1555 exempted up-and-down land while still penalising permanent grass, but it transpired defendants were often able to pass off permanent pastures as temporary leys. A new attempt in 1597 to frame workable statutes unfortunately resulted in over-complicated enactments. 'They were so like labyrinthes, with such intricate windings and turnings, as little or no fruit proceeded of them.' The only solution was to repeal all the Acts, which was finally done in 1624. Not only were they 'obsolete, and in time grown apparently impossible or inconvenient to be performed', they were also, as they had always been, 'snares whereupon the relator, informer or promoter did vex and entangle the subject'.[52]

A few statutes ordered the general cultivation of limited acreages of flax and hemp, mainly with a view to increasing supplies of naval stores. These laws proved unnecessary and no one took much notice of them (except in vexatious suits), so they were repealed in 1593. An attempt to revive then in 1601 failed after Raleigh had voiced the general opinion by saying, 'I do not like this constraining of men to manure or use their grounds at our wills; but, rather, let every man use his ground to that which it is most fit for, and therein use his own discretion.'[53]

Usury was a sin and always an offence in law, but interest (which arose from the lender's risk or loss of money or opportunity or from the borrower's failure to repay on time) was neither sinful nor illegal, so the usury laws, even at their strictest, could hardly have impeded industry or commerce; and, anyway, usury up to rates roughly half those earned in ordinary trades was openly tolerated in England from 1571, as it had been in Geneva since 1538 and in Antwerp since 1546.[54]

Even were we to expand this admittedly brief conspectus of early modern England, it would only be to lend additional detail to a picture whose broad outlines are already clearly discernible. There was nothing that in modern parlance could be classed as government economic policy. The Crown saw to its own economy, to its own estates and revenues, and to the affairs of the Church it headed; its subjects saw to the economies of their own families, firms and associations. The subjects had economic policies, but they were not national; the government had national policies, but they were not economic. In short, this was basically a free society.

But free societies survive only if they can defend themselves against attacks from without and within, and this defence must often take the form of righteous coercion, force and killing. Early modern English society survived two great assaults from without and two from within.

Notwithstanding that depopulating enclosure was an offence to be tried by due course of law, Cardinal Wolsey, who was seeking to override the common law and make do without Parliament, set up inquisitions of depopulation in 1517–18. Protector Somerset followed his example in 1548–9. Both seem to have tried to kill two birds with one stone: to raise money and to divert the populace from real grievances. Disregarding allegations that immunity from prosecution could be obtained 'by giving money to Wolsey' and that Somerset did 'gape after the fruitless breath of the multitude', it still remains that these inquisitions were unlawful, if only because they allowed a man to be falsely accused and yet have no remedy by ordinary course of law. As Lord Darcy put it, 'None shall lack that be over marvellous and odible for any goodman to hear — yea, and that in great and sundry specialities.'[55] Even more menacing were the successive debasements of the coinage in 1543, 1545, 1546, 1548, 1549 and 1551. The Crown effectually purloined its subjects' precious metals from their coins and left them with no real money. Economic and political chaos followed, and even armed rebellion. But inflation in those days was self-limiting, for the end of it was, the king was paid back in his own coin, and then true coinage had to be restored.[56]

After a long period of good government, the next assault opened in much the same way as the first. In 1607 King James commissioned an inquisition of depopulation and so started a prolonged conflict with the common law. The bench of judges condemned the commissions as unlawful:

> The said commissions were against law for three causes: 1. For this, that they were in *English*. 2. For that the offences enquirable were not certain within the commission itself, but in a schedule annexed to it. 3. For this, that it was only to enquire, which is against law, for by this a man may be unjustly accused by perjury, and he shall not have any remedy. 4. For this, that it is not within the statute of 5 Elizabeth etc. Also the party may be defamed and shall not have any traverse to it.

In further explanation, the judges instanced a dangerous anomaly that could result from James's way of proceeding: 'Such a commission may be only to enquire of treason, felony committed etc. And no such commission ever was seen to enquire only.'[57] Charles I tacitly conceded this point when, in 1634, he took up a proposal to raise money from enclosures by bringing alleged offenders to composition. Between 1635 and 1638, in one part of the Midland Plain alone, £44,000 was raised from just under 600 alleged depopulators; the grand total was enormous. Archbishop Laud went round the country with fellow commissioners holding kangaroo courts where alleged enclosers and depopulators were subjected to summary fines and penalties. Two men, falsely accused, protested against the allegations both in point of fact and in that they had not been made on oath. When they asked for a commission to examine witnesses on oath, 'whereby the truth might better appear', His Grace replied, 'Since you desire it and are so earnest for it, you shall not have it.' When they refused Laud's sentence, they were hauled before the Star Chamber, which first James and then Charles had been perverting from a good court of criminal equity into an instrument of tyranny. It had become, as Maitland says, 'a court of politicians enforcing a policy, not a court of judges administering the law'.[58] And this policy, contemporaries said, was to find 'depopulation where never any cottage was built' and levy fines 'from depopulation where never any farm was decayed and from inclosures where never any hedges were set.'[59]

Partly by his promise 'to make a free trade' (by ending exactions and concessions), James managed to persuade Sir Edward Coke to oppose the Merchant Adventurers' Company. But what the king actually did, in 1614, was to revoke the company's charter and hand over their rights in the export of cloth to a new King's Merchant Adventurer's Company headed by Alderman Cockayne. Moreover, the new company was granted the right to export coloured cloths, whereas the old had only had a grant to vend white ones. James was hoping to increase his revenues by shifting the weight of customs and other taxes from whites to coloureds. But his move was grossly premature. He was trying to make the coloured cloth industry run before it could walk, and only for his own benefit. The white cloth trade, already ailing, was almost killed, and no fillip was given to the coloured cloth one. As far as Cockayne and the other Eastland Company members who ran the scheme were concerned, their real object was to seize the white cloth trade from the old company. When Cockayne's scheme collapsed, which it soon did, the king graciously allowed the old company to pay through the nose to recover its former rights and licences. This they could only do by borrowing £50,000 and more, so they had to be given leave to recoup themselves by placing further impositions on their exports. The king thus succeeded in playing both ends against the middle. To line his own and his courtiers' pockets, he had 'set the trade itself in debt'. As the trade continued to shrink, so did the number of adventurers in it. No more than about 50 substantial traders, in a dozen or a score of firms, now remained. Their opponents were quick to point out, 'It gives them an inevitable opportunity of combynacion to sett what price they please on cloth to the clothier, of wooll to the grower.' But we have no evidence of any such combination. Export prices were now higher, and volumes lower, but the obvious cause was the debt the company had incurred in ransoming its charter. The worst reorganisation undertaken by the company was their abandonment of the quota system by which young merchants had been helped to enter the trade and rise within it. But, then, it was no longer a trade for an ambitious young man. The real culprit in the Cockayne scheme was James himself. Coke was cozened and realised it too late. Sir Julius Caesar, who knew better, lacked the courage of his convictions, but he was by no means alone in this. The Privy Councillors quailed before a king who thought he was 'a little god to sit on his throne and rule over other men'. Even the better informed Councillors only told him what they knew he liked to hear.[60]

Then there were the monopolies. Their nature was clearly recognised in law:

> A monopoly is an institution or allowance by the king by his grant, commission or otherwise, to any person or persons, bodies politique or corporate, of or for the sole buying, selling, making, working or using of anything, whereby any person or persons, bodies politique or corporate, are sought to be restrained of any freedome or liberty that they had before, or hindered in their lawfull trade.

It followed 'that a monopolizer is either an officer in the creation or the execution'. Also, 'incident to a monopoly is, that after the monopoly granted, the commodity is not so good and merchantable as it was before; for the patentee, having the sole trade, regards only his own private benefit, and not the commonwealth'. Moreover, a monopoly

> tends to the impoverishment of divers artificers and others, who before, by the labour of their hands in their art or trade, had maintained themselves and their families, who now will of necessity be constrained to live in idleness and beggary.

Monopolies were ungodly, but not so patents of invention. Patents of monopoly, what we nowadays call simply 'patents', were granted for new inventions, for these were the property of the inventors. As long as William Cecil examined applications for patents, the system worked well; but in the 1590s abuses started to creep in, patents being granted for all manner of things, new and old, provided the applicant paid enough. Hearing complaints, Elizabeth had been content to let the courts and the common law decide which patents were lawful and which not. But James pushed the sale of patents regardless. People were beset by swarms of agents demanding composition. Loud popular protests found an echo in Parliament, and eventually, in 1624, an Act restricted patents of monopoly to new inventions and to terms of 14 years, leaving the courts to decide what was a new invention. But Charles I found a way round this. He granted charters of monopoly to corporations and stopped the charters being contested in the courts. The corporations had to pay large sums for their charters, for which they levied their members, who in turn passed on the cost to their customers, so the whole operation amounted to unlawful and oppressive indirect taxation. Moreover, the monopolists were empowered to destroy the business, and even the machines and workshops, of those who refused to submit to extortion under a name of licence fees. As Coke said, 'A mans trade is accounted his life, because it maintaineth his life; and therefore the monopolist that taketh away a mans trade, taketh away his life'. Monopolies hurt the poor more than the rich, which was why journeymen were among their most vocal opponents. This was what Coke was driving at in his comment in 1621, after the House of Lords rejected a Bill of Monopolies along the lines of the Act of 1624. As hastily recorded in a parliamentary report, his words were: 'The Lords have no inconvenience by monopolies, but the poor cedars and shrubs have danger by it.' Courtiers and lords (the old oaks) took no harm from monopolies, and might even gain from one or more of them, but new and rising firms (the cedars) and small men (the shrubs) were blighted by them.[61]

James and Charles also extorted money from improvements like the draining of fens and the disforesting of forests. In 1621 James tried to set himself up as the nominal undertaker of the drainage of the fens south of the Humber, wanting in return 120,000 acres of rich land. When nothing came of this, he turned elsewhere, particularly to Sedgemoor, but with hardly greater success. He claimed the local proprietors had agreed to cede him a third of the whole area; but after hearing the members for those parts, the House of Commons concluded consent had never been given. Charles found pretexts for annulling common rights in Hatfield Chase and enclosed the land. He then took the draining of the Great Level out of the hands of the Bedford Company and claimed 152,000 acres for himself; but the commoners destroyed his works. In placing contracts for engineering work in the level, Charles showed himself in his true colours. A tender entailing a 6s rate on occupiers was rejected in favour of another needing a 10s one. Bargaining for contracts was perverse; contracts went to the highest bidder, so as to provide for the largest possible land grant to the king.[62] The two kings also cast their covetous eyes on the foreshores and on relicted lands like coastal marshes and Severn warths; but James was thwarted by the 1621 Parliament, and Charles left it too late, for by 1636–8 his intended victims, and notably Lord Berkeley, were emboldened to stand up to him.[63]

As a result of much earlier struggles over afforesting, many royal forests were left with two sets of boundaries, one restricted and legally accepted, the other marking the height of royal pretensions. Now James and Charles planned to enrich themselves by two successive moves. First, wherever possible, they enlarged the forests to the outer and unaccepted boundaries, 'making forrests when never any deere fedd there'. Secondly, they disforested the land. The extensions drew in wide areas of pretended assarts, whose proprietors were compelled to compound in large sums for leave to take what was theirs in the first place. In this way, 17 townships were newly drawn into the Forest of Dean, Salcey Forest was expanded to include 42 towns instead of six, the compass of Rockingham Forest was increased from six to 60 miles, and Waltham Forest was widened to cover half Essex.[64]

All these confiscations and attempted confiscations were accompanied by the overruling of the common law and the corruption of the judiciary.[65] Only by the most truculent and dictatorial methods were the justices of the forests able to browbeat juries at the justice seats. As the inhabitants of Alice Holt Forest stated afterwards, the justices got their way, 'there beeing none found in those oppressing tymes so hardy as to oppose them'.[66] In the matter of foreshores and relicted grounds, judges Weston and Trevor, who were Charles's creatures, were able to obtain some verdicts in his favour, though more went the other way. The pliant bishop of Llandaff included packed juries of inquisition to find for the king. The Gloucester jury was just about to decide against the Crown, when the attorney-general withdrew some of the jurors, forcing the impanelling of a new jury; but then this one found against the king. In the Slimbridge case, the inquisition jury was not believed impartial, and John Smyth of Nibley, who was counselling the defendant, Lord Berkeley, declared it had been packed by the high sheriff and that the principal promoter and projector, under the Crown, namely Sir Sackvile Crow, had corrupted the undersheriff and paid the diet and expenses of both jurors and witnesses.[67] The royal enclosures of the fens were carried out under seemingly legal forms intended to cloak gross illegalities. Having been turned off the bench, Coke seized the opportunity in 1621 to speak out in the House against 'the Bill of the Fens', saying any lawful enclosure could easily have been proceeded with simply by writ of *De admeasuratione pasture*, under the Statute of Merton, and that the Bill itself was a danger to property; it would have allowed six commissioners of sewers, or even a quorum of three, with a jury of twelve, to override all opposition.[68] In practice, the consents of freeholders and commoners were not freely given; they were not given at all. Commissions and juries were packed, suborned or ignored, and the laws stretched and broken. In 1613 Coke had declared, 'The commission of sewers is as necessary as may be, but no commission is more abused than this is; for they do pretend the good of the commonwealth, but do intend their own proper good.' Having packed the commissions, James or Charles ordered the commissioners to disregard presentments from local sewers' courts and juries, overruled or overawed the judges, and even assembled all the commissioners in the Star Chamber, where they could be swayed by a minister appointed to preside over them. It was by such means that the commissioners were drawn to act *ultra vires* in undertaking new rivers and in laying excessive rates on both flooded and unflooded ground on the pretence that it was all flooded and on whole townships instead of on individuals. Then those unable or unwilling to bear the exorbitant rates were distrained upon to pay for the draining, so that the beneficiaries might be granted lands some of which were newly drained and some dry in the first place.[69]

No wonder the Grand Remonstrance denounced

> the enlargement of forests, contrary to *Carta de Foresta*, and the composition thereupon; the taking away of mens right, under

colour of the kings title to land between high and low water marks . . . large quantities of common and several grounds . . . taken from the subject by colour of Statutes of Improvement and by abuse of the Commission of Sewers, without their consent and against it.[70]

James and Charles between them wrongfully appropriated hundreds of thousands of acres in and about the fens and forests and took huge sums by way of composition,[71] all for themselves or their courtiers and favourites.[72]

And this is only the half of it. We have no room to relate how Charles in 1640 arbitrarily seized £200,000 or so of coin and bullion confided by merchants for safekeeping in the Mint vaults in the Tower,[73] nor to deal with ship-money and the rest. Suffice to say that James and Charles could not keep their fingers out of their subjects' pockets. They undermined the rule of law, freedom of trade, and so the whole of English society.

Having embarked on a war against his own subjects in Scotland, with his power sapped by unrest and disorder in England, Charles was defeated and forced to concede constitutional government to his subjects in England until such time as he would be ready to take up arms against them. And raise arms he did, only to be defeated in the name of Parliament by the New Model Army under Oliver Cromwell. This army rescued the rule of law and handed it down to immediate posterity. In 1704 Holt, CJ, was still able to declare,

It is the law gives the queen her prerogative; it is the law gives jurisdiction to the House of Lords; and it is the law limits the jurisdiction of the House of Commons . . . If the ecclesiastical court exceed their jurisdiction, a prohibition will lie; and even the king's acts, if contrary to law, are void.

Indeed, the rule of law now seemed secure against all but external enemies, so much so that vigilance against internal ones was somewhat neglected. Nevertheless, throughout the remainder of the early modern period, the rule of law and freedom of trade were preserved.[74]

Let us keep in mind England as she was under the rule of law. We have it on Sir Walter Raleigh's testimony that, 'Learned writers abroad have declared, that of all the seigniories of the world, the realm of England was the country where the commonwealth was best governed.' Under the rule of law, the English people became the most affluent and powerful in the world. Under the rule of law, not even the poorest man had any political axe to grind. 'Those that live by their own labour . . . have never been displeased where they have been suffered to enjoy the fruit of their own travails. *Meum* and *Tuum*, Mine and Thine, is all wherein they seek their certainty and protection.' And, 'Men well governed should seek no other liberty, for there can be no greater liberty than good government.'[75] Indeed, 'It is not the sharing of government that is for the liberty and benefit of the people; but it is how they can have their lives and liberties and estates safely secured under government.'[76]

Under the rule of law, a free people enjoyed freedom of trade in free markets at fair and just prices.

Notes

1. This is a slightly revised version of my paper.
2. L. von Mises, *Human Action* (London, 1949), p. 324; *Theory and History* (London, 1958), pp. 29, 30; L. E. Read, 'The Miracle of the Market' in *Champions of Freedom* (Hillsdale, 1974), p. 61.
3. N. S. B. Gras, *A History of Agriculture in Europe and America* (London, n.d.), pp. 133–5, 137; *The Evolution of the English Corn Market* (Cambridge, Mass., 1915), pp. 77, 95ff., 111ff., 245, 256–8, 437; D. G. Barnes, *A History of the English Corn Laws from 1660 to 1846* (London, 1930), p. 299; A. H. John, 'English Agricultural Improvements and Grain Exports 1660– 1765' in D. C. Coleman and A. H. John (eds), *Trade, Government and Economy in Pre-Industrial England* (London, 1976), pp. 49, 56; W. Camden, *Britannia*, Gibson (ed.) (London, 1695), p. 367; R. B. Westerfield, *Middlemen in English Business 1660–1760* (Transactions of the Connecticut Academy of Arts and Sciences, vol. 19, New Haven, 1915), pp. 135–7, 145, 149, 152, 189–90, 205–6, 208, facing p. 328; A. P. Usher, *History of the Grain Trade in France 1400–1710* (Cambridge, Mass., 1913), frontis., pp. 3ff., 37ff., 299, 362; D. Davis, *A History of Shopping* (London and Toronto, 1966), pp. 60–3, 68–70, 74, 93–5, 100ff., 146ff., 181ff.; T. S. Willan, *The Inland Trade* (Manchester, 1976), pp. 59ff., 79ff.; W. B. Stephens, *Seventeenth Century Exeter: A Study of Industrial and Commercial Development, 1625–1688* (Exeter, 1958), pp. 80–1; R. Reyce, *The Breviary of Suffolk*, F. Hervey (ed.) (London, 1902), p. 32, 41; R. Blome, *Britannia* (London, 1673), p. 207; E. Leigh, *England Described* (London, 1659), pp. 181, 184; D. Woodward (ed.), *The Farming and Memorandum Books of Henry Best of Elmswell 1642* (London, 1984), pp. 105–6; E. Kerridge, *Textile Manufactures in Early Modern England* (Manchester, 1985), pp. 218ff.; *Commons Journals* vol. 13, pp. 570, 720; F. J. Fisher, 'The Development of the London Food Market, 1540–1640' in E. M. Carus-Wilson (ed.), *Essays in Economic History* (London, 1954), pp. 149–50.
4. F. J. Fisher, 'London Food Market', pp. 136, 138–9, 144, 148; Gras, *Corn Market*, pp. 47, 105ff., 121–2, 124, 186–9, 223, 300–1, 310ff., 319–20, 330ff., 342ff., 350ff., 357–60, 363; E. Kneisel, 'The Evolution of the English Corn Market', *Journal of Economic History*, vol. 14 (1954), pp. 46ff.; T. S. Willan, *The English Coasting Trade* (Manchester, 1938), pp. 79ff., 148; *Inland Trade*, pp. 27–8, 33–4, 36; Westerfield, *Middlemen*, pp. 169–70, 172–3, 178–80, App., map i.

5. Westerfield, *Middlemen*, pp. 190, 199, facing p. 328; F. J. Fisher, 'London Food Market', pp. 144–5; R. Baxter, 'The Poor Husbandman's Advocate', *Bulletin of the John Rylands Library*, vol. 10 (1926), p. 186; B. Winchester, *Tudor Family Portrait* (London, 1955), pp. 173, 179; J. Aubrey, *The Natural History of Wiltshire* J. Britton (ed.) (London, 1847), p. 37; J. Morton, *The Natural History of Northamptonshire* (London, 1712), p. 483; [J.] Coker, *A Survey of Dorsetshire* (London, 1732), p. 4; British Library, Harleian MS 570, fo. 15; Reyce, *Suffolk*, p. 37.

6. Reyce, *Suffolk*, p. 41; Willan, *Coasting Trade*, pp. 84–7, 118, 122, 124, 126, 132, 134–6, 185; *Inland Trade*, pp. 28–9, 33–4, 137; Westerfield, *Middlemen*, pp. 204–6, 208; F. J. Fisher, 'London Food Market', pp. 137, 139, 144–5; R. Plot, *The Natural History of Staffordshire* (Oxford, 1686), p. 108; Leigh, *England Described*, pp. 42, 165, 181, 184; Blome, *Britannia*, p. 207; T. Gerard, *The Particular Description of the County of Somerset* (Soms. Record Society, vol. 15 (1900), p. 172; Bodleian Library, Aubrey MSS, vol. 2, fos. 99v. ff., 148, 151; vol. 3, fo. 84 v. (p. 83).

7. Kerridge, *Textile Manufactures*, pp. 149–50, 214ff.

8. W. H. B. Court, *The Rise of the Midland Industries 1600–1838* (London, 1938), pp. 135ff.; Willan, *Coasting Trade*, pp. 97–8; M. G. Davies, *The Enforcement of English Apprenticeship: A Study in Applied Mercantilism 1563–1642* (Cambridge, Mass., 1956), pp. 136–7.

9. J. U. Nef, *The Rise of the British Coal Industry* (2 vols., London, 1932), vol. 1, facing p. 19, pp. 81–2, 110–11, 444–5; Willan, *Coasting Trade*, pp. 60ff., 210–11.

10. J. Youings, *The Dissolution of the Monasteries* (London, 1971), pp. 126ff.; S. J. Madge, *The Domesday of Crown Lands: A Study of the Legislation, Surveys, and Sales of Royal Estates Under the Commonwealth* (London, 1938), pp. 59, 210, 216, 220–1, 224; J. Thirsk, 'The Sales of Royalist Land during the Interregnum', *Economic History Review*, 2nd ser., vol. 5 (1952), pp. 191–4, 196–7, 204; D. C. Coleman, 'London Scriveners and the Estate Market in the later Seventeenth Century', ibid., vol. 4 (1951), pp. 222ff.

11. See my forthcoming work on money and banking in early modern England.

12. Gras, *Corn Market*, pp. 77, 113–14, 116; Barnes, *Corn Laws*, p. 299; John, 'Agricultural Improvements', pp. 49–56.

13. E. Kerridge, *The Agricultural Revolution* (London, 1967); *Textile Manufactures*; Nef, *Coal Industry*; 'The Progress of Technology and the Growth of Large-scale Industry in Great Britain, 1540–1640' in Carus-Wilson (ed.), *Essays*, pp. 88ff.; E. S. Godfrey, *The Development of English Glassmaking 1560–1640* (Oxford, 1975); L. A. Harper, *The English Navigation Laws* (New York, 1939), pp. 322, 326, 335–6, 339; R. Davis, *The Rise of the British Shipping Industry* (London, 1962), pp. 7, 10, 15, 27, 45, 48–9, 52–3.

14. B. W. Dempsey, *Interest and Usury* (London, 1948), pp. 149ff.; J. T. Noonan, *The Scholastic Analysis of Usury* (Cambridge, Mass., 1957), p. 88; J. A. Schumpeter, *History of Economic Analysis* (London, 1972), pp. 60–2, 93, 98–9, 359–60; R. De Roover, *Business, Banking and Economic Thought in Late Medieval and Early Modern Europe* (Chicago and London, 1974), pp. 24, 278, 290, 303.

15. Deut. xxiv. 6; Matt. xx. 15; E. Plowden, *The Commentaries or Reports* (Pl. Comm) (London, var. eds), p. 315; J. Dodderidge, *The Lawyers Light* (London, 1629), pp. 68–70; E. Coke, *The Reports* (Co. Rep), 13 parts (London, var. eds), 8 Rep., fo. 86v.; 12 Rep., p. 65; *The Institutes of the Lawes of England* (Co. Inst.), 4 parts (London, 1628–44 and var. eds), pt. 3, p. 181.

16. 3 Co. Inst., p. 205; Pl. Comm., pp. 303–4; T. B. Howell (ed.), *A Complete Collection of State Trials etc.* (21 vols., London, 1816–28), vol. 2, col. 670; vol. 5, col. 172; J. W. Gough, *Fundamental Law in English Constitutional History* (Oxford, 1955), pp. 20–1, 30, 39, 41, 46, 214, 216–17; W. M. Cooper, *Outlines of Industrial Law* (London, 1954), p. 1; *Commons' Journals*, vol. 1, p. 254.

17. A. V. Dicey, *Introduction to the Study of the Law of the Constitution*

(London, 1948), p. 184; T. Smith, *De Republica Anglorum* (London, 1583), p. 45; 1 Co. Inst., fo. 97v.; S. E. Thorne (ed.), *Discourse upon the Exposicion and Understandinge of Statutes* (San Marino, Calif., 1942), pp. 168–9; cf. F. A. Hayek, *The Constitution of Liberty* (London, 1960), p. 163.

18. T. F. T. Plucknett, *A Concise History of the Common Law* (London, 1956), pp. 15, 16; S. F. C. Milsom, *Historical Foundations of the Common Law* (London, 1969), p. 1ff.; S. R. Gardiner (ed.), *Parliamentary Debates in 1610*, Camden Society, vol. 81 (1862), p. 75; S. A. Moore, *A History of the Foreshore and the Law relating thereto* (London, 1888), p. 292; J. M. Holden, *The History of Negotiable Instruments in English Law* (London, 1955), p. 34; 1 Co. Inst., fo. 110.

19. 1 Co. Inst, fo. 110v.; R. Brownlow, *Reports (A Second Part) of Divers Famous Cases in Law* (2 Brownl.) (London, 1652), pp. 197–8; Gough, *Fundamental Law*, pp. 11, 14, 19, 20, 143, 177–8; E. Kerridge, *Agrarian Problems in the Sixteenth Century and After* (London, 1969), pp. 66–9.

20. Holden, *Negotiable Instruments*, pp. 33–6, 78; 1 Co. Inst., p. 182; *Reports of Sir Humphrey Winch* (Winch) (London, var. eds), p. 24; T. Carthew, *Reports of Cases adjudged in the Court of King's Bench from the Third Year of King James the Second to the Twelfth Year of King William the Third* (Carth.) (London, var. eds), pp. 369–70; R. D. Richards, *The Early History of Banking in England* (London, 1929), pp. 47–9; Plucknett, *Common Law*, pp. 246, 668–9; *The Reports of Sir George Croke knt . . . during the Reign of James the First* (Cro. Jac.) (London, var. eds), p. 306; J. Keble, *Reports in the Court of King's Bench from XII to XXX year of King Charles II* (Keb.) 2 parts (London, var. eds), pt. 1, pp. 592, 636; pt. 2, pp. 105, 132–3; W. Dalison, *Les Reports des divers Special Cases* (London, var. eds), p. 104; F. Moore, *Cases Collect & Report* (Moo., KB) (London, var. eds), p. 667. The Court of Admiralty dealt with extra-territorial law merchant cases.

21. T. Leach (ed.), *Modern Reports or Select Cases* (Mod.) (12 vols., London, var. eds), vol. 12, pp. 687–8; 4 Co. Inst., pp. 36–7; 2 Co. Inst., proem.

22. 2 Co. Inst., proem; 4 Co. Inst., p. 25; J. R. Tanner, *Constitutional Documents of the Reign of James I, 1603–25* (Cambridge, 1930), p. 341; G. W. Prothero, *Select Statutes and Constitutional Documents Illustrative of the Reigns of Elizabeth and James I* (Oxford, 1906), p. 341; Howell (ed.), *State Trials*, vol. 2, col. 389.

23. 8 Co. Rep., p. 118; 2 Brownl., pp. 265–6; 12 Mod., pp. 672, 687; R. Skinner, *Reports of Cases Adjudged in the Court of King's Bench* (Skin.) (London, var. eds), pp. 526–7, Gough, *Fundamental Law*, pp. 10, 11, 17, 19ff., 216; Thorne, *Statutes*, pp. 84ff.

24. Thorne, *Statutes*, pp. 29, 36, 51–4, 56–8, 60–1, 64–5, 67–9, 75, 77, 79ff., 123ff., 134, 136, 139ff., 154ff., 171, 214–15.

25. Ibid., pp. 53, 61–3, 72–4, 79, 85–8, 92; B. C. Hunt, *The Development of the Business Corporation in England 1800–1867* (Cambridge, Mass., 1936), pp. 6, 7, 41; Gras, *Corn Market*, pp. 132–3, 138; Davies, *Apprenticeship*, p. 253; H. Heaton, *The Yorkshire Woollen and Worsted Industries* (Oxford, 1965), pp. 140–3; E. M. Leonard, *The Early History of English Poor Relief* (Cambridge, 1900), p. 51; 1 Co. Inst., p. 379, 383; 2 Co. Inst., pp. 61–2, 199; 3 Co. Inst., p. 204; 4 Co. Inst., pp. 29, 31, 76, 174; 8 Co. Rep., fo. 118v.; J. Vaughan, *Reports and Arguments* (London, var. eds), p. 337.

26. Vaughan, *Reports*, p. 336; W. H. Price, *The English Patents of Monopoly* (London, Boston and New York, 1906), pp. 11, 12, 142; Smith, *De Republica Anglorum*, p. 45; Thorne, *Statutes*, pp. 168–9; E. Misselden, *Free Trade or the Meanes to make Trade Florish* (London, 1622), p. 62 recte, 42 erron.; 3 Co. Inst., pp. 181, 196; 4 Co. Inst., p. 63.

27. 2 Co. Inst., p. 63; 4 Co. Inst., p. 172; Gough, *Fundamental Law*, pp. 11, 31–3, 143, 178; G. R. Elton, *Studies in Tudor and Stuart Politics and Government* (2

vols., Cambridge, 1974), vol. 1, pp. 261, 265; W. J. Jones, *Politics and the Bench* (London, 1971), pp. 45–7; J. E. Neale, *The Elizabethan House of Commons* (Harmondsworth, 1963), pp. 290ff.; J. H. Gleason, *The Justices of Peace in England 1558 to 1640*, (Oxford, 1969), pp. 83, 86–8, 94; M. Dalton, *The Countrey Justice* (London, 1618), p. 62 *et passim*; J. Fortescue, *A Learned Commendation of the Politique Lawes of England* (London, 1567), pp. 116–17; W. Raleigh, *The Cabinet-Council, Containing the Chief Arts of Empire and Mysteries of State Discabineted* J. Milton (ed.) (London, 1658), p. 129; cf. D. O. Wagner, 'Coke and the Rise of Economic Liberalism,', *Economic History Review*, vol. 6 (1936), pp. 30ff.; 'The Common Law and Free Enterprise', ibid., vol. 7 (1937), pp. 217ff.

28. D. North, *Discourse upon Trade* (London, 1691), postscript pp. i, ii; and see H. M. Robertson, *Aspects of the Rise of Economic Individualism* (Cambridge, 1935), p. 73.

29. W. Notestein, F. H. Relf and A. Simpson, *Commons Debates 1621* (7 vols., New Haven, 1935), vol. 2, pp. 252–4, 318, 423; vol. 3, pp. 66–7; vol. 5, pp. 94, 346; vol. 6, p. 94; S. Kramer, *The English Craft Gilds; Studies in Their Progress and Decline* (New York, 1927), pp. 161, 205–6.

30. Statute 5 & 6 Ed. VI c. 14; 3 Co. Inst., pp. 196–7.

31. 3 Co. Inst., p. 219; Statutes 4 Hy VII c. 11; 22 Hy VIII c. 1; 33 Hy VIII c. 16; 37 Hy VIII c. 15; 1 Ed. VI c. 6; 3 & 4 Ed. VI cc. 9, 21; 5 & 6 Ed. VI cc. 7, 14; 2 & 3 P. & M. c. 13; 1 Eliz. c. 18; 13 Eliz. c. 25; Cheshire Record Office (RO), Quarter Sessions Records 19: Miscellaneous List of Informations etc. 27–9 Eliz. nos. 1–4, 14, 15, 19–21, 23–6, 31, 38; F. G. Emmison, *Elizabethan Life: Home, Work and Land* (Chelmsford, 1976), pp. 178 ff., 184–6; B. H. Cunnington, *Records of the County of Wiltshire* (Devizes, 1932), pp. 26, 31, 96, 109–10, 285; A. H. A. Hamilton, *Quarter Sessions from Queen Elizabeth to Queen Anne* (London, 1878), p. 103.

32. Notestein *et al.*, *Commons Debates*, vol. 2, pp. 317–8; vol. 3, p. 66; vol. 5, pp. 93–4; vol. 6, p. 94.

33. 2 Co. Inst., p. 47.

34. Ibid., pp. 47, 63; 11 Co. Rep., fos. 53v–4, 84–8.

35. 11 Co. Rep., fos. 53v–4; H. Hobart, *The Reports* (Hob.) (London, var. eds), pp. 210–11; *The Reports of Sir George Croke knt . . . during the reign of Charles I* (Cro. Car.) (London, var. eds), p. 499; *Commons' Journals*, vol. 13, pp. 376, 404, 657, 664, 783; vol. 14, pp. 31–2, 67–8; Statutes 11 Hy VII c. 11; 12 Hy VII c. 1; 19 Hy VII c. 17; 14 & 15 Hy VIII c. 3; 21 Hy VIII c. 21; 3 & 4 Ed. VI c. 22; 5 & 6 Ed. VI cc. 8, 24; 2 & 3 P. & M. c. 11; 4 & 5 P. & M. c. 5; 5 Eliz. c. 4; 8 Eliz. c. 11; 14 Car. II c. 15; 22 & 23 Car. II c. 8; 5 & 6 W. & M. c. 9; 1 Anne stat. 2 c. 18; 1 Geo. c. 41; Davies, *Apprenticeship*, pp. 2, 8, 11, 210–11, 226, 241–2, 262, 264–6 *et passim*; Heaton, *Yorks.*, pp. 35–6; O. J. Dunlop, *English Apprenticeship in History* (London, 1912), pp. 213ff., 222; G. W. Hilton, *The Truck System, Including a History of the British Truck Acts, 1465–1960* (Cambridge, 1960), pp. 64, 73, 89; G. D. Ramsay, *The Wiltshire Woollen Industry in the Sixteenth and Seventeenth Centuries* (London, 1965), pp. 60–2; 'Industrial *Laissez-faire* and the Policy of Cromwell', *Economic History Review*, vol. 16 (1946), p. 97; M. James, *Social Problems and Policy during the Puritan Revolution* (London, 1930), p. 173; G. Unwin, *Industrial Organisation in the Sixteenth and Seventeenth Centuries* (London, 1963), pp. 117–18, 252; H. Stewart, *History of the Worshipful Company of Gold and Silver Wyre Drawers* (London, 1891), pp. 70, 91.

36. J. R. Burton, *A History of Kidderminster* (London, 1890), p. 176; W. Hudson and J. C. Tingey, *The Records of the City of Norwich* (2 vols., Norwich and London, 1906–10), vol. 2,p;. 376–7; P. Morant, *The History and Antiquities of Colchester* (London, 1748), p. 75.

37. Ramsay, 'Industrial *Laissez-faire*', pp. 105–6; J. de L. Mann, 'Clothiers and Weavers in Wiltshire during the Eighteenth Century' in L. S. Pressnell (ed.), *Studies*

148 Early Modern English Markets

in the *Industrial Revolution presented to T. S. Ashton* (London, 1960), p. 86; W. Money, *The History of the Ancient Town and Borough of Newbury* (Oxford and London, 1887), pp. 242–3; A. Lynes, *History of Coventry Textiles* (Coventry, 1952), p. 11; Davies, *Apprenticeship*, pp. 115–17, 131, 133–4, 139; Emmison, *Home, Work and Land*, p. 195; M. Bateson, *Records of the Borough of Leicester* (3 vols., Cambridge, 1899–1905), vol. 3, pp. xviii, xxxvii–viii, 91, 156, 409–10; W. G. Benham, *The Oath Book or Red Parchment Book of Colchester* (Colchester, 1907), pp. 92–3, 96–8, 102–3, 111, 114, 117, 120, 127, 130, 132–3, 136, 147ff., 154, 156, 158, 160, 162–3, 172–3, 175ff., 182, 233, 236–7; Dunlop, *Apprenticeship*, pp. 58–9; Stephens, *Exeter*, pp. 73–5, 79; P. Millican, *The Register of the Freemen of Norwich 1548–1713* (Norwich, 1934); *A Calendar of the Freemen of Great Yarmouth 1429–1800* Norfolk and Norwich Archaeological Society (1910); *A Calendar of the Freemen of Lynn 1292–1836*, idem (1913); J. H. E. Bennett, *The Rolls of the Freemen of the City of Chester*, Record Society for Lancashire and Cheshire, vol. 51, 55 (1906–8); 11 Co. Rep., fos. 53–4; Hob., pp. 210–11.

38. Morant, *Colchester*, pp. 74–5; W. J. C. Moens, *Register of Baptisms in the Dutch Church at Colchester from 1645 to 1728*, Publications of the Huguenot Society of London, vol. 12 (1905), pp. xl, 146; J. May, *A Declaration of the Estate of Clothing* (London, 1613), pp. 50–1; Hudson and Tingey, *Records of Norwich*, vol. 2, pp. lxvii–viii, 105–6, 108, 145–6, 150–1, 408–9; A. D. Dyer, *The City of Worcester in the Sixteenth Century* (Leicester, 1973), pp. 96, 114–15; Burton, *Kidderminster*, pp. 174–5; Public Record Office (PRO), State Papers Domestic (SPD), Eliz. vol. 106 no. 48; vol. 242 no. 75; Jas. vol. 120 no. 95; vol. 130 nos. 140–1, 144; vol. 133 no. 35; Chas. vol. 293 no. 86; vol. 341 nos. 100–1; Interreg. vol. 124 no. 97; Supplementary vol. 80 fos. 104ff.; E. Misselden, *The Circle of Commerce* (London, 1623), p. 61.

39. Misselden, *Circle*, p. 62; *Free Trade*, pp. 42, 55, 62–3 recte, 47 erron., 64, 70, 74, 76–7; A. C. Wood, *A History of the Levant Company* (Oxford, 1935), pp. 64, 67, 72, 138; G. Unwin, *Studies in Economic History* (London, 1958), pp. 149ff., 170, 176–7, 180, 183–5; J. Wheeler, *A Treatise of Commerce* (London, 1601), pp. 24–5, 31–3, 36, 46, 56, 58–9, 101, 103; A. Friis, *Alderman Cockayne's Project and the Cloth Trade* (Copenhagen and London, 1927), pp. 77ff., 81, 88–9, 92–3, 95, 99, 100; H. Parker, *Of a Free Trade* (London, 1648), pp. 28–9; M. James, *Social Problems*. pp. 149ff., 157; G. D. Ramsay, *The City of London in International Politics at the Accession of Elizabeth Tudor* (Manchester, 1975), pp. 44–5, 48, 73, 134, 136–9; T. S. Willan, *Studies in Elizabethan Foreign Trade* (Manchester, 1959), pp. 45–6; J. Haynes, *Great Britain's Glory* (London, 1715), p. 16; Anon., *Reasons Humbly Offered by the Governour, Assistants and Fellowship of the Eastland Merchants against the Giving of a General Liberty* (sine loco, 1689), pp. 4, 9, 12–14; A. F. W. Papillon, *Memoirs of Thomas Papillon of London, Merchant (1623–1702)* (Reading, 1887), pp. 61–3; W. Noy, *Reports and Cases taken in the time of Queen Elizabeth, King James, and King Charles* (Noy) (London, var. eds), p. 182.

40. Noy, p. 182; 8 Co. Rep., p. 125; 11 Co. Rep., fo. 54.

41. Noy, p. 182; Cooper, *Industrial Law*, pp. 348–9; M. D. Harris, *The Coventry Leet Book A.D. 1420–1555* Early English Text Society, vol. 134–5, 138, 146 (1907–13), pp. 687, 694; Unwin, *Industrial Organisation*, pp. 50, 120, 132–3, 199, 210, 216ff., 226, 245ff.; Nef, *Coal Industry*, vol. 2, pp. 177–9; Dyer, *Worcester*, p. 116; Historical Manuscripts Commission (HMC), *12th Rep.*, App., pt. 9, pp. 416–18; HMC, *Various Collections*, vol. 8, pp. 581ff.; Stewart, *Wyre Drawers*, p. 91; M. Dunsford, *Historical Memoirs of the Town and Parish of Tiverton* (Exeter, 1790), pp. 205–6, 208–9, 226ff., 238–9, 247ff., 253; A. P. Wadsworth and J. de L. Mann, *The Cotton Trade and Industrial Lancashire 1600–1780* (Manchester, 1931), pp. 343ff., 361.; Statues 12 Geo. c. 34; 29 Geo. II c. 33; 39 Geo. III c. 81; 39 & 40 Geo. III c. 106; K. H. Burley, 'A Note on a Labour Dispute in Eighteenth Century Colchester', *Bulletin of the Institute of Historical Research*, vol. 29 (1956), pp. 225–8; J. Latimer,

The Annals of Bristol in the Eighteenth Century (Bristol, 1893), p. 70; A. Plummer, *The London Weavers' Company 1600–1970* (London, 1972), pp. 166, 292ff., 320 ff., 327; J. de L. Mann, *The Cloth Industry in the West of England from 1640 to 1880* (Oxford, 1971), pp. 108, 123, 125ff., 140–1; 'Clotheries and Weavers', pp. 67–8, 70–2, 93–4; Cunnington, *Records of Wilts.*, pp. 259–60; E. Hughes, *North Country Life in the Eighteenth Century: The North-East 1700–1750* (London, 1952), p. 16; W. Cunningham, *The Growth of English Industry and Commerce* (3 vols., Cambridge, 1907), vol. 2, p. 508; J. L. and B. Hammond, *The Skilled Labourer 1760–1832* (London, 1936), pp. 145–6, 149, 196; M. F. L. Prichard, 'The Decline of Norwich', *Economic History Review*, 2nd ser., vol. 3 (1950), p. 372; M. D. George, 'The Combination Laws Reconsidered', *Economic History*, vol. 2 (1929), pp. 214ff.; *Commons' Journals*, vol. 9, p. 375; vol. 15, pp. 312–13; vol. 18, p. 715; vol. 20, pp. 268–9, 598–9, 647–8; vol. 27, pp. 503, 683, 730–2; W. E. Minchinton, 'The Beginnings of Trade Unionism in the Gloucestershire Woollen Industry', *Transactions of the Bristol and Gloucestershire Archaeological Society*, vol. 70 (1951), p. 131.

42. Minchinton, 'Trade Unionism', p. 131; *Commons' Journals*, vol. 27, pp. 503, 683, 730–2; Statutes 11 Hy VII c. 22; 4 Hy VIII c. 5; 6 Hy VIII c. 3; 5 Eliz. c. 4; 39 Eliz. c. 12; 1 Jas c. 6; 29 Geo. II c. 33; 30 Geo. II c. 12; S. T. Bindoff, 'The Making of the Statute of Artificers' in S. T. Bindoff, J. Hurstfield and C. H. Williams (eds), *Elizabethan Government and Society: Essays Presented to Sir John Neale* (London, 1961), pp. 75ff.; R. K. Kelsall, *Wage Regulation under the Statute of Artificers* (London, 1938), pp. 3, 6–9, 16ff., 23–5, 27–8, 56–8, 62–4, 78ff., 84–5, 99, 104–5; R. H. Tawney, 'The Assessment of Wages in England by the Justices of the Peace', *Vierteljahrschrift fuer Sozial-und Wirtschaftsgeschichte*, vol. 11 (1913), p. 336; vol. 12 (1914), pp. 539, 549–51, 556–7, 560, 562, 564; Hamilton, *Quarter Sessions*, pp. 249, 265–6; Hammond, *Skilled Labourer*, pp. 57–9; M. James, *Social Problems*, pp. 175–7; Ramsay, '*Industrial Laissez-faire*', p. 102; Mann, *Cloth Industry*, pp. 110–13, 117; 'Clothiers and Weavers', pp. 69–71, 79; Hilton, *Truck System*, pp. 45, 74–5, 77–8, 89; Plummer, *London Weavers' Co.*, pp. 324ff.; Cunnington, *Records of Wilts.*, pp. 43, 93–4, 105–6; Emmison, *Home, Work and Land*, p. 165; Woodward, *Henry Best*, pp. xxxvii–xl, xlix, 73, 83, 139–41, 178–81, 184–6, 188ff.; HMC, *Various Collections*, vol. 1 pp. 94, 162ff., 167ff.; Unwin, *Industrial Organisation*, pp. 119–20, 223, 252.

43. Unwin, *Industrial Organisation*, pp. 82, 183–6; T. S. Willan, *A Tudor Book of Rates* (Manchester, 1962), pp. xlvii, xlixff.; N. S. B. Gras, *The Early English Customs System* (Cambridge, Mass., 1918), pp. 128–9; E. E. Hoon, *The Organisation of the English Customs System 1696–1786* (Newton Abbot, 1968), pp. 2, 243; Ramsay, *City of London*, pp. 151–4, 157, 163, 167, 170–3, 178, 189ff.; 202–3; R. Davis, 'The Rise of Protection in England, 1689–1786', *Economic History Review* 2nd ser., vol. 19 (1966), pp. 307ff.; M. Priestley, 'Anglo-French Trade and the "Unfavourable Balance" Controversy, 1660–1685', ibid., vol. 4 (1951), pp. 37ff.; H. Hall, *A History of the Custom-Revenue in England from the Earliest Times to the Year 1827* (2 vols., London, 1892), vol. 1, pp. 17–19, 151ff.; T. Birch (ed.), *A Collection of the State Papers of John Thurloe* (7 vols., London, 1742), vol. 1, pp. 199, 200; J. James, *History of the Worsted Manufacture in England* (London, 1857), pp. 178–81, 204–5; F. Warner, *The Silk Industry of the United Kingdom* (London, n.d.), p. 490; F. W. Cross, *History of the Walloon and Huguenot Church at Canterbury*, Publications of the Huguenot Society of London, vol. 15 (1898), pp. 245–6, 253; N. B. Harte, 'The Rise of Protection and the English Linen Trade, 1690–1790' in N. B. Harte and K. G. Ponting (eds), *Textile History and Economic History: Essays in Honour of Miss Julia de Lacy Mann* (Manchester, 1973), pp. 76ff., 92, 97–8; Mann, *Cloth Industry*, pp. 15, 16; C. W. Cole, *Colbert and a Century of French Mercantilism* (2 vols., London, 1939), vol. 1, pp. 427ff.; vol. 2, pp. 566–7; W. T. Morgan, 'Economic Aspects of the Negotiations at Ryswick' in I. R. Christie (ed.), *Essays in Modern History* (London, 1968), pp. 181, 185, 187, 190, 193; Papillon, *Memoirs*, pp.

140-2; Friis, *Cockayne's Project*, pp. 193ff.; H. Horwitz, *The Parliamentary Diary of Narcissus Luttress 1691–1693* (Oxford, 1972), pp. 239, 361; Bodleian Library, Rawlinson MSS, A.478 fos. 79, 80, 99ff.; Statutes 5 Eliz. c. 7; 39 Eliz. c. 14; 3 Chas c. 4; M. B. Donald, *Elizabethan Monopolies: The History of the Company of Mineral and Battery Works from 1565 to 1604* (Edinburgh and London, 1961), p. 134; M. Prestwich, *Cranfield: Politics and Profits under the Early Stuarts* (Oxford, 1966), pp. 1ff., 22, 25–6, 30–1, 119–20, 187–90, 205; R. H. Tawney, *Business and Politics under James I: Lionel Cranfield as Merchant and Minister* (Cambridge, 1958), pp. 132–4.

44. P. F. Tytler, *England under the Reigns of Edward VI and Mary* (2 vols., London, 1839), vol. 1, p. 341; Gras, *Corn Market*, pp. 134ff., 155–6, 226, 230–1, 243; Barnes, *Corn Laws*, pp. 3, 9; V. Ponko, Jr, 'N. S. B. Gras and Elizabethan Corn Policy: A Re-examination of the Problem', *Economic History Review*, 2nd ser. vol. 17 (1964), pp. 34, 36, 38–41; John, 'Agricultural Improvements', p. 47; W. Camden, *The History of the Most Renowned and Victorious Princess Elizabeth, late Queen of England* (London, 1688), pp. 56, 82; Statutes 25 Hy VIII c. 2; 1 & 2 P. & M. c. 5; 1 Eliz. c. 11; 5 Eliz. c. 5; 13 Eliz. c. 13; 35 Eliz. c. 7; 1 Jas c. 25; 21 Jas c. 28; 3 Chas c. 5; 12 Chas II c. 4; 15 Chas II c. 7; 22 Chas 2 c. 13; 25 Chas II c. 1; W. Notestein and F. H. Relf (eds), *Commons Debates for 1629* (Minneapolis, 1921), p. 107; Notestein *et al.*, *Commons Debates*, vol. 2, pp. 29, 177–9; vol. 7, pp. 108–10.

45. Notestein *et al.*, *Commons Debates*, vol. 2, p. 177; vol. 5, p. 171; Barnes, *Corn Laws*, pp. 9, 10; B. D. Henning, *The Parliamentary Diary of Sir Edward Dering 1670–1673* (New Haven, 1940), pp. 100, 126; *Acts of the Privy Council 1627*, pp. 148, 173; Statutes 15 Chas II c. 7; 25 Chas II c. 1; 1 Jas II c. 19; 1 W. & M. c. 12; Gras, *Corn Market*, pp. 144ff.

46. Gras, *Corn Market*, pp. 152ff., 183–4, 186; Notestein *et al.*, *Commons Debates*, vol. 7, pp. 213ff.; Emmison, *Home, Work and Land*, p. 176; *Victoria County History (VCH) of Leicestershire*, vol. 4, p. 79; Hamilton, *Quarter Sessions*, pp. 26–7; H. C. Johnson, *Wiltshire County Records: Minutes of Proceedings in Sessions 1563 and 1574 to 1592*, Wilts. Record Society, vol. 4 (1948), pp. 1ff.; C. H. Firth and R. S. Rait, *Acts and Ordinances of the Interregnum 1642–1660* (3 vols., London, 1911), vol. 2, pp. 442–3; W. Harrison, *The Description of England*, New Shakespeare Society (1877), pp. 295–6; Statutes 5 & 6 Ed. VI c. 14; 1 Eliz. c. 18; 5 Eliz. c. 12; 13 Eliz. c. 25; 21 Jas c. 22; 3 Chas c. 5; Cunnington, *Records of Wilts.*, pp. 25, 28, 86, 105, 107, 124, 199.

47. Cunnington, *Records of Wilts.*, pp. 182–3; Ponko, 'Gras', pp. 27ff.; Emmison, *Home, Work and Land*, pp. 178ff.; Hamilton, *Quarter Sessions*, p. 103; J. Kirshner in De Roover, *Business, Banking and Economic Thought*, p. 24; Leonard, *Poor Relief*, p. 334; *VCH Leics.* vol. 4, p. 95; Firth and Rait, *Acts and Ordinances*, vol. 2, p. 442; Gras, *Corn Market*, p. 228, 233ff.

48. Gras, *Corn Market*, pp. 223, 240–1; Leonard, *Poor Relief*, p. 333; *VCH Leics.* vol. 4, p. 108; *VCH Soms.* vol. 2, p. 308; H. Stocks, *Records of the Borough of Leicester 1603–1688* (Cambridge, 1923), p. 74; S. R. Gardiner (ed.), *Reports of Cases in the Courts of Star Chamber and High Commission*, Camden Society, new ser., vol. 39 (1886), p. 83; R. H. Tawney, *The Agrarian Problem in the Sixteenth Century* (London, 1912), p. 22; PRO, SPD, Jas vol. 113, no 22; vol. 137, no. 16; Chas vol. 177, no. 50; vol. 189, no 12; *Acts of the Privy Council* vol. 30, pp. 733–5; vol. 33, pp. 457–8, 652–3; 1629–30, p. 373; 1630–1, p. 240.

49. Harper, *Navigation Laws*, pp. 9, 10, 19ff., 41, 48–9, 53–4, 58–61, 233–6, 273, 319–20, 356, 361–3, 377, 389; Willan, *Coasting Trade*, pp. 15, 17; O. A. Johnsen, 'The Navigation Act of 9 October 1651', *History*, vol. 34 (1949), pp. 89ff.; Statutes 1 Jas II c. 18; 9 Geo. II c. 37.

50. H. Gurney (ed.), 'Extracts from a Manuscript containing Portions of the Proceedings of the Corporation of Lynn Regis, in Norfolk, from 1430 to 1731, taken from the Hall Books', *Archaeologia*, vol. 24 (1832), pp. 325–6; J. Latimer, *The*

Annals of Bristol in the Seventeenth Century (Bristol, 1900), p. 393; P. McGrath, *Merchants and Merchandise in Seventeenth Century Bristol* Bristol Record Society, vol. 19 (1955), pp. 163–6; Heaton, *Yorks.*, p. 124; 4 Co. Inst., p. 273; M. James, *Social Problems*, pp. 162–4; A. H. Johnson, *The History of the Worshipful Company of the Drapers of London* (5 vols., Oxford, 1914–22), vol. 1, pp. 166–7; Ramsay, *Wilts.*, p. 53; W. B. Willcox, *Gloucestershire: A Study in Local Government 1590–1640* (New Haven, 1940), p. 165; R. Thoresby, *The Diary of Ralph Thoresby*, J. Hunter (ed.) (2 vols., London, 1830), vol. 2, p. 18; Neale, *House of Commons*, pp. 369ff.; Gough, *Fundamental Law*, p. 42; Burton, *Kidderminster*, pp. 176–7; T. C. Mendenhall, *The Shrewsbury Drapers and the Welsh Wool Trade in the XVI and XVII Centuries* (London, 1953), pp. 124–6, 128, 142–3, 164, 167–8, 172–3, 176, 181, 183–4, 187; Hudson and Tingey, *Records of Norwich*, vol. 2, pp. lxxv–vii, 150–1, 408–10; Dyer, *Worcester*, p. 114; Mann, *Cloth Industry*, p. 108; Statutes 14 & 15 Hy VIII c. 5; 21 Hy VIII c. 21; 26 Hy VIII c. 16; 27 Hy VIII c. 12; 1 & 2 P. & M. c. 14; 14 Eliz. c. 10; 27 Eliz. c. 18; 4 Jas c. 2; 12 Chas II c. 22; 14 Chas II cc. 5, 15, 32; 22 & 23 Chas II c. 8; 7 Anne c. 13; 10 Anne c. 16; 1 Geo. stat. 2 c. 15; 12 Geo. c. 34; 11 Geo. II c. 28; 14 Geo. II c. 35; Firth and Rait, *Acts and Ordinances*, vol. 2, pp. 451ff., 775ff., 1137.

51. 3 Co. Inst., pp. 204–5; Statute 4 Hy IV c. 2; J. Rushworth, *Historical Collections for the year 1639–40* (London, 1680), App., p. 107; my *Agrarian Problems*, pp. 120–1.

52. Kerridge, *Agrarian Problems*, pp. 124–7, 200–3; *Agricultural Revolution*, pp. 108ff., 181ff.; J. E. Neale, *Elizabeth I and her Parliaments* (2 vols., London, 1965), vol. 2, pp. 337ff.; Notestein et al., *Commons Debates*, vol. 4, p. 359; S. D'Ewes, *A Compleat Journal of the House of Lords and House of Commons throughout the whole Reign of Queen Elizabeth* (London, 1693), pp. 674–5; 3 Co. Inst., pp. 192, 204–5; 4 Co. Inst., p. 171; J. Bridgman, *Reports of that Grave and Learned Judge Sir John Bridgman* (Bridg.) (London, var. eds), pp. 89–90; Statutes 1 Ed. IV c. 1; 4 Hy VII cc. 16, 19; 6 Hy VIII c. 5; 7 Hy VIII c. 1; 27 Hy VIII cc. 22, 28; 5 & 6 Ed. VI c. 5; 2 & 3 P. & M. c. 2; 1 Eliz. c. 18; 5 Eliz. c. 2; 13 Eliz. c. 25; 14 Eliz. c. 11; 27 Eliz. c. 11; 29 Eliz. c. 5; 31 Eliz. c. 10; 35 Eliz. c. 7; 39 Eliz. cc. 1, 2; 43 Eliz. c. 9; 1 Jas c. 25; 21 Jas c. 28; H. Townshend, *Historical Collections or an Exact Account of the Proceedings in the Last Four Parliaments of Queen Elizabeth* (London, 1680), pp. 188–9, 299, 300.

53. Townshend, *Historical Collections*, pp. 188–9; Statutes 24 Hy VIII c. 4; 5 Eliz. c. 5; 35 Eliz. c. 7.

54. Dempsey, *Interest and Usury*, pp. 134, 141–4, 165–6, 171ff., 189; Firth and Rait, *Acts and Ordinances*, vol. 2, pp. 548ff.; Statutes 3 Hy VII cc. 5, 6; 11 Hy VII c. 8; 37 Hy VIII c. 9; 5 & 6 Ed. VI c. 20; 13 Eliz. c. 8; 35 Eliz. c. 7; 21 Jas c. 17; 3 Chas c. 4; 12 Chas II c. 13; 12 Anne stat. 2 c. 16; R. Ehrenberg, *Capital and Finance in the Age of the Renaissance* (London, 1928), pp. 246–7, 312, 323–4; J. F. Bergier, 'Taux de l'Interet et Credit a court Terme a Geneve dans la seconde moite du XVIe siecle' in *Studi in Onore di Amintore Fanfani*, vol. 4 (Milan, 1962), pp. 101–2, 119; M. Grice-Hutchinson, *Early Economic Thought in Spain 1177–1740* (London, 1978), p. 48.

55. 3 Co. Inst., p. 124; 4 Co. Inst., pp. 89, 92; R. W. Chambers, *Thomas More* (London, 1951), p. 272; Plucknett, *Common Law*, pp. 696–7; *The* Anglica Historia *of Polydore Vergil, A.D. 1485–1537* D. Hay (ed.), Royal Historical Society, Camden 3rd ser., vol. 74 (1950), pp. xxix, 276–9; *Letters and Papers, Foreign and Domestic, of the Reign of Henry VIII*, vol. 4, pt. 3, no. 5749; E. Kerridge, 'The Returns of the Inquisitions of Depopulation', *English Historical Review*, vol. 70 (1955), pp. 214ff.; *Lord Nottingham's 'Manual of Chancery Practice' and 'Prolegomena of Chancery and Equity'*, D. E. C. Yale (ed.) (Cambridge, 1965), p. 10.

56. C. E. Challis, *The Tudor Coinage* (Manchester, 1978), pp. 83ff., 312ff.; J. D.

Gould, *The Great Debasement: Currency and the Economy in mid-Tudor England* (Oxford, 1970), pp. 43ff.; R. De Roover, *Gresham on Foreign Exchange* (Cambridge, Mass. and London, 1949), pp. 51ff.; Smith, *De Republica Anglorum*, p. 45; 3 Co. Inst., p. 171.

57. 12 Co. Rep., p. [31]; Kerridge 'Returns', pp. 222–3.

58. Kerridge 'Returns', pp. 216ff., 225; Rushworth, *Historial Collections*, App., p. 107; H. R. Trevor-Roper, *Archbishop Laud* (London, 1940), pp. 168–70; E. C. K. Gonner, *Common Land and Inclosure* (London, 1912), pp. 166–7; E. M. Leonard, 'The Inclosure of Common Fields in the Seventeenth Century', *Transactions of the Royal Historical Society*, new ser., vol. 19 (1905), p. 129; S. R. Gardiner, *History of England from the Accession of James I to the Outbreak of the Civil War* (10 vols., London, 1884), vol. 8, p. 77; F. W. Maitland, *The Constitutional History of England* (Cambridge, 1909), p. 263; H. Phillips, 'The Last Years of the Court of Star Chamber, 1630–41' in Christie, *Essays*, pp. 93, 101ff.

59. W. Notestein, *The Journal of Sir Simonds D'Ewes from the Beginning of the Long Parliament to the Opening of the Trial of the Earl of Strafford* (New Haven, 1923), p. 11.

60. Friis, *Cockayne's Project*, pp. 58, 94, 99, 129, 135, 138, 220–2, 230–3, 239, 241–2, 244–7, 255, 260, 267, 270, 278–9, 292–3, 343, 353, 383, 396, 458–9; Prestwich, *Cranfield*, p. 188; Parker, *Free Trade*, p. 29; E. Hughes, *Studies in Administration and Finance 1558–1825* (Manchester, 1934), pp. 67–8; Notestein et al., *Commons Debates*, vol. 2, pp. 75, 290, 325; vol. 4, p. 150; vol. 6, p. 72; M. James, *Social Problems*, p. 148; S. R. Gardiner (ed.), *Debates in the House of Commons in 1625*, Camden Society, new ser., vol. 6 (1873), pp. 39, 40; G. Malynes, *The Maintenance of Free Trade* (London, 1622), pp. 54, 68–9; Anon., *Discourse consisting of Motives for the Enlargement and Freedome of Trade* (London, 1645), pp. 18, 28, 42–3; S. D. White, *Sir Edward Coke and the Grievances of the Commonwealth* (Manchester, 1979), pp. 102–5, 107–10; Unwin, *Industrial Organisation*, p. 182.

61. Unwin, *Industrial Organisation*, pp. 144–7, 168–9, 203–4; 2 Co. Inst., pp. 47, 51; 3 Co. Inst., p. 181; 4 Co. Inst., p. 41; 8 Co. Rep., fos. 84v.–6; 11 Co. Rep., fos. 53v.–4; Price, *Patents*, pp. 7, 15ff., 71–3, 76–7, 100–1, 152–3, 160–3; D. S. Davies, 'Acontius, Champion of Toleration, and the Patent System', *Economic History Review*, vol. 7 (1936), pp. 63ff.; Notestein, *D'Ewes Journal*, p. 537; Notestein et al., *Commons Debates*, p. 509.

62. Notestein et al., *Commons Debates*, vol. 3, pp. 186–7; vol. 5, pp. 148–9; Notestein, *D'Ewes Journal*, pp. 19, 429; H. C. Darby, *The Draining of the Fens* (Cambridge, 1940), pp. 29, 30, 38ff., 44, 58–61; *VCH Lincs.*, vol. 2, p. 333; L. E. Harris, *Vermuyden and the Fens* (London, 1953), pp. 31, 37–8, 41ff., 49, 50, 60–1, 71–2, 85, 118–20; K. Lindley, *Fenland Riots and the English Revolution* (London, 1982), pp. 23ff., 39ff.; Gardiner, *Reports*, pp. 59ff.; W. R. Scott, *The Constitution and Finance of English, Scottish and Irish Joint Stock Companies to 1720* (3 vols., Cambridge, 1910–11), vol. 2, pp. 354–5; W. Dugdale, *The History of Imbanking and Drayning* (London, 1662), pp. 110–12; J. T. Rutt, *The Diary of Thomas Burton Esq.* (4 vols., London, 1828), vol. 1, p. 259; G. Stovin, 'A Brief Account of the Drainage of the Levells of Hatfield Chase and parts adjacent', *Yorks. Archaeological Journal*, vol. 37 (1948–51), pp. 385ff.; M. Williams, *The Draining of the Somerset Levels* (Cambridge, 1970), pp. 96–9.

63. S. A. Moore, *Foreshore*, pp. 169ff., 175, 180–2, 215, 256, 258–9, 281–2, 284ff., 290–2, 306; J. Thirsk, *English Peasant Farming: The Agrarian History of Lincolnshire from Tudor to Recent Times* (London, 1957), pp. 147–8; *Fenland Farming in the Sixteenth Century* (Leicester, 1953), pp. 17, 18; Notestein et al., *Commons Debates*, vol. 7, pp. 89–91; J. Smyth, *A Description of the Hundred of Berkeley*, J. Maclean (ed.) (Gloucester, 1885), pp. 69, 337ff.; Kerridge *Agricultural Revolution*, p. 128.

64. Jones, *Politics*, pp. 97–8; Notestein, *D'Ewes Journal*, pp. 11, 151; Nef, *Coal Industry*, vol. 1, p. 317; *VCH Derbys.*, vol. 2, p. 174; *VCH Leics.*, vol. 4, pp. 108–9; J. Wake, *The Brudenells of Deene* (London, 1954), pp. 124–5; G. Goodman, 'Aulicus Coquinariae' in W. Sanderson (ed.), *The Secret History of the Court of King James the First* (2 vols., Edinburgh, 1811), vol. 2, p. 152; P. A. J. Pettit, *The Royal Forests of Northamptonshire: A Study in Their Economy 1558–1714*, Northants. Record Society, vol. 23 (1968), p. 175; F. H. Manley, 'The Disafforesting of Braden', *Wilts. Archaeological Magazine*, vol. 45 (1932), pp. 549ff.; Gardiner, *History of England*, vol. 7, pp. 362–5; vol. 8, pp. 86, 282.

65. S. A. Moore, *Foreshore*, pp. 175, 258, 288, 303–4; J. Bruce (ed.), *Liber Famelicus of Sir James Whitelocke*, Camden Society (1858), pp. 51, 53–5, 57–8, 66; S. R. Gardiner (ed.), *Constitutional Documents of the Puritan Revolution 1625–1660* (Oxford, 1906), pp. 211–12.

66. Gardiner, *History of England*, vol. 7, p. 365; Pettit, *Royal Forests of Northants.*, p. 84; Notestein, *D'Ewes Journal*, p. 150; T. Birch, *The Court and Times of Charles the First* (2 vols., London, 1848), vol. 2, p. 106; A. F. Upton, *Sir Arthur Ingram* (Oxford, 1961), pp. 196–9; W. R. Fisher, *The Forest of Essex* (London, 1887), pp. 38, 42, 45.

67. S. A. Moore, *Foreshore*, pp. 180–2, 258, 285ff., 303–4, 306–7, 310, 312–13, 316, 414, 419, 424–5, 461; Smyth, *Hundred of Berkeley*, pp. 337, 346.

68. Notestein *et al.*, *Commons Debates*, vol. 3, pp. 186–7; vol. 5, pp. 148–9; E. Payton, 'The Divine Catastrophe of the Kingly Family of the House of the Stuarts' in Sanderson (ed.), *Secret History*, p. 440.

69. Moo., KB, pp. 824–5; E. Bulstrode, *The Reports* (3 pts, London, var. eds), pt. 2, pp. 197–9; Jones, *Politics*, pp. 40, 49–52; Rutt, *Diary*, vol. 1, p. 259; Notestein, *D'Ewes Journal*, p. 19; Thirsk, *English Peasant Farming*, p. 190; L. E. Harris, *Verymuyden*, p. 28; Cunningham, *Industry and Commerce*, vol. 2, p. 113; M. Albright, 'The Entrepreneurs of Fen Draining in England under James I and Charles I', *Explorations in Entrepreneurial History*, vol. 8 (1955), pp. 56ff.; 10 Co. Rep., pp. 141–3.

70. Gardiner, *Constitutional Documents*, pp. 211–12.

71. Madge, *Crown Lands*, p. 444; Pettit, *Royal Forests of Northants.*, p. 80; F. H. Manley, 'Parliamentary Surveys of the Crown Lands in Braden Forest (1651)', *Wilts. Archaeological Magazine*, vol. 46 (1933), pp. 176ff.; Upton, *Ingram*, p. 198; R. G. Albion, *Forests and Sea Power* (Cambridge, Mass., 1926), pp. 124–7; Gardiner, *History of England*, vol. 8, p. 282; *VCH Leics.*, vol. 4, pp. 108–9.

72. S. A. Moore, *Foreshore*, p. 304; Lindley, *Fenland Riots*, pp. 46–7; L. E. Harris, *Vermuyden*, pp. 43, 63–4; Price, *Patents*, p. 42; Stovin, 'Brief Account', p. 386; J. Tomlinson, *The Level of Hatfield Chace* (Doncaster, 1882), p. 290; J. E. Jackson, 'On the History of Chippenham', *Wilts. Archaeological Magazine*, vol. 3 (1856), p. 35.

73. W. R. Bisschop, *The Rise of the London Money Market 1640–1826* (London, 1910), p. 43; A. V. Judges, 'The Origins of English Banking', *History*, vol. 16 (1931), p. 142; R. D. Richards, *The Early History of Banking in England* (London, 1929), pp. 35–7.

74. Gough, *Fundamental Law*, pp. 9–11, 24, 159, 167, 172, 177–8, 188–91; C. G. Robertson, *Select Statutes, Cases and Documents to Illustrate English Constitutional History 1660–1832* (London, 1928), p. 418; Howell (ed.), *State Trials*, vol. 14, col. 860; 12 Mod., pp. 672, 687–8; Skin., pp. 526–7.

75. W. Raleigh, *Observations Touching Trade and Commerce with the Hollander, and Other Nations, as it was presented to King James* (London, 1653), pp. 69, 70; *Three Discourses of Sir Walter Raleigh*, P. Ralegh (ed.) (London, 1702), pp. 141–2.

76. Howell (ed.), *State Trials*, vol. 5, col. 992.

6 ENTREPRENEURSHIP, MARKET PROCESS AND THE INDUSTRIAL REVOLUTION IN ENGLAND

B. L. Anderson

The considerable literature on the subject of entrepreneurship in economic history testifies to the importance that has been attached to it as an explanatory factor in the study of the Industrial Revolution and economic growth in general. This chapter is not intended to review that literature but to approach the concept of entrepreneurial activity in a rather different way in order to apply it more closely to some of the evidence relating to the onset of the Industrial Revolution in England. As a generalisation it seems that the historical work on the function of the entrepreneur has been of two types. Either it has been interpreted as biographical (usually with the subject deeply embedded in the context of a particular firm or industry study), or the entrepreneurial role has been seen as a catch-all term for the whole gamut of functions — innovating, managing, marketing, etc. — within a production organisation, whether firm or farm.[1] Moreover, both types of approach, whether intentionally or not, usually locate the entrepreneurial function within a fairly circumscribed social category, assumed to possess common class or cultural characteristics.

One reason for the persistence of these approaches to the question of entrepreneurship may be a lack of stimulus from the side of theory. Certainly the fact that modern economic analysis has been concerned with final equilibria under different conditions, and especially in the perfect competition model, has tended to minimise or remove the entrepreneurial factor. Another reason may be that because the entrepreneur in eighteenth- and nineteenth-century economic history is conventionally associated with large enterprise-employers of a perceived social status, it has been difficult to avoid subsuming any distinctive entrepreneurial quality under the capitalist or managerial functions. Recent contributions to the theory of entrepreneurship from certain quarters in the economics profession indicate a revival of interest. They offer some encouragement for the economic historian to break away from conventional treatments, where the entrepreneurial element tends to be indistinguishable from its institutional setting, and to shift the emphasis to the individual actor *per se*. In what follows there is no suggestion that the entrepreneur does not in fact operate within a particular set of arrangements like a firm arising out of a wider legal-institutional framework. Rather the argument will be that this is not the most important thing about him.[2] To treat entrepreneurship as a feature of individual action, to trace it to individual perceptions and actions, as the source and spring of events and arrangements in economic history, provides some fresh insights into a qualitative factor in English economic growth whose importance is widely acknowledged but which has proved difficult to specify clearly. In the context of the early modern English economy three problem areas invite attention. One is the extent and type of market activity obtaining in the economy. Second, the growth of large firms employing wage labour thereby internalising some market transactions. Third, the question of the ownership and use of land and, linked with this, the constitutional arrangements within which economic life is carried on. We begin by briefly reviewing some new points of departure in the theory of the entrepreneur and his function in the market process.

For the economic historian, concerned as much with what evidence does not reveal as with what he believes it shows, there are difficulties in accepting literally the economist's general equilibrium concept of the entrepreneur as a decision-maker allocating and economising *known* means (factors) in the pursuit of *given* ends (output). If in theory the entrepreneur's role consists essentially in making a specifying decision, in history it seems clear that in order to specify the entrepreneur must first perceive how it is that his envisaged ends are to be achieved — he must *discover* the means. The difficulty is that the kind of entrepreneurs known to economic history are, for the most part, only successful ones, that is, those who with benefit of hindsight we can be reasonably sure had better *ex ante* expectations of how to reach *ex post* ends. In history, however, much entrepreneurial activity must have run into the sand leaving little evidence and, perhaps, having little influence on events. Clearly the entrepreneurial function cannot be defined simply in terms of its successful manifestation. This is not to deny that some skills usually associated with entrepreneurs, for example the possession of various managerial and accounting techniques, etc. may well be explicable simply in terms of 'learning by doing' or as a consequence of the deliberate acquisition of knowledge.

If, instead of considering entrepreneurship as a reaction to maximising possibilities implied or inherent in a given set of economic data, the emphasis is switched to the idea of an entrepreneur as the active originator of what has been overlooked by others, then the conventional problem of entrepreneurship can be looked at in a different way. Instead of posing the static question, what do entrepreneurs do?, we can ask the dynamic one, where does entrepreneurship come from? In practice of course, no observer could ever identify with any exactitude an ends-means situation, much less the decision-making processes which prefaced and prompted the entrepreneurial activity associated with it. But when in economic theory the optimum course of action relevant to the known, because prescribed, circumstances is identified it is by no means clear that the historian can simply follow on the theorist in predicting that the outcome of entrepreneurial action necessarily conforms to that optimum course. That could only happen if the world of history was like the general equilibrium world of perfect (complete) knowledge. Instead entrepreneurship seems to arise from the fact that profit opportunities need to be discovered before they can be exploited; indeed their exploitation may well be conceptually separable from the essential entrepreneurial element which is not simply a matter of the capacity to maximise *given* market data but of the alertness to *new* possibilities.

If the entrepreneurial element in economic action and organisation can be usefully disentangled in this way then it offers a different point of departure for relating the concept of entrepreneurship to historical change in economic organisation. It now becomes a factor that is not learnt or deliberately acquired at all; it is, in other words, not merely a typological or class category of individuals, but a function or faculty that potentially inheres in *all* individuals. Furthermore, once the equilibrium assumptions (that the entrepreneur's goal and means are both given and that prices and incomes in the relevant markets are known with certainty) are relaxed, then the manner of the entrepreneur's proceeding cannot be likened to mechanical maximising calculation alone. It cannot be characterised simply as 'learning by doing' or as 'the acquisition of knowledge deliberately sought' The entrepreneurial element in a market procedure must also depend on a 'propensity to sense' what options are actually available in existing and likely future conditions.

There is an important paradox to notice in this approach to the problem; that the unique aspect of entrepreneurship is that it is not learnt or acquired in any systematic way. In a market economy undergoing rapid change, such as that obtaining in late seventeenth- and eighteenth-century England, knowledge was certainly very incomplete, not to say highly partial and uncertain, though it was changing more quickly. As recent work on the period has shown there was at the same time growing scope for extending both domestic and overseas markets through entrepreneurial activity exploiting a widening range of demand opportunities, either hitherto unnoticed or newly capable of being taken advantage of.[3] The emergence of a 'consumer society', as it has been called, in the period 1680–1780 seems to be attributable to a major shift in economic decision-making activity at every level. The paradox lies in considering the two most obvious facets of economic decision-making in such an environment of more rapid information change accompanied by heightened uncertainty. One aspect is the 'calculative' (rational) by means of which the entrepreneur methodically arrives at the solution to a 'constrained maximisation problem' as in neoclassical microtheory; here any faulty decision-making becomes an accounting error. The other is the 'entrepreneurial' (imaginative) by means of which what is required by the market is originally noticed. Much business history characterises the businessman largely in such inspirational, even heroic, terms; here he becomes a backer of hunches, the lucky gambler catching windfalls from aloft. In principle these facets can be considered separately, but in the minds of real world economic agents it is difficult to see how the exercise of imagination can ever properly be made distinct from the use of reason.[4]

There is a further ambivalence to be noticed when considering the function of entrepreneurship in a period in which information, opportunity and risk are all extending together. In the usual sense of the word, 'calculation' (optimisation) is not itself sufficient for selecting relevant information, noticing profit opportunities and assessing likely risks. Much of the economic decision-making in the consumer revolution that preceded industrialisation in England after 1780 occurred in the exchange and distribution sectors of the economy. In other words much entrepreneurial activity in that period is in danger of being overlooked if one looks only for the forerunners of the new industries and products whose output growth and technical transformation revolutionised the economy from the end of the eighteenth century. From much earlier most entrepreneurial opportunity for gain lay in the arbitrage situations that had opened up in the train of transport improvements and easier communication of prices, product varieties and other commercial information. In this context what the decision-maker requires to have is not so much *given* means but rather perception of opportunity, a sensibility to be aware that price discrepancies, between different local markets say, can be bridged and removed. It is at the lowest level of such activity, in the actions of dealers and middlemen of all sorts, that we see how entrepreneurship is quite unlike the other resources that are manipulated in the economic process. Conventionally, entrepreneurship is almost always associated with the means of production, if not always with the capitalist proprietor *per se*. The virtue of the approach adopted by Kirzner and others lies in its emphasis on entrepreneurship as a function that is, in principle, quite independent of *any given* means.

A final irony that arises from this ambivalent quality of entrepreneurship as beginning without means is that, because on this view economic decision-making cannot simply be read off from given data, entrepreneurial decisions cannot be implied in the evidence of the circumstances obtaining. For the entrepreneur history is indeed bunk! Information is important, of course, because in actual market situations information errors yield opportunities for profitable activity on the part of entrepreneurs; these in turn call further entrepreneurial alertness into play and eventually signpost investment flows in the direction of consumer requirements yielding higher profit rates. In this way the entrepreneurs become the prime movers in the data of the markets in which they operate. In pursuing profits (pure gains) the entrepreneurs are seeking to capture the most volatile of all forms of income. In this they may possess foresight but not foreknowledge (full knowledge) in a world of historical change. Thus it turns out that they are, in essence, creatures of ignorance and indeterminacy and could not exist without them.

It is almost three-quarters of a century since R. B. Westerfield pointed to the role of middlemen in the organisation and extension of English internal trade in the century or so before the Industrial Revolution.[5] Subsequent work, more recently by Everitt especially, has generally confirmed the importance of such figures in making and remaking markets, in formal (official) ·markets serving manufactured products in towns, and fairs trading livestock in country locations. Alongside these, and increasingly supplanting them by the first half of the eighteenth century, were the informal marts such as inns and the direct, wholesale, links between factors and producers.[6] Westerfield generalised the organisation of the main internal trades as consisting of a 'five-fold succession of middlemen' — buyers of raw materials — jobbers and merchants in these materials — factors — wholesale and manufacturing merchants — and retailers.[7] Further investigation of the marketing arrangements in the home trades has revealed a much more complex picture as well as pointing up the importance of inter-neighbourhood as well as occupational specialisation in promoting internal trade, and the growth of road-carriage and newspaper circulation, in particular, for reducing transport and information costs.[8]

The enormous growth in numbers and rapid differentiation of middlemen, brokers, agents, etc. in the century or so after the Restoration, as evidenced in contemporary directories, for example, is indication enough of the profits to be earned in making markets more articulate. But the advantage of the approach to entrepreneurship adopted here is that *all* changes in prices, quantities and qualities of input used, and outputs produced, are capable of being explained in terms of pure entrepreneurial activity, whether in the form of a distinct market function for the entrepreneur as a result of the growth of specialisation, an arbitrager say; or else as an entrepreneurial element in the make-up of market participants with other primary roles, such as capitalist, manager, etc. In short, entrepreneurship becomes the active agent, wheresoever located, in explaining how prices, quantities and qualities of inputs and outputs are systematically changed over time in the direction of greater coherence.

Recent historical research has shown how uniquely favourable was the post-Restoration English economy for the exercise of pure entrepreneurship (arbitrage) in three main directions. Commenting on a wide range of evidence relating to the remarkable expansion in the numbers and variety of craftsmen as a proportion of the populations of county towns and provincial urban centres, Everitt points to the high order of physical diversity of which seventeenth- and eighteenth-century England was made up. The process by which entrepreneurial competition creates and extends markets was greatly facilitated in '. . . a landscape, a society, an economy, and in some respects a culture, that in every area was sharply divided into contrasting *pays* . . . rarely delimited by county boundaries'. The economic significance of this kaleidoscopic character of English regional development lies in the way these constellations of interfacing localities (neighbourhoods) prompted mounting specialisation of small units in crafts, services, professions, etc., all showing different degrees of specialisation in time and place.[9] In turn this economic differentiation offered increasing opportunities for noticing and removing buying-selling price spreads. Another aspect of English society which invited entrepreneurial initiative was its closely packed social strata and barely perceptible transitions from rank to rank. The relative openness of the English social order to vertical and lateral mobility might have been expected to expand the scope for emulative consumption even if the real disposable incomes of the mass of the population were not growing. But as the work of McKendrick in particular has shown the commercialisation of leisure and fashion on the basis of a sustained, if uneven, growth of real incomes in the period 1680–1780 was not less socially extensive for being hierarchical. The reverse side of these gradations of consumption growth was a pecking-order of entrepreneurs, ranging from the Wedgwoods and Boultons to the pedlars and packmen, each addressing different segments of their markets.[10]

Underpinning this unprecedented extension of the eighteenth-century markets, by geographical and social interplay revealing arbitrage opportunities, was transport development. Here recent work has shown how unbalanced is the available evidence, especially the statistical data, relating to the relative importance of the overseas and home trades as sources of English economic growth. The relative lack of tolls, duties, etc. on domestic trades, by contrast with most other European states, has left much less evidence of the undoubted freedom of the internal trades than is the case with the much more regulated foreign trades. But estimates of the capacity of the road-carriage industry indicate an approximate doubling of scheduled services output between the 1630s and 1715. Beginning at the Restoration the turnpiking of England's major roads was virtually completed by the middle of the eighteenth century. The cost advantage of inner and coastal transport was considerable, perhaps 50 per cent, over road and it seems that the carrying capacity of England's inland waterways may have doubled in the century and a half before 1700. Certainly up to the late eighteenth century the most extensive markets in England's internal trades were being served by water carriage, including coastal trade as an extension of river and canal traffic; it was in the carriage of lower value/higher bulk commodities like coal and the inferior grains that the comparative cost advantages of water transport had already produced very considerable cost reductions and market expansions over the century or more before 1700.[11] No more effective challenge was offered to the survival of local monopoly and restrictive trading practices than the corrosive power of lowering transport costs in the eighteenth century.[12]

In the long run the survival of centralised fixed location markets, of the type which grew up in the high Middle Ages, were vulnerable to their tendency to promote monopolistic practices. In medieval markets very high search and information costs doubtless represented powerful inducements to centralise traders' transactions if only in order to identify them to buyers. Market tolls and regulations such as those prohibiting the purchase and sale of designated goods within a given radius of the market, or on non-market days, may well have increased the efficiency of such markets and indicates the value of access to them for both buyers and sellers in the circumstances of that time. But the geographical concentration of transactions also seems likely to facilitate market sharing and price agreements among dealers. This is even more likely at a time when dealers were not very numerous and when there were difficulties in the way of new dealers entering the market. There seems to be firm evidence that by the eighteenth century the number of known markets had reduced by more than 50 per cent from a figure of 1,500 or more in the late thirteenth century; though numbers of official markets have almost certainly never been coincident with the total number of trading points at any given time.[13] Costly and more difficult communications and much less product differentiation would appear to justify the expectation of more numerous centralised markets in earlier times and this appears to have been the case in England. During the early modern period these old markets and fairs were being supplanted by a network of informal regional markets, frequently focusing on county towns and, of course, London from where by the eighteenth century commercial information was concentrated and disseminated and where the professions and ancillary personnel located themselves. Patterns of shires, different kinds of countrysides ('countrys') and neighbourhoods overlaid and interacted one with another through the county towns and other urban centres leading to a very complex but unmistakable increase in interregional specialisation in agriculture and craft skills.

Direct evidence of the growing trade among these heavily

variegated physical environments is difficult to document adequately and impossible to quantify precisely, if only because market arrangements and procedures had come to depend less on institution and place and much more on interpersonal relationships. This was largely a consequence of the enormous multiplication and variegation of craft skills which by the early eighteenth century had expanded the craft element in the principal English provincial towns to around half of their populations; craftsmen were several times more numerous than labourers, servants and even retailers whose numbers had also been increasing rapidly. These large numbers of small, diverse, craft firms, typically comprising a master and his family and three or four journeymen and apprentices, were obviously not catering for an overseas or even a national market in most cases, but for their own extensive regional and rural hinterlands. To describe these firms as specialist producers or as batch producers, while not inaccurate, fails to capture the wide ranges of product types and qualities which fell within (or could be and were introduced into) the practical capability of any particular craft. Such descriptions also fail to appreciate the degree to which batches and short runs of output were manipulated (enhanced, deteriorated, eventually standardised) by these firms in a constant interplay with the preferences of the final consumers to whom they were so close. These workshop firms were nurseries of entrepreneurship as much as of skill. Indeed, their character was as entrepreneurial as the consumers in the markets they served; their existence in such large numbers tells a good deal about the structure of demand in the consumer revolution of the eighteenth century, for they and their dependants constituted an important segment of it. Moreover the numbers of these kinds of firms continued to increase during industrialisation and it is quite misleading to think of them as merely 'surviving' that process.

It was to such firms, located as they were in the entrepôts of internal trade in London and the provincial centres, that merchants and middlemen turned for making up their 'assortments' of goods. It would be wrong to see these craft firms and general merchants of the home trades as being completely specialised. Modern occupational classifications are notoriously unreliable guides for comprehending and comparing economic activities in historical situations of incomplete specialisation. Though impossible to assess in quantitative terms, it seems highly probable that the common tendency to attach too precise and exclusive occupational labels to people before and during the eighteenth century has led to gross underestimation of the numbers actually involved in trade, transport and distribution. With settlement in the countryside *relatively* dispersed, towns outside of London *relatively* small, improving communications *relatively* long and difficult, the problems of assembly, storage and distribution must have absorbed much more resources of working time and effort, not to mention capital, than is commonly allowed. Sharp distinctions between agriculture, trade and services in the pre- and early-industrialisation period, for example, ignore the fact that trade and transport were important and integral parts of agricultural activity.[14] Similarly, much agricultural work in early modern England was accompanied by industrial employment which varied over time and with the seasons; indeed there seems no reason to doubt that trading was an important adjunct of industrial work in town and country, and of agricultural work as far back as the Middle Ages. Moreover, incomplete specialisation meant not just part time or 'by-employment'; workers were often involved in several specialities at the same time and at certain times of the year they may not even have been subsidiary, so that 'multi-specialised' may be a better description.[15]

Specialisation of function was not just incomplete it was also uneven across the eighteenth-century economy, with 'mixed' incomes probably more important on the land than in the towns; so that while the prevailing structure of demand may have reflected itself in the available macroestimates of income and output growth during the century, and in what we know of their sectoral distribution, it did not do so completely. Furthermore, mixed occupational pursuits and income receipts were not confined to any single section of English society. Real incomes appear to have grown more in the first half of the eighteenth century, as does agricultural productivity, while agricultural prices fell considerably relative to industrial prices. In the second half renewed population growth seems to have been expanding demand while slowing down real wages growth; on the other hand there is some evidence to think that household incomes were at least being maintained by increased work on the part of wives and children, perhaps greater regularity of labour participation offset real wage pressure, and this permitted industrial prices to fall relatively to those in agriculture. The whole question of the growth rates and distribution of *per capita* incomes in pre- and early-industrial England, however, is confounded by an awkward fact of long-standing; that households were hardly ever coterminous with natural families.[16]

The latest re-estimates of the macro-dimensions of British growth provide only indirect support for the role of the home market before and during industrialisation. Assertions in this area need to be as approximate and liable to revision as the underlying figures themselves. But it seems that growth rates of real national product were rather slower during the eighteenth century than was previously believed, not attaining a sustained 2 per cent per annum until the 1820s. No 'take-off' in the investment ratio is apparent for the later decades of the eighteenth century and total factor productivity growth and consumption per head in the second half rose only marginally above rates for the first half of the century. The impact of the cotton industry on the composition of industrial output in the later decades remains — as does its unique dependence on imports and exports — but it appears that throughout the eighteenth century investment was rising only enough to counteract population pressure on living standards, and that total exports are confirmed as not being important for the growth of national income before the last decade.[17] Taken together with the latest revisions of agricultural productivity growth, which indicate improvements of crop yields by more than 30 per cent over the period *before* 1770, there is good reason to believe that the growth of incomes prior to the middle of the eighteenth century may have been consistently underestimated.[18]

At the same time there is now detailed evidence of just how considerable was the growth of consumer wants across a wide range of the English population in the century after 1680. As yet the capital goods sector of the economy was small and largely concerned with replacement rather than with technical change and expansion; but it is clear that consumer tastes had become much more dynamic, that above the level of necessities a significant proportion of the population was experiencing a proliferation of wants, and that these were more difficult to satisfy than in the seventeenth century. This means that the returns to entrepreneurial search and discovery of market opportunities could be high. In pre-industrialised economies buying and selling activity is characterised by the investment of considerable amounts of time in information search and bargaining. It is not easy to say whether this phenomenon necessarily becomes more important during periods when discretionary incomes increase, as in eighteenth-century

England, though it is not clear that its importance should diminish. Given that English social segmentation was close and interpenetrating this would have offered incentives to entrepreneurial arbitrage activity and thus facilitated the diffusion of information across the social spectrum. In fact trading and related transport and service activities seem to have been particularly attractive to small entrepreneurs just because they could be commenced with relatively small investments of capital compared with time. Thus it seems likely that just as the absolute numbers employed in agriculture increased during industrialisation so did those engaged in internal trade, transport and distribution. But unlike local trading, capital outlays in transport seem to have become considerable quite early on and especially in the provinces where larger firms were needed to conduct more distant trading. In fact distribution seems likely to have been expensive in terms of all factors before industrialisation; but it was a vital prerequisite to furthering the completion of specialisation in exchange and production at every stage.

The point is, however, that entrepreneurial competition could be expected to make much local and interregional trading activity fairly unremunerative over time if entry conditions were reasonably easy. Of course in eighteenth-century markets price adjustment never approached spontaneity; buyers and sellers made and received over- and under-payments depending on their entrepreneurial skill or lack of it, and on their good or bad luck. In all market economies some production and consumption, and therefore some market-making activity, must always be experimental; it is only in the long run that the competitive process averages out returns. Thus when wide price ranges were frequent, as they often were in eighteenth-century agricultural market such as for wheat, buyers and sellers often attempted to reduce the risks of short-run fluctuations in supply and demand by attempting to nurture special trading relations with an opposite number; and, of course, demands for government intervention were vociferous from time to time. There is no doubt of a growing market economy in consumer goods in the eighteenth century, but where communications lagged behind effective demand at certain times or were inadequate at certain times of the year, then price differences could be considerable.[19] Moreover, this was an economy well-placed to attract arbitrage activity not just from specialist merchants but from itinerants and from the many service activities that existed to cater for most sections of society. Most of them seem to have been fairly labour-intensive, notably domestic service; and no doubt they attracted the under-employed and were a symptom of insufficiently remunerative alternative employment. But even among the small craft producers with little in the way of cash resources and storage facilities, many must have needed to trade their outputs frequently and turn over their meagre capital rapidly.

If the large numbers of intermediaries and middlemen were a consequence of the extent to which differentiation and decentralisation of economic activity had developed by the eighteenth century, they were also essential for it to proceed further. The first object of this elaborate distribution system would have been the gathering and dissemination of information about prices. We really know very little about eighteenth-century price formation. But even relatively uncomplicated farming and industry throw up wide arrays of prices when product variation is increasing. Buyers choose different quantities; some producers make in volume, others hardly ever; and each quantity/class has its own price. In a pre-industrial economy transport costs and credit terms produced considerable price disparities. Different markets arrived at prices in different ways — spot, arbitration, bargaining and auction — and weights and measures were often peculiar to particular activities and areas. About the importance of second-hand markets and their prices virtually nothing seems to be known, apart from the growing market in art; yet even a brief acquaintance with an undeveloped country today suggests that the refurbishing and inferior copying of many types of goods is an important means of transmitting more complex consumption patterns at lower prices. How typical are the prices that make up the available price indices, especially when one recalls that they are all sellers' prices? In fact from the standpoint of entrepreneurial competition a price index may well be the least helpful information around, projecting as it does the idea that there is only one price in a market at any given time and leaving no clue as to how prices are changed. Much more could be said concerning the importance of the nature and frequency of transactions in price formation. But price signals were rarely unambiguous and complete. If they required interpretation, additional search, to transform them into usable information, then the entrepreneurial function was essential.

A price is a highly concentrated information capsule, but it has always required interpretation. What is remarkable about the consumer revolution of the eighteenth century, however, was that product differentiation was proceeding so rapidly that it too, and not just prices, was requiring greater inputs of entrepreneurial activity. For, to a degree without precedent in earlier times, even at the start of the century the evidence shows that the product itself had become a variable. The price system alone could never be fully informative for that would remove any incentive to seek further information. Put another way profits are earned in the market process not just because prices convey *information* but also because they contain a return to entrepreneurial experiment, to *risk-taking*. Recently economic models of competition have begun to take account of this view of the market as being at any given time in process of becoming more efficient, with the result that such models, in order for incentive to remain for participants to go on collecting information, have no final equilibrium.[20] If the market is a metaphor for a series of interpersonal relations based on changing perceptions of product opportunities and valuations, then who but the entrepreneurs can ensure that markets tend to operate efficiently; and what can their reward be for this activity if it is not the profits earned in the intervals of adjustment? Kirzner's approach to this insight is to distinguish between 'alertness' and superior command over information. His idea of entrepreneurship is not fully comprehended by the notion of already possessing substantive knowledge of market data such as prices; alertness is the recognition of where to find and how to use appropriate data.[21] Mere possession of knowledge without the conviction to exploit its profit possibilities is *not* entrepreneurial; this is *not* a question of obtaining or affirming a property right in information.

If competition is the method of the market, generalising the economic aspect of behaviour across all the activities and institutions in a society to some degree, then because there is a risk as well as an information dimension in competition, pricing and price changes are only one facet of it. The idea that competition also works through product differences, contracting, institutional change, etc., that is, that it occurs in real time and in the face of uncertainty is evident in the work of Demsetz and others. They emphasise that the perfect competition model is better for showing how prices co-ordinate decentralised activities, rather than for analysing the essentially rivalrous process of competition, because the model assumes away transactions and information costs. It also neglects an important aspect of decentralisation — the division of knowledge in an economy — that decentralised institutions such as firms and families use their specific knowledge to engage in production, consumption and trade.[22] Moreover, as has been emphasised by Shackle in particular, lack of complete knowledge cannot be made up by any precise calculation of risk. Strictly speaking risk cannot be calculated, but only insured against; and if risk did not exist neither would choice. This is why the distinction between trading, organisational innovation and technical change, is to some extent artificial and misleading. It is the manner in which such forms of information are appraised that is decisive, and why the pure entrepreneurial element as distinct from calculation in economic decision-taking is often best revealed at the level of basic trading. In the final analysis it is not *how* to proceed but *whether* to act at all that is decisive for action. Or in Shackle's words, 'If "calculable risk" is meant to suggest that calculation can be a substitute for evidence and not merely an exploitation of it, then this phrase is a muddle and merely covers a pretence.'[23]

This brings us to a further aspect of the role of entrepreneurship in creating and extending markets for consumer goods and in speeding up the process of taste change. There seems to be no reason for thinking that entrepreneurship is a scarce resource in the usual economic sense of requiring incentives to raise its supply; so that under the right conditions it is not 'class-bound' at all but potentially socially extensive with only the prospect of pure gain needed to trigger it. Furthermore, the need for changes in the co-ordination and organisation of economic activity is not demanded as such, except perhaps by the facts of a situation; the need for such interventions is perceived to be necessary. Entrepreneurship is a supply-side phenomenon and does not require incentives to see solutions. In addition it is clear that by the eighteenth century there was a hierarchy of entrepreneurship which reflected the different types and levels of demand. Whether or not there is such a thing as a hierarchy of alertness, there was considerable entrepreneurial specialisation. London, with its uniquely large population (increasing from 200,000 in 1600 to 900,000 in 1800) was the chief focus of entrepreneurial activity, and it played a vital role in transmitting fashion changes and leisure activity to provincial centres. The pace of fashion change in the growth of home demand was very rapid and it was propelled by entrepreneurial advertising using all the modern techniques. Those who have developed the idea of a major expansion of home consumption being emulated down from the upper and middle ranks to the lowest orders tend to characterise it purely in terms of an expansion of demand, resulting from the growth of more disposable income among more sections of society. But of course 'the eager advertising, active marketing and inspired salesmanship' which figures so largely in explanations of the growth of demand in the eighteenth century is precisely the input of entrepreneurship.[24]

The role of middlemen, dealers, etc. in extending price competition and emulative consumption patterns should not be taken too far, of course; there is no doubt that for long periods, especially in remote localities, shortages and surpluses may have remained the response to short-run changes in supply and demand rather than signalling by price changes. And by the late eighteenth century much more disturbing competitive influences were building up in the form of even more new products, different technologies, sources of supply and changes in organisation. Nevertheless, greater price stability does seem to have coincided with a secular expansion in the numbers and types of market intermediaries in the century or so after the Restoration. What seems to have been distinctive about this entrepreneurial activity, compared with other European countries at the same time, was that it occurred in agriculture and the craft economy when division of labour, product type, and information channels were all increasing together. Towards the smaller entrepreneurs especially, there was often a good deal of resentment, as there always is to those who trawl for price and quality discrepancies, and a number of eighteenth-century commentators are reminiscent of modern critics of rivalrous advertising and the wasteful creation of products for which consumers are supposed to have artificial demands. But it is clear, for example, that the advantage of the petty chapmen (cheap men) over many of the local village and town shops that were also growing rapidly in number lay in their rigorous competition. They were criticised for escaping apprenticeship, taxation, rents, and public office duties; they evaded licensing or borrowed or hired licences, yet in many localities they were key figures in bringing new consumption habits to the very poor.[25] Another practice commonly protested was that of middlemen buying up goods and crops at fixed prices, in advance or in arrears of production. But this was either to finance the production and distribution of goods where the producer had little capital, or because he had already discovered what he could offer for an output already produced.[26]

It is important to note that the growth of this kind of entrepreneurial competition in the eighteenth century, especially at its leading edge in the consumer goods markets, does not depend on any prior or concurrent growth in real income, even where this may have resulted simply from fortuitous falls in agricultural prices coinciding with a period of little population change.[27] Effective demand, purchasing power currently available, is important, of course, if only because it is the only form of demand that is even approximately measurable. But behind it, and of much more immediate interest to the entrepreneur are all the latent and potential wants that make up the fine structure of demand. At prevailing income levels these may be low-preference wants, they may be ill-defined and going unsatisfied for lack of demonstration to make them realisable. Even at low income levels there may be purchasing power not currently buying anything, or there may be exchange possibilities that would improve the personal substitution rates of groups of consumers perhaps unknown to each other. Certainly, above the level of some 'minimum of necessities', final demand across a wide range of incomes is much more fickle than is commonly credited.

Consumers indeed do seek to maximise their own satisfaction, but this cannot simply be defined in terms of solely objective criteria such as price and quantity. Purchasers gain varying amounts of subjective satisfaction from what is involved in buying different kinds of goods; and they develop a subtle and tilting awareness of difference (of choice) that has its counterpart in the often slight physical differentiation of products. Moreover it is not just that different people have combinations of goods to which they attribute different personal (subjective) valuations that makes exchange possible, and thereby introduces arbitrage and the entrepreneur. Exchange exists because choice exists, not because surpluses and deficits exist. It only takes one person to make an exchange — not two. This is why people gain from trade even though the middleman-entrepreneur does as well.

Mokyr has shown by examining the various formulations of the demand side explanation for industrialisation that the standard reasons offered to account for a shifting of the demand curve for industrial goods in eighteenth-century England, such as agricultural growth, overseas demand and population increase, do not stand up to close analysis.[28] This indicates an explanation that runs from cost reductions and output growth towards demand, not the other way round; such as more effective entrepreneurial activity improving the efficiency of the market process. A study of the consumer revolution in eighteenth-century England highlights an important truth about the function of the entrepreneurial element, as not being given and known in advance, in the market process. That 'the product' consists of *everything* the purchaser receives in exchange for his money. It also leads on to a second. That 'production' is not just about making things, but about making things *useful*.

The concept of entrepreneurship outlined above is basically an arbitrage theory. In other words entrepreneurship is about relative prices; it is inseparable from the idea of profit. It sees entrepreneurial profits as always being available in a market process in the form of a permanent income stream arising out of the fact of the imperfection of knowledge. These profits have nothing to do with any specialist function in the market; they are pure gains resulting from the perception that prices are adjusting at different rates on different markets. Thus in production, for example, to the extent that the entrepreneur *also* may contribute a necessary resource in the form of capital, say, or the managerial organisation of a factor combination, then the entrepreneur is just another resource-owner to that extent. On the other hand, if the producer is buying resources and selling products, then the points of contact between the resource market and the product market is an area where pure entrepreneurship is offered scope for its initiative without, in principle, contributing any resources of its own at all.[29]

This applies whether or not the entrepreneur happens also to be a producer at the time and irrespective of whether he possesses capital, which he may anyway borrow; if he is a producer it is the pure entrepreneur in him that prompts him to hire all the talents needed to organise the factor combination and to buy, perhaps with loans, all the resource requirements needed to realise the production plan. On the other hand if the producer simply contributes his own managerial capability as its owner to the enterprise for a return equal to its implicit cost there is nothing entrepreneurial here. Simply to maximise the return on whatever resources are contributed on straightforward price-taking lines, and choosing the optimum mix of inputs in the light of technically feasible courses of action, is the activity of a constrained resource-owner, not an entrepreneur as such. It is only when the resource-owner is viewed solely as an entrepreneur, commencing his decision-making with no resource contribution to the enterprise, in other words, when there is nothing as yet to allocate and organise, that the distinction made earlier between *adaptive economising* and *creative alertness* becomes fully apparent. Hence, what is entrepreneurial in production, on this view, consists not in the least-cost input arrangement of a production plan; it inheres in the realisation that such a production possibility exists at all. Alertness is innate and independent of economic resources.

Production can be looked upon as a more complex arbitrage operation, more complex than exchange for instance, because usually the passage of time being much longer it is attended by much more uncertainty. It might be thought that business risk would always be higher in earlier times, as it often seems to be in undeveloped countries today, because of greater uncertainty in respect of such things as personal catastrophe, famine, natural disaster, political upheaval and disease. Rudimentary capital markets with few investment alternatives, and a greater preponderance of small firms with more liability to failure, might seem to make for much higher risks associated with economic activity than in industrialised countries. Whether or not this is the case it does seem to be the uncertainty associated with production, rather than the specialisation which is also characteristic of it, that exposes this activity to risk. The reason for this, it has been suggested, is that there can be no presumption that a non-specialist has more knowledge of what the future holds for him than does a specialist.[30]

Production is also much more likely, it seems, to take place in a firm than is exchange. On almost any reasonable view of what entrepreneurship is, it seems clear that it is in principle quite independent of the idea of a firm and that historically, however we choose to define it, entrepreneurship predates it. Whatever else may be said about the notion of a firm, this seems to be the most important thing about it; that it could not exist without the entrepreneur and that entrepreneurship alone is the necessary and sufficient condition for the origin of firms. The industrial structure of pre-industrialised England, to the extent that it can be sensibly distinguished in what was essentially an agricultural economy, had evolved a broadly tripartite system of organisation by the eighteenth century. This comprised handicrafts, putting-out, and the centralised production of mining, milling and shipbuilding; there was little difference in the level of technique and fixed capital between handicrafts and putting-out, but the latter was far more intensive of labour and credit. Centralised production was generally less important in terms of output and employment though fixed capital requirements were often considerable. Craft industry was to be found in town and country, putting-out usually in the rural areas; they overlapped and were internecessary, and whereas small firms were the rule in crafts, putting-out arrangements were more flexible and quite large concerns could develop to exploit possibilities for the greater division of labour.[31]

Both the craft economy and putting-out arrangements expanded more rapidly, side by side during the early modern period, the former especially in more skilful higher value-added trades and the latter particularly in textiles, underpinned by a growth of population. Some historians have attempted to characterise the expansion of putting-out in particular as a preliminary stage to the Industrial Revolution proper. Dubbed 'proto-industrialisation', it ignores the fact that putting-out industries, and for that matter craft ones as well, have experienced periods of expansion and contraction over many centuries in England down to the nineteenth. They cannot be considered peculiar to any period from at least the fourteenth century and, as Coleman has pointed out in a neat disposal of the idea, periods of expansion and contraction of putting-out simply fail to coincide with periods of rising population or falling real wages.[32] An idealised 'peasant household' or 'communal family' plays a vital role in the proto-industrialisation model; the essential point is that peasant production is considered to be almost wholly for direct consumption and that this is broken down by a 'post-feudal' development of putting-out industry which introduces the peasantry to wages and the labour market. But the English evidence is extensive and quite unequivocal that smallholders were working for wages for the local lord or wealthy villager as early as the thirteenth century.[33] Even then farmers and farm labourers were often at the same time craftsmen and traders, and in many villages wage-earners were often as numerous as other village groups. It may be that the English experience has been markedly different from that of the Continent, and especially from Eastern Europe, in these respects; and there is some reason to think that this was so.[34] In fact even at the Conquest English society seems to have been far more variegated than Norman, possessing different legal and personal relations as the difficulties of the Domesday compilers show.[35]

The point is that neither the firms conducting putting-out arrangements in the sixteenth and seventeenth centuries, nor the larger centralised firms of the late eighteenth and nineteenth centuries were uniquely characterised by a wage nexus, when comparison is made with English economic organisation of earlier times. In fact it seems that wage payments and living-in servants from outside the nuclear family were a common feature of English economic life for as far back as records permit us to see. There is no doubt, of course, that wage labour expanded with the more rapid extension of putting-out in early modern England, so that by the eighteenth century not just textiles but other major industries had become similarly organised, and that this development was part of an interaction with agricultural change especially in pastoral areas of the country.[36] There is no doubt either that wage labour grew even more rapidly during the Industrial Revolution with the advent of the factory system. But neither of these historical developments was *necessary* for the advent or emergence of wage labour; neither was an *essential condition* for its existence. In the English context, at least, the dispersal of the offspring by parents — the decentralisation or 'putting-out' so to speak, of children, in-laws, etc. — already involved wage payments and seems to have been a practice as ancient as it was in the processing of commodities. This is one reason why in the case of England it seems preferable to use the evidential phrase 'putting-out' to describe decentralised production, rather than the historiographical concept of 'domestic system' with its possible implication of an exclusively familial household as the basic unit of economic organisation.[37]

The nature and functions of the firm have been analysed by Coase, in a classic article, and more recently by Alchian, Demsetz and others in terms of property rights, information and transactions costs.[38] A very brief summary of what this now extensive economics literature seeks to explore is necessary. Before very recent times it has almost certainly been more costly, not least in terms of human time and effort, to sort and co-ordinate economic activity. More resources have been used up in arrangement than in production. Consequently, to specify and make as exclusive as possible, and then to protect as far as allowable in law, the ownership of resources has been seen as a primary spur to getting them used more efficiently. Since only individuals can maximise the value of any available resource, there is need for some method that will enable the transfer of such rights. Such a method might be a market. In a market it is important that what is to be exchanged is well specified, is clear to the parties concerned. Furthermore, the terms of the exchange and the costs of enforcing them — that we mean and will do what we say — need to be resolved. Rights and the terms of their exchange have never been completely exclusive and specific; and over time they are redefined and adjusted as the relative values of their uses change. In this way resources in general are made to be more or less mobile away from lower value and towards higher value uses through the mechanism of voluntary exchange.

Drawing on this body of theory, Milward has analysed the putting-out system in the early modern English context. He suggests that neither the relative simplicity of technique, the geographical dispersal of production units, nor market widening or capital requirements would necessarily have been inconsistent with a development of industry by means of direct market exchanges between independent raw material suppliers, producers and merchants. Surveying the historical literature on the subject, he finds that its discussion of the various factors associated with the superiority of putting-out over other possible arrangements has produced no conclusive explanation for its widespread existence historically and its undoubted longevity. By focusing on the merchants' ownership rights in the raw material, product and residual income and the need to achieve a standardised high volume output, he concludes that it was the input control factor which explained the particular contractual features of the putting-out system's vertical integration; and that this presaged the merchant/ manufacturer's contracting for all co-operant inputs under the factory system. It was the necessity for direct work supervision that accounts for the ownership and contractual characteristics of putting-out piece-work and which, in due course, led to the change to centrally located wage labour.[39]

The property rights and transactions costs analysis can undoubtedly shed fresh light on the changing forms of economic organisation, and provide insights into why entrepreneurs subsume more or fewer direct market exchanges within firms at all, as well as why there are different forms of firms. But it cannot provide a complete explanation for the existence of firms because, we suggest, that would have to include the entrepreneurial perspective. Only when the analysis is extended to include the role of knowledge or information change and its associated search costs can the full significance of the existence of firms be appreciated, and be seen to be about more than just the contractual or control element. From the standpoint of the entrepreneur the firm is always an institution of the market; it never becomes unrelated from the fabric of relative costs and prices which faces him. For the entrepreneur there will be at any given time an optimum (right) degree of planning influenced by the quality and extent of his information (and ignorance) and the costs of searching for more. (Certainly, of course, there will also be an optimum (best) use of organisation influenced by the type and extent of individual property rights and the costs of exchanging them.) To the entrepreneur a firm is simply a unit of organisation to enable him to deal with the specialisation that is taking place in the economy, and its structure will be that which is best adapted to reducing *all* the costs involved in his use of the price system.

The contractual arrangements of firms are important, of course, but the entrepreneur is interested in the firm as an economic not a legal institution. Knowing that value can only be added by a change in the consumer's taste for a thing or by a change in the means of providing it, he locates where he can best influence either or both. The firm is a vehicle of opportunity for the entrepreneur, enabling him to be interactive between what is happening to consumption and what is happening to production. For the view of entrepreneurship adopted here means that the real anatomy of the market lies deeper than the institutions and rules that are its manifestations. Thus once entrepreneurship has left a firm it does not disappear, there is always some capacity to survive by trial and error, by imitation and inertia; such firms may survive for long periods, perhaps preserved by government or vested interests not alert to new profit opportunities. However, they cannot be said to lack *control*. Entrepreneurship, though not completely unrelated to control in practice, is not about control as such. Controllers and monitors can be hired in the market. In putting-out, for example, firms with very extensive arrangements could divide the control function among a hierarchy of monitors at each process stage and receiving payment which included a return to that function. It is certainly not a matter of *current control* since the operations of a firm settle into habituation for long periods and even control becomes routine. Moreover, in small firms, perhaps family firms, and even in families as such, control can be implicitly exercised because of the close proximity of the members engaged in their activity.

It seems to have been Knight who first pointed to the fact that ultimate control is never to be found separate from ultimate responsibility.[40] Changes in the ownership and hiring arrangements of firms arise out of earlier errors of judgement that have been seen as such; they are changes made to improve a situation. Entrepreneurship is about putting resources, whether owned or hired, to use in the most profitable way that has been perceived by the firm's ultimate decision-maker, its final hirer. The replacement of specific contracts requiring specific performance between separate principals across the market, by a firm in which the entrepreneur pays wages for the right to direct performance, has a pure entrepreneurial or information dimension. Control is not appropriate to change, indeed, it may be positively inimical to it; change means the shouldering of responsibility. Introducing change into economic organisation means bringing knowledge into the picture. And this means taking account of information change specific to the situation, the action counterparts of which are *uncertainty* and *risk-bearing*.

Another implication that springs from distinguishing, in principle, the role of the entrepreneur from those other functions to be found in firms, such as manager and capitalist, should be noticed. This is that entrepreneurship alone among the functions to be found in firms requires no prior ownership. What the entrepreneur seeks — profit — is not a payment for an owned or hired factor service. It is not a compensation required in order for a firm to commence production. Profit belongs entirely to the future. Every entrepreneurial opportunity for gain — the excess of the value of outputs over the costs of inputs — every prospect of profit must always contain the threat that it will not be realised, or that not enough of it will be realised. As Kirzner puts it, 'only in a world in which men make mistakes (in the sense of not perceiving the best opportunities) can there arise those opportunities for pure gain which offer scope for entrepreneurial activity'.[41] Thus it is uncertainty giving rise to risk which requires someone to take final responsibility, and this responsibility may involve varying degrees of ownership and hiring. But at the outset entrepreneurial activity is predicated on uncertainty and risk-bearing. The incentive to maximise profits does not arise out of ownership; in fact the particular property and contractual arrangements of a firm may deflect attention from the fact that a firm only exists when the owners of some productive services have sold them to the entrepreneur. Entrepreneurial profits do not accrue to him because he now owns a firm, but because of his decision to purchase its services in the first instance. He could make the same profits by hiring the resources of someone else's firm. Entrepreneurial profits originate in the *decision* to purchase or hire, irrespective of which form of 'right to use' is chosen. Entrepreneurial decision is different from acquiring ownership, or even control. As Shackle puts it: 'Decision, in the origin of this word, means an act of cutting, and it is the appropriate and precise word for the psychic act of cutting the future from the past, for discarding the existing policy and many of its preconceptions in favour of novelties and unfamiliar implications.'[42]

There may be no doubt that the merchant's retention of ownership of the material, and the indirect control this provided, was the important contractual feature distinguishing putting-out from an organisation based on independent firms making external market transactions. But a full explanation of the system should include a recognition that pre-specification and ownership of the material by the entrepreneur also represented a very flexible system for risk-shifting for all the parties. Over the long history of putting-out there were periods, not just in the sixteenth and seventeenth centuries, when the recruitment of putting-out workers became much easier than at others. At such times there were always entrepreneurs to take advantage of the pool of potential workers who were easier to recruit, required less pay, and, because for them it was *additional* employment, worked amounts and at times of their own choosing. Entrepreneurs who adapted their production arrangements to such labour conditions and preferences outcompeted those who insisted on retaining different work practices, such as the non-specialised small firm. One such period seems to have occurred in the mid-fifteenth century when a wool glut produced particularly low prices. At the same time working out of Bristol can be found a number of very large putting-out firms extending their operations far into the hinterland counties. Also in the same port the shipowner William Canynges owned nearly half of Bristol's fleet at one stage, the kind of specialised firm which is not supposed to have emerged in England before the second quarter of the nineteenth century.[43]

But there were limits to competitive responses of this kind. For example, various forms of buy-back arrangement seem to have been more common earlier on in the evolution of putting out. But the risks, of production delays, substandard output, inadequate quantities, and of prices changing in the interim, resulted in frequent miscalculation for both merchant and maker. This seems to explain the contractual alteration that became a feature of the system during its expansion of the sixteenth and seventeenth centuries. Not only can a new method of organisation be given no property right through patenting; but the fact that innovation in organisation was at least as scarce as in technique meant there was no ready-made market for new ideas.[44] Entrepreneurial perception was necessary to carry them into action. At any time in the history of putting-out, specialising too early, too far, or for too long, in either the trading or the manufacturing function left a man vulnerable to competition; and this competition came not simply from new entrants, but from existing less-specialised firms and from cross entrants. Thus on the eve of the great technical transformation of the cotton industry in the mid-eighteenth century the small country manufacturers selling direct to the Manchester merchant, or on commission, were actually gaining ground at the expense of the large putting-out employers.[45]

No doubt there are many reasons to explain why, at any particular time in any given situation, the costs of organising exchanges between independent market participants outweigh the costs of organising them within firms. It is clear that under the putting-out system, where labour was a high proportion of total costs, the remuneration for a costly pattern of working, involving considerable travelling time, embezzlement, etc., was for that reason alone lower than under a more regular and supervised regime. But there is little evidence of any long-run or deep-seated preference for leisure, or for irregular, specialised work of low skill among the labour force over that for increased money incomes.[46] So that at all times there was a strong presence of small firms; nor were by any means all of these non-specialised; and they should certainly not be considered as 'survivals'. In textiles as much as in other industries, product differentiation was never so slight nor markets so narrow, as to preclude the continuing existence of substantial numbers of small firms in good times and bad. Even after the critical period of mechanisation in cotton, in the second quarter of the nineteenth century, '. . . large firms were still few, and small to middling (and single-process) firms were preponderant'.[47] Moreover, while changes in a particular firm or type of firm may have economic significance, they need not have; a change in rank may imply a real change in firm size or market share, but if there is any tendency for firms in a market to bunch together in size then changes in rank have little significance. Markets indeed may experience economic changes of far-reaching importance without any change in the ranking of their firms.

Large firms, like new men of wealth, the gentry, and much else besides, have been rising only to fall again for many centuries in England; and it is almost never safe to apply even approximate dating to the emergence of such phenomena.[48] In practice there were few arbitrary barriers preventing an entrepreneur acting on an opportunity once perceived. Again, however, it should be stressed that such alertness was not simply a question of possessing information. The operation of the division of knowledge is more subtle. Knowledge and changes in knowledge as such are important; but individual skills are often based on the learning and experience of practical rules in such a way as to become routine; they are deeply embedded in individuals and incapable of being acquired simply by the passage of information.[49] Such specialised knowledge can be hired in the market. It would be wrong to see the entrepreneur as an expert in any similar sense, though it might be said of him that he has expertise in hiring the right experts. The point is that there are always many small firms existing at any time which lack this kind of entrepreneurial alertness to opportunity, as distinct from having knowledge of something, and are failing to act to secure an available profit.[50] In the limit entrepreneurship means a propensity to sense what is wanted, to *know* what *will* be *useful*.

It is a commonplace that English industrial expansion, and changes in economic organisation in general, occurred in a pervasively agricultural economy and that its government and constitutional arrangements broadly reflected that fact. Taken together with the fact that the 'political nation' was extremely small — perhaps little more than 200,000 in a population of something over five million people at the beginning of the eighteenth century — this must have represented a powerful conditioning influence on the exercise of entrepreneurship in the market. If the framework of rules and rights have some bearing on the way market processes work in practice, then the fact that the eighteenth-century economy and state was dominated by landed interests whose property rights were strongly entrenched in the constitution is of great relevance. The costs of entrepreneurial activity under uncertainty are high and the willingness of entrepreneurs to take risks cannot depend solely on the expectation of profit; it must also depend on the type and extent of property rights, how well they are protected in law, and whether some are better safeguarded than others.

But there is another point to make in this connection. If the idea of entrepreneurial competition for pure profit is essential to the market process but at the same time, as an aspect of human perception, exists independently of whether the society is market-ordered or not, then presumably there is no reason to think it would not find outlets in some other directions if market procedures were unavailable. The fact that entrepreneurship has a tendency to display itself in even the most unpromising environments does seem to confirm its durability; or perhaps it is just that in those situations the gains from some co-ordinating activity are so palpable that even a dying ember of alertness will rekindle in response to them. In any event, in relation to the questions of landholding and the polity an entrepreneurial approach might be thought to raise special problems.

There has always been a widespread assumption that land should be considered differently from other assets, if only because its quantity cannot be significantly increased. Strictly this is not the case, though Alfred Marshall believed it;[51] drainage and reclamation have increased its quantity over time, even in England and certainly in The Netherlands. More important the economic value of land has obviously increased considerably through the expenditure of labour and capital to bring more of it into cultivation and to change its uses. Again, while land is not fixed in quantity an ancient building above ground or mineral reserves below clearly may be. Nevertheless it seems reasonable to treat land as one of a small group of assets whose supply increases only slowly in relation to the current stock. There seem to have been active land markets at least in some parts of England since the thirteenth century.[52] And Loyn comments that the ' . . . fact of alienation warns against the ascription of too powerful a mystique to land. There is evidence indeed for something approaching a land-market in late Anglo-Saxon England'. Tenancy for lives, usually three, and for years appears to have been very common also.[53] The landlord-tenant system, which is said to be at the root of the different course of agricultural change compared with France, was clearly a much older difference than could be accounted for simply in terms of medieval explanations concerning stronger English control of tenure. Moreover, it is often remarked how the French peasants' attachment to land is seen in their willingness to defend infringements of rights by outbreaks of organised violence, even where tenancy operated, over many centuries.[54] In England, by contrast, whatever the social consequences associated with enclosure at particular periods, organised and prolonged opposition to it for reasons pertaining to rights, as distinct from rents, wages and employment, is difficult to substantiate.

The superior efficiency of the landlord-tenant system is commonly attributed to the greater security for the tenant that could be written into the lease in respect of conditions, term, etc. Yet in an early study of this question Habakkuk took the view that, while the length of term was important, ' . . . leases promoted agriculture more by the covenants they omitted than by those they included'.[55] What is more in Ireland where the landlord-tenant system was widely used and leases were often long, it clearly did not help to turn that economy from the fate of famine.[56] It is clearly not the landlord-tenant system as such which is so important as its context; its success depended on how the parties to it perceived the arrangement at any given time and place. That it was not just the institution and its rules *per se* which mattered, but the expectations which were held of it, receives confirmation from Adam Smith's comment that 'In England the security of the tenant is equal to that of the proprietor.' He is quite clear that it is not simply the legal position but the force of custom as well that accounts for the fact that there is ' . . . nowhere in Europe, except in England, any instance of the tenant building upon the land *of which he had no lease*, and trusting that the honour of his landlord would take no advantage of so important an improvement'.[57] We are obviously in the realm of speculation in offering any explanation of such a phenomenon. But it seems to be important for explaining why over many centuries the enclosure movements, involving the taking in of common and waste, the buying up of small freeholders and variations in tenancy agreements, proved a superior method of adapting the uses of land to changing agricultural opportunities.

In France there appears to have been some tendency for large estates to increase in size by purchase in the three centuries before 1789, a trend which seems to have had little effect on agricultural productivity and which was reversed after the Revolution. But it is the intensity with which the ownership of land in France is endowed that seems significant; the fact that even when taken out of common all sorts of egalitarian abridgements hedged its use; and the fact that tenants took every opportunity to purchase and expected no change in their terms and continuing family possession. In England, on the other hand, the long-term trend in the agglomeration of great estates seems to have been reinforced at certain times by the influx of new wealth from outside of agriculture as in the sixteenth century with the Dissolution; in fact the whole process of a landed society dominated by large and politically powerful landholders began with a massive land consolidation following the Conquest. In the same way the Revolution Settlement of 1688 reasserted this element of continuity and had the effect of entrenching politically the great Whig magnates as brokers for balancing the competing claims of present and future generations in the ownership and use of the land.

The rights of a landholder in the theory of property rights are absolute where they do not derive from another party's right. Translating this into the English context throws up a peculiar, perhaps surprising, fact. All the land in England for as far back as one can find evidence is owned, in the ultimate and superior sense of that word, by the Crown. Even today what an English freeholder thinks he owns, and the same applies to all other interests, is in fact a derivative right. Of course, there is no practical distinction between an English freehold and the absolute right in land existing in other countries today; in the same way as there is no practical significance in the fact that a UK passport holder finds that he is a subject as well as, indeed before, being a citizen. But this may well have been important in the early evolution of the relations between the Crown, its great landholders and the smaller owner-occupiers and tenants. It may have much to do with the fact that the landlord-tenant system, working at its best, developed as a highly reciprocal relationship in which both interests in the land were acknowledged. This kind of arrangement, where the perceptions of its nature and the expectations of its possibilities, is so important to the parties concerned may well owe something to the fact that such a tenure is actually just as derivative as a freehold.

It is easy to overdraw this sort of difference and to generalise it too readily to particular national circumstances. But it is clear that these arrangements evolved over a long time-span in an agricultural system that shows marked contrasts with Continental developments even at an early date. The Crown's superior ownership right to the land of England can be seen as an original and highly entrepreneurial act to secure a permanent resource monopoly; its rarity suggests that it should also be regarded as a strategic innovation. It seems to be in the nature of the case that once the essential elements of what was literally a huge confidence trick were widely understood — that is, the monopoly and the permanence — the process of entrepreneurial competition could only work through dynastic change after a long time interval, if the object of such competition were not to be destroyed. The long-term maintenance of the monopoly position required a control arrangement, and an institutionalised rights system that would reinforce the controlling interests by the force of custom, and give the unique resource ownership a high degree of immunity. It is, of course, more costly, but in this case unavoidable, to have a situation where control and management of the property is exercised by people other than the owner. The control group could not become too large, if the power and privileges of control are not to become diffused and degraded; at the same time its members — the great landholders — know that the monopoly arrangement, being in the nature of a crucial experiment, could only be retested in order to reaffirm its validity notwithstanding any change of personnel.

The most important validation occurred at the Conquest when '. . . some four to five thousand Anglo-Saxon thegns were replaced by no more than a hundred and eighty Norman barons . . .', of whom ten held almost a quarter of the country.[58] Subsequently the Crown and its great landholders appear to have functioned essentially as a rationing mechanism for the release of land into the market process over the long term. For example, the fifteenth century seems to have been a period of fairly rapid release. There is no suggestion that the development worked evenly or in a single direction over time, or that the constitution of the group did not change. On the contrary, the mechanism seems to have continued to operate despite major and often violent changes in its personnel, and it operated alongside a continuously active market in land and land use. Indeed the long-run viability of this superior ownership and control of the land seems to have depended on its capacity to generate derivative interests and arrangements in and for the use of land that offered flexible substitutes for the monopolised resource ownership. Maintaining the integrity of this entry-blocking resource ownership and its control group led to the growth of a broad range of lesser landlords who in their turn needed to keep their tenure arrangements flexible. The mobility of labour and rents seems to have been considerable throughout the middle ages and as early as the thirteenth century '. . . the tenant became the *verus dominus* (true lord) of the fee, with much freedom to dispose of it and with the protection of the royal courts for a possession which was verging upon property'.[59] There seems no reason to think that over time these changing perspectives on tenure did not reach the lower level of society.

By the seventeenth century if not earlier it does seem that English agriculture had developed along lines that were more likely to produce security of tenure at approaching a market clearing rent. An important consequence of this was a variety of arrangements between landlord and tenant, not all of them contractual. In due course this meant that the Tulls, Bakewells and Collings could address the problems of agricultural improvement without the excess baggage of an absolute ownership obsession that characterised the French peasantry. Another result of the development of the agricultural economy in this way was the early and prolonged stimulus it gave to trade and service intermediaries throughout the economy. In France the eighteenth-century seigneurs, being often absentee and lacking much interest in farming, diverted the activity of entrepreneurial middlemen into maximising the rents and dues from the land. In England it expanded local trade. As late as the 1860s 10 per cent of the land in 33 French departments was in communal holdings.[60] The latest estimate for English enclosures suggests that already by 1500 about 45 per cent of the land was enclosed; and about 75 per cent by 1760.[61] If the development of English agriculture encouraged a situation at the level of the farming unit which tended to balance the interests of landlords, sitting tenants and potential tenants, what of the highest level of landed society — the peerage?

Ever since the Conquest the great territorial nobility, with some changes in its membership, managed to retain a degree of separateness (peerage) from the rest of landed society. Its distinctiveness as a group, its dominance of the House of Lords, and its closeness to the Monarchy, all survived relatively unscathed into the nineteenth century. Although it suffered some dynastic changes and experienced a severe breakdown in the civil wars of the seventeenth century, Kingship and its control elements have been an important ingredient of political stability, even if at times they have also contributed to its breakdown. One could argue that in countries which industrialised later than England, where the process was one of emulation, of catching up on the competition, political arrangements must adjust to the economic imperative. Indeed it may be that in such countries the pace of economic change forces a political response. In the case of England, however, it seems unlikely that industrialisation could have occurred without adequate political arrangements already being in place. Political historians have begun to reveal just such a period centring on the second quarter of the eighteenth century.

After the turbulence and political breakdown of the seventeenth century the achievement of political stability in the early eighteenth century appears remarkable; and essential if the processes leading to industrialisation were not to be impeded. The nature of stability in the political sphere was no less remarkable, and consisted of a monopoly of power *without* its normal accompaniment of arbitrary power. It was not unrelated to the economic changes taking place in English society in the century after 1660 — demographic stability and growing real wages gave it a surer basis — perhaps they were indispensable to it. Nevertheless the growth of stability also depended on a successful outcome to the exercise of entrepreneurship in the business of politics. It was firmly established during the 1720s and lasted almost 50 years. Its main elements were single party government (the Whigs) within a 'mixed' constitution (Crown, Lords and Commons); this balance of interests representing the political nation had the effect of 'limiting' government, as did the common law, though there was strictly no separation of powers. The means by which stability was achieved and sustained were intense, continuous power-broking and the extensive application of patronage. The seventeenth century had shown that it was not just the potential of monarchical power for absolutism, but the potential of Parliament, especially the Commons, for party faction and anarchy that had to be controlled for stable government. A change of dynasty on terms which enabled the great landholders and most of the gentry to support its, and therefore their own, authority was one prop to stable government. The other, perhaps the most telling fact of English political history in the first half of the eighteenth century, was that the franchise which had been considerably extended during the seventeenth century was reduced.

Under the leadership of that most alert of political entrepreneurs, Robert Walpole, the new Whig party negotiated the threat of monarchy to the power of the landed interests and shed its more populist radical leanings from the seventeenth century. It became the party of the major interests in the state and the only basis on which stable government could be built. Walpole ensured that these interests were expressed through a strong executive government which was acceptable to the Crown, which dominated the Lords and controlled the Commons. Moreover the achievement long survived his ministry. As Plumbe comments: '... he made the world so safe for Whigs that they stayed in power for a hundred years'.[62]

This chapter takes a particular view of the role of the entrepreneurial factor in human action. Without denying the importance of institutional arrangements the intention has been to show how the entrepreneurial factor is at the root of changes in such arrangements. The chapter has looked at three areas of the English pre-industrial economy. In two — the growth of the domestic consumer market and the role of the firm in the market process — it finds at least indirect evidence of considerable entrepreneurial activity extending back long before the late eighteenth century. In English landed society and the political institutions of the country, which were intimately related, it also finds an important entrepreneurial element in their development and functioning. It may be that the Scientific Revolution and the Enlightenment had an important role in sharpening entrepreneurial alertness in English society prior to the Industrial Revolution. Both were clearly proximate changes that raised aspirations and the possibilities for greater material progress. On the other hand the chapter also points to the effectiveness of competitive pressures in the relevant parts of the economy from an early date. Conjecture, and the control of conjecture, or rationality, do not seem to have been lacking in earlier centuries; though perhaps they were more widely diffused by the eighteenth century. The aspiration to industrialise may indeed be in Landes' phrase, 'the puberty of nations'; but to do it at a period when there are no precedents seems to require some of the qualities usually associated with maturity, even middle age.[63]

In conclusion what answer can be offered to the question of entrepreneurship posed at the beginning? Are there any fresh insights to be gained from asking where does entrepreneurship come from, rather than what do entrepreneurs do? Two kinds of answer seem possible. One is that entrepreneurship springs from knowledge, specifically information and especially formal or scientific information. There is much to be said for adopting this position and falling in with the central explanation that figures in so much of the literature on the industrial revolution. Leaving aside some differences of emphasis concerning the precise nature of the links, this would mean broadly accepting the focus on the Scientific Revolution to account for the technological change which most of the textbooks see as the unique element in the industrial revolution.[64]

The other possible answer is that entrepreneurship springs from ignorance. Adopting this position means much more than simply looking at the other side of the coin from knowledge. It is not just a question of how a major shift in the quantity and quality of *new* knowledge arising out of the Scientific Revolution was carried into technical innovation. This way of looking at the phenomenon of entrepreneurship makes its field of action much wider than the science-technology linkage. It includes as well harnessing the economic benefits of what others know already, perhaps have long known; and one should expect to see it manifesting itself far outside the areas of scientific advance and technical application. Accepting the premise of this paper, that an entrepreneurial culture existed in eighteenth-century England, means that entrepreneurship brings to bear on problem-situations not only existing but presently unavailable information in areas remote from the realm of purely scientific enquiry and its application. It is surely no accident that contemporary writers across diverse fields seem to have been so occupied with illustrating, charting, and explaining the proliferating specialisation that was the expression of the market process taking place around them. It extended into literature and the arts, and into social theory, as well as into the natural sciences. It was not only the social analysts like Bernard Mandeville, Daniel Defoe, Adam Ferguson and, of course, Adam Smith, who sought to represent and explain the growing division of labour; the same urge can be seen in Samuel Johnson's periodical literature and in the eighteenth-century novel, such as Henry Fielding's *Tom Jones* and Tobias Smollet's *Roderick Random*. Occupational and product differentiation seized the imagination of the Age.

By itself the idea of a Scientific Revolution seems inadequate to encompass the many different corners of this entrepreneurial culture that contemporaries explored. In fact the rapid division of the sciences during the course of the eighteenth century suggests that the rise of experimental science itself was part of the accelerating market process in response to the action of entrepreneurial competition. It may be necessary to recover the concept of the English (and Scottish) Enlightenment from the History of Ideas for a better understanding of the environment necessary for generating the incentives for increased entrepreneurial activity in the eighteenth century. It was not simply the quality of Enlightenment ideals, nor even the new channels of communication for transmitting much more than scientific information alone, that was significant in England. It was the fact that they could be used that matters, that they were actively disseminated through the market process, or, in other words, attracted the notice of entrepreneurs. If in the case of England it is possible to speak of a Practical Enlightenment, then what activates the entrepreneurial perception that lies behind it? In particular, what activates it more frequently and to better effect in some societies than in others? Part of the answer must lie in the society's prevailing rules for action. This means not so much the resolutions of the legislative authority as such, but the substantive body of law governing the relations between persons, and between them and government. Unlike elsewhere in Europe, England does seem to have had the ground rules in place for a Practical Enlightenment to occur. As Porter confirms:

> The cardinal fact is that in England, and in England almost alone, the realization of Enlightenment hopes was not thwarted at every turn by the existing order of state and society. Quite the reverse. In England after 1688 the constitution itself incorporated central Enlightenment demands such as personal freedom under Habeus Corpus, representative government, religious toleration and the sanctity of property.[65]

However, it does seem that something more is required than just having the appropriate rules of action in place, and defining the arena within which entrepreneurial action can proceed. To commence in the first place there must be reasonably sure expectations that such action can proceed to fruition by ground rules that are not vulnerable to the caprice of authority. At the same time, for these rules of conduct to attain long-run stability, the society as a whole must have become habituated to them by virtue of respect, fear or a mixture of both. Otherwise compliance with them would become so low and the costs of enforcing them so high that their operation would become so uncertain as to defeat their purpose. The Rule of Law — that the law not men, including the monarch, govern conduct — and the role of precedent — that the law is certain, does not change, but only extends its certainty case by case — were both particularly important in the evolution of the English common law. During the seventeenth century English society had experienced the abuses of arbitrary power by *both* sources of authority, Crown and Parliament. The reassertion of the Rule of

Law following the Settlement of 1688 needed to be vigorous and single-minded if it was to serve to prevent *all* the institutions of government from coercing individuals except in the enforcement of a known, general rule. Conditions were favourable in several respects. By the second decade of the eighteenth century a rare equipoise had been established between Crown and Parliament in which the competitive tension between monarch and ministry was the chief domestic preoccupation of government, rather than their relations with the electorate and society as a whole. In one sense eighteenth-century government was not so different from that of the Tudors, accommodating factions and interceding with the monarch rather than involving itself with frequent and complex legislative enterprises. In another sense it was very different. Both elements of government had revealed and confirmed the limits of their utility in the previous century in the only way that really instils conviction; by breaching those limits time after time. Against that background the eighteenth-century fear of arbitrary power is easily understood.

This also helps explain the need of government and judiciary to recover and restore the common law. In the law, as in politics, the concern is not to reform, or even to rebuild, but to find again what had seemed so recently to have been lost beyond recall. Only the experience of how easy it is to fail, the sense of holding fast to what little they are sure of and how much they are not, can explain the preoccupation with certain rules and historical precedent that is characteristic of both constitutional thought and judicial decision from Locke to Blackstone. It was in this context of a successful re-establishment of the rules of conduct in government, as well as in society at large through the separate operation of judicial process, that an entrepreneurial climate of economic activity was possible. William Paley's watchword, 'Whatever is expedient, is right', expresses the entrepreneurial attitude of the times very well; but taken out of context it might be taken to mean that any and all actions are inevitably right, whereas for contemporaries it meant that those activities that make up the custom and usage of society are seen to be the best way of proceeding because over time they have proved to be the most successful.[66] The Enlightenment analysis of the importance of rules of conduct did not carry the implication that they antedated market activity, but that their evolution enabled the market in suspense to articulate increasingly effectively as a 'process'.[67] However, it also revealed an ultimate paradox that hinted at the kind of freedom that was required for the market process to be sustained.

If the extension of the division of labour had the effect of constantly enlarging the scope for entrepreneurial action, the parallel process of division of knowledge could only increase awareness in the individual person of the partiality of his own knowledge and the extent of his ignorance. It is just because each person can hold only a fragment of knowledge to the backcloth of his own ignorance that entrepreneurship is necessary at all. Those like Johnson and Smith, for whom the Enlightenment offered the possibility of comprehensive knowledge, were very well aware of the lure of intellectualism that it could offer; that freedom of thought might in the end subordinate freedom of action. Ferguson, in particular, saw to where rationality might lead when 'thinking itself becomes a craft'.[68] Even as they wrote the Newtonian calculus, the central idea of the Scientific Revolution, would soon be brought into service for the analysis of society. Because it seemed possible that the actions of the individual were now capable of calculation in terms of the balance of pleasure and pain (utility) which flow from them, then it was also possible that the individual will could replace the higher rationality of abstract rules.

The emphasis given to the importance of certain rules and customary usage by the Enlightenment writers arose from their direct observation of the consequences of freedom of action in the entrepreneurial culture of their time. An entrepreneurial perspective of the market process reinforces their insight that the freedom to pursue ideas into action was the most important kind of freedom for sustaining economic progress. It is the idea of freedom as the ground of discovery that is significant for an entrepreneurial culture. The role of entrepreneurship then is not simply optimising among available means; it is to bring to the support of flawed rationality that fertility of imagination which alone can conjure new alternatives and, perhaps, create different ends from those apparent in the here and now. This suggests that the freedom to sustain change through regular innovation can only derive from a particular tradition. In this sense some degree of stability seems to be an important accompaniment of constructive change. Innovation and tradition are not mutually exclusive but, on the contrary, reliant on each other.

Notes

1. The generalisation is based on the following works of business history relating to the period of the Industrial Revolution: T. S. Ashton (1939) *An Eighteenth Century Industrialist: Peter Stubs of Warrington*; C. Wilson (1957) 'The Entrepreneur in the Industrial Revolution', *History*, 62; S. Pollard (1965) *The Genesis of Modern Management. A Study of the Industrial Revolution in Great Britain*; R. Church (1969) *Kenricks in Hardware: A Family Business 1791–1966*; N. McKendrick (1975) *Josiah Wedgwood 1730–1795*; P. Payne (1974) *British Entrepreneurship in the Nineteenth Century*.
2. On the theory of entrepreneurship I have drawn on the work of I. Kirzner, especially the following: (1973) *Competition and Entrepreneurship*; various articles collected under (1979) *Perception, Opportunity and Profit. Studies in the Theory of Entrepreneurship*; (1980) 'The Primacy of Entrepreneurial Discovery' in *Prime Mover of Progress. The Entrepreneur in Capitalism and Socialism*. Alongside the Austrian tradition proper there are Shackle's contributions, most notably the following: (1972) *Epistemics and Economics. A Critique of Economic Doctrines*; 'Marginalism: The Harvest' in R. D. Collison Black, A. W. Coats *et al.* (1972) *The Marginal Revolution in Economics*; (1979) *Imagination and the Nature of Choice*. Earlier contributions along similar lines are F. A. Hayek (1948) *Individualism and Economic Order*; L. M. Lachmann (1943) 'The Role of Expectations in Economics as a Social Science', *Economica*, 10; L. v. Mises (1949) *Human Action: A Treatise on Economics*; and J. A. Schumpeter (1934) *Theory of Economic Development*. From a neoclassical standpoint the following are useful: S. J. Grossman and J. E. Stiglitz (1976) 'Information and Competitive Price Systems', *American Economic Review*, 66, and (1980) 'The Impossibility of Informationally Efficient Markets', *American Economic Review*, 70; H. A. Simon (1979) 'Rational Decision Making in Business Organizations', *American Economic Review* 64; J. M. Buchanan and R. L. Faith (1981) 'Entrepreneurship and the Internalization of Externalities', *Journal of Law and Economics*, 24. Finally, there is in Shackle and some of the Austrians a French influence ('entrepreneur' is after all French in origin) that seems to be traceable via Bergson and Poincaré back to J. B. Say. On the latter's emphasis on entrepreneurship see C. Gide and C. Rist (1915) *A History of Economic Doctrines*, pp. 113–14.
3. On the role of the merchant function and the growth of overseas markets see the following: W. Minchinton (1957) 'The Merchants of England in the Eighteenth Century', *Explorations in Entrepreneurial History*, 10; (1969) *The Growth of English Overseas Trade*; R. Davis (1967) *A Commercial Revolution*, (1979) *The Industrial Revolution and British Overseas Trade*; F. Crouzet (1980) 'Towards an Export Economy: British Exports During the Industrial Revolution', *Explorations in Economic History*, 17. Also see K. Berrill (1960) 'International Trade and the Rate of Economic Growth', *Economic History Review*, 12; and J. Sperling (1962) 'The International Payments Mechanism in the 17th and 18th Centuries', *Economic History Review*, 14. Until very recently knowledge of the organisation and extent of the domestic market had not greatly surpassed, and still does not supersede, the valuable contemporary accounts of D. Defoe (1724–7) *A Tour Through England and Wales*, 2 vols.; (1728) *A Plan of the English Commerce* and (1745) *The Complete English Tradesman*. Also see J. D. Marshall (ed.) (1967) *The Autobiography of William Stout of Lancaster 1665–1752*; and T. S. Willan (1970) *An Eighteenth-Century Shopkeeper*. The most important modern contributions for understanding the organisation of, and trends in, the internal market are N. S. B. Gras (1915) *The Evolution of the English Corn Market from the 12th to the 18th Century*, and R. B. Westerfield (1915) *Middlemen in English Business 1660–1760*. For the agricultural commodity trades see A. M. Everitt, 'The Marketing of Agricultural Produce' in

J. Thirsk (ed.) (1967) *The Agrarian History of England and Wales*, vol. 4; A. H. John 'The Course of Agricultural Change 1660–1760' in L. S. Pressnell (ed.), (1960) *Studies in the Industrial Revolution: Essays Presented to T. S. Ashton*; P. J. Bowden (1962) *The Wool Trade in Tudor and Stuart England*; J. A. Chartres 'Markets and Marketing in Metropolitan Western England in the Late 17th and 18th Centuries' in M. A. Havinden (ed.) (1973) *Husbandry and Marketing in the South-West 1500–1800*; C. W. J. Granger and C. M. Elliott (1967) 'A Fresh Look at Wheat Prices and Markets in the Eighteenth Century', *Economic History Review*, 20; B. A. Holderness (1976) 'Credit in English Rural Society Before the 19th Century, with special reference to the period 1650–1720', *Agricultural History Review*, 24. On trade in industrial commodities and manufactures see T. S. Willan (1976) *The Inland Trade*; A. P. Wadsworth and J. de L. Mann (1931) *The Cotton Trade and Industrial Lancashire 1600–1780*; M. M. Edwards (1967) *The Growth of the British Cotton Trade*; W. H. B. Court (1938) *The Rise of the Midland Industries 1600–1838*; M. B. Rowlands (1975) *Masters and Men in the West Midlands Metal Ware Trades Before the Industrial Revolution*; H. Hamilton (ed.) (1967) *The English Brass and Copper Industries to 1800*; J. R. Harris (1964) *The Copper King*; T. S. Ashton and J. Sykes (ed.) (1964) *The Coal Industry in the 18th Century*; M. W. Flinn (1983) *History of the British Coal Industry 1700–1830*; M. W. Flinn (1958) 'The Growth of the English Iron Industry 1660–1760' *Economic History Review*, 11; C. K. Hyde (1977) *Technological Change and the British Iron Industry 1700–1870*; L. A. Clarkson (1966) 'The Leather Crafts in Tudor and Stuart England', *Agricultural History Review*, 14.

4. According to Kirzner ' . . . the task of making the consumer "notice" the opportunity turns out to be an integral part of making that opportunity available'. The suggestion seems to be that the distinction between the provision (production) of a product and the comprehension of the need for it (selling/buying) is from the standpoint of the entrepreneur misleading and distracts not just from what entrepreneurial activity really means but how it is successful. Thus there is no justification for distinguishing between production cost and selling costs because for the entrepreneur to be successful he must have correctly anticipated the opportunity for which the consumer has a conscious requirement, without any distinct entrepreneurial selling effort being needed. The point is worth pursuing because distinctions of the latter kind may be symptomatic of a more fundamental fallacy, frequently encountered, concerning the nature of economics. For example, it is commonly believed that economics has to do with a particular kind of behaviour — rather than with a particular aspect of all behaviour — and that it represents an attempt to generalise the so-called 'material' or 'physical', or 'external' or 'objective' world from the standpoint of an abstract 'economic man'. This seems to be a variant of historicism, of the idea that economic facts are historical facts and that there are such things as peculiarly economic events which may be studied in the past and from which lessons for current action can be discovered. But economics, no more than any other science, could make 'man' its subject matter irrespective of any adjective applied to him, simply because 'man' is not a scientific concept.

In the case of the production costs/selling costs dichotomy (which seems to be an attempt to justify charges of excessive advertising creating redundant products) the assertion of value, the entrepreneurial attribution of a valuation to a product, can ultimately only mean that the product exists in a certain way, has particular characteristics, that recommend it to consumers' tastes. Thus it is difficult to see how there could be independently determined ('objective') consumer wants. There is no question, of course, that in everyday language the subjective/objective distinction is useful to a degree and as far as it goes. But beyond that values, being essentially ideas, perhaps even informed ideas or appraisals, cannot be unrelated to consciousness. Accordingly, in Kirzner's instance of the point, it is not a question of a 'subjective' consumer interpreting the value of an 'objective' product, but rather of the evaluation of what is given or available (or may become available), in the light of his practical experience. So there is no presumption either that selling effort has not improved the product or that consumer tastes prior to sale were in any sense superior to those that followed entrepreneurial selling activity. If anything the situation may be to the contrary, because it is difficult to see why there should be any such sequence of entrepreneurial action and consumer evaluation if it is not an interactive effort to alter what is to what ought to be. Kirzner (1973), p. 150 and n. 17.

The problem raised by this approach to entrepreneurship has a number of implications, for example in respect of risk and uncertainty, and property rights, which we return to later. For the moment, however, it is worth noting that if valuation is a necessary condition of all entrepreneurial activity, whether on the part of entrepreneur or consumer, then such activity could never be brought to a final conclusion (general equilibrium). Even if it was assumed that it could be such a state could be no more than momentary. If the trigger for action is the expectation that it will make more coherent, improve on current experience, what from the entrepreneurial standpoint is an unsatisfactory state of things; then every achievement of coherence would bring a new prospect of coherence entailing a new sequence of re-evaluation. If the essence of the entrepreneurial quality is what Kirzner calls 'alertness' then it is clearly a part, or a form, of perception. Possibly the difficulty this raises for neoclassical models could be answered by saying that 'alertness' is a 'pre-analytic' concept, meaning it belongs to our common sense and is operative in the practical world. But there does seem to be reasonably firm scientific evidence that sense data are not literally parts of the external (objective) world; instead they seem to be facets of consciousness brought about by a complex of causes of which the physical objects perceived are only a part: see D. J. O'Connor and B. Carr (1982) *Introduction to the Theory of Knowledge*, p. 100. This also has a bearing on the difficult question of an appropriate concept of rationality in economics. A useful account of the different approaches to this issue and a review of the literature is S. M. Sheffrin (1983) *Rational Expectations*. For present purposes the assumption is that entrepreneurial expectations encompass some measure of rational calculation but that they are inevitably bounded by time and place and always, and most importantly, by the fact of uncertainty or incomplete knowledge. In other words entrepreneurial 'alertness', a form of sense perception, does provide knowledge for the creation of expectations as a prelude to action, but it is limited knowledge — not what we *might* know — after all.

 5. Westerfield (1915).

 6. See D. Davis (1966) *A History of Shopping*; D. Alexander (1970) *Retailing in England During the Industrial Revolution*; A. M. Everitt, 'The English Urban Inn 1560–1760' in Everitt (ed.) (1973) *Perspectives in English Urban History*; and J. A. Chartres (1977) *Internal Trade in England 1500–1700*.

 7. R. B. Westerfield (1915), p. 324.

 8. For these aspects see A. H. John (1971) 'Aspects of English Economic Growth in the First Half of the Eighteenth Century', *Economica*, 28; R. Davis (1967) *A Commercial Revolution*; R. M. Hartwell, 'Economic Growth in England before the Industrial Revolution' in Hartwell (ed.) (1971) *The Industrial Revolution and Economic Growth*; D. E. C. Eversley, 'The Home Market and Home Demand 1750–1780' in E. L. Jones and A. H. John (ed.) (1967) *Land, Labour and Population in the Industrial Revolution*; A. Everitt (1975) 'The Primary Towns of England', *The Local Historian*, 11, and (1979) 'Country, County and Town: Patterns of Regional Evolution in England', *Royal Historical Society Transactions*, 29; P. Borsay (1977) 'The English Urban Renaissance: the Development of Provincial Urban Culture c. 1680–1760', *Social History*, 5; J. A. Chartres (1977) 'Road Carrying in England in the Seventeenth Century: Myth and Reality', *Economic History Review*, 30; G. L.

Turnbull (1976) 'Provincial Road Carrying in England in the Eighteenth Century', *Journal of Transport History*, 32; G. A. Cranfield (1962) *The Development of the Provincial Newspaper*.

9. Everitt (1979).

10. N. McKendrick, 'Home Demand and Economic Growth: A New View of the Role of Women and Children in the Industrial Revolution' in McKendrick (ed.) (1974) *Historical Perspectives: Studies in English Thought and Society*; (1960) 'Josiah Wedgwood: An Eighteenth Century Entrepreneur in Salesmanship and Marketing Techniques', *Economic History Review*, 12. On the acceleration of fashion change in the eighteenth century in comparison with earlier times see N. B. Harte 'State Control of Dress and Social Change in Pre-Industrial England' in D. C. Coleman and A. H. John (ed.) (1976) *Trade, Government and Economy in Pre-Industrial England*, Ch. 8. F. Braudel (1973) *Capitalism and Material Life 1400–1800*; N. McKendrick et al. (1982) *The Birth of a Consumer Society. The Commercialization of Eighteenth-Century England*. On the powerful consequences of increased family leisure and its very varied uses see J. H. Plumb (1975) 'The New World of Children in Eighteenth Century England', *Past & Present*, 67; (1973) *The Commercialization of Leisure*; (1977) *The Pursuit of Happiness* and (1980) *Georgian Delights*. On a more theoretical level also see H. Leibenstein (1950) 'Bandwaggon, Snob and Veblen Effects in the Theory of Consumers' Demand', *Quarterly Journal of Economics*, 64; D. E. Robinson (1963) 'The Importance of Fashions in Taste to Business History', *Business History Review*, 37, and (1960) 'The Styling and Transmission of Fashions Historically Considered', *Journal of Economic History*, 20; E. L. Jones, 'The Fashion Manipulators: Consumer Tastes and British Industries 1660–1800' in L. P. Cain and P. J. Uselding (eds) (1973) *Business Enterprise and Economic Change*; G. Vichert, 'The Theory of Conspicuous Consumption in the Eighteenth Century' in P. Hughes and D. Williams (ed.) (1971) *The Varied Pattern: Studies in the Eighteenth Century*; P. Mathias, 'Leisure and Wages in Theory and Practice' in Mathias (1979) *The Transformation of England. Essays in the Economic and Social History of England in the Eighteenth Century*.

11. See T. S. Willan (1936) *River Navigation in England 1600–1760* and (1967) *The English Coasting Trade*; R. Davis (1972) *The Rise of the English Shipping Industry in the Seventeenth and Eighteenth Centuries*; J. R. Ward (1974) *The Finance of Canal Building in Eighteenth-Century England*.

12. The loss of influence of local gild and borough authorities and the reduction of their ability to restrict local trade and craft demarcations by means of by-laws and group pressure did not mean, of course, that by the eighteenth century markets were any less liable to attract the efforts of vested interests attempting to rig their functioning and restrict their extent. In the case of the gilds their influence — and it was always at bottom an influence to restrict entry — declined very unevenly across the country over a long period. Many had become little more than institutional 'shells' by the end of the sixteenth century; others, such as in old centres of gild organisation like Exeter, appear to have collapsed relatively suddenly during the Civil War; whereas in Newcastle a degree of gild control appears to have been effective until well into the eighteenth century: S. Kramer (1927), *The English Craft Gilds*, p. 150. In fact the latter instance can be taken as an example of how deceptive evidence of gild activity can be, as well as of the more general point that the formal institutional arrangements existing in a market at any given time, frequently obscure much more than they reveal about its actual operational procedures. By the beginning of the eighteenth century the Newcastle coastal trade in coal with London had effected an almost complete transition from wood to coal as the source of energy for London's households and manufacturers. The country's oldest and most productive coalfield was the object of constant complaints of price control levelled at the 'Hostmen' of Newcastle during the seventeenth century. In fact, however, the

North-east coalfield's distribution system involved detailed specialisation of function and numerous middlemen between the Newcastle coal owners and the London consumers. It was, however, the shipping sector of the distribution chain which was the most competitive part of the trade and prevented any long-run monopoly influences developing. All attempts by ship masters — whether independent or acting for other interests such as mine owners who often owned shares in several ships — to control prices in the trade were confounded. The main reason for this failure was the ease of entry into the coastal trade in coal due to the relatively low capital cost of colliers and the frequency with which such shipping could be switched away from the Baltic and Archangel trades to coasting. Probably also sea risks of all sorts were lower in the London coal trade and a recent estimate suggests that, notwithstanding the scope for competition, profit rates of the order of 6–12 per cent p.a. were earned in the eighteenth century: see W. J. Hausman (1977), 'Size and Profitability of English Colliers in the Eighteenth Century', *Business History Review*, 51. Since this is higher than the best estimates of 1–5 per cent p.a. in overseas, and especially colonial, trades he concludes that Adam Smith's belief that monopoly elements in colonial trade had redirected capital out of both domestic industry and other overseas trades, and had increased thereby profitability in colonial trade and lowered it elsewhere, was without foundation.

13. Everitt (1967) and (1979).

14. See, for example, J. Thirsk 'Industries in the Countryside' in F. J. Fisher (ed.) (1961) *Essays in the Economic and Social History of Tudor and Stuart England*; and M. Spufford (1974) *Constrasting Communities: English Villages in the Sixteenth and Seventeenth Centuries*.

15. On the difficulties of relating statistical analyses of occupational specialisation to employment changes during economic development see P. T. Bauer and B. S. Yamey (1968) *Markets, Market Control and Marketing Reform*, pp. 3–29.

16. See especially the chapters by R. D. Lee and R. S. Schofield, and by W. A. Cole in R. Floud and D. McCloskey (eds) (1981) *The Economic History of Britain since 1700*, vol. 1, 1700–1860; and T. P. R. Laslett (1969) 'Size and Structure of the Household in England, over Three Centuries', *Population Studies*, 23.

17. N. F. R. Crafts (1983) 'British Economic Growth 1700–1831: A Review of the Evidence', *Economic History Review*, 36.

18. M. Turner (1982) 'Agricultural Productivity in England in the Eighteenth Century: Evidence from Crop Yields', *Economic History Review*, 35. He quotes unpublished work by B. A. Holderness. See also E. Kerridge (1967) *The Agricultural Revolution of the Seventeenth Century*. If productivity and income growth was much more marked, especially in agriculture, before the onset of population growth then this indicates a supply-side role for agriculture and would confirm the importance of entrepreneurial initiatives on the land; see P. K. O'Brien (1977) 'Agriculture and the Industrial Revolution', *Economic History Review*, 30. Enclosure is the most obvious, and most studied, of the sources of agricultural productivity growth and the consensus seems to be that not only could it raise yields substantially but that much more of these gains were made in the century or more before 1760 than after. Also tenant farmers for life or on long leases who farmed most of English land by the mid-eighteenth century benefited much more than landowners; see J. A. Yelling (1977) *Common Field and Enclosure in England 1450–1850*; C. J. Dahlman (1980) *The Open Field System and Beyond*; and J. R. Wordie (1981) 'Rent Movements and the English Tenant Farmer, 1700–1839', *Research in Economic History*, 6, and (1983) 'The Chronology of English Enclosure 1500–1914', *Economic History Review*, 36.

19. For the stimulus to demand given by improved communications see W. Albert (1972) *The Turnpike Road System in England 1663–1840*; A. W. Skempton, 'Canals and River Navigation Before 1750' in C. Singer (ed.) (1957) *History of Technology*, 3; E. Pawson (1977) *Transport and Economy; the Turnpike Roads of*

18th Century England.
20. Grossman and Stiglitz (1980).
21. Kirzner (1973), pp. 137–50.
22. H. Demsetz (1982) *Economic, Legal, and Political Dimensions of Competition*, p. 8.
23. Shackle (1979), p. 137.
24. F. J. Fisher (1935) 'The Development of the London Food Market 1540–1640', *Economic History Review*, 5; (1948) 'The Development of London as a Centre of Conspicuous Consumption in the Sixteenth and Seventeenth Centuries', *Royal Historical Society Transactions*, 30; E. A. Wrigley (1967) 'A Simple Model of London's Importance in Changing English Society and Economy 1650–1750', *Past and Present*, 37; A. M. Everitt (1973 edn.) *Perspectives in English Urban History.*
25. Westerfield (1915), pp. 315ff.
26. The grain market was traditionally the major object of government intervention, but for whatever reason there is no doubt that in this as in other areas of the economy its influence was small by the end of the seventeenth century; see A. B. Appleby (1979) 'Grain Prices and Subsistence Crises in England and France 1590–1740', *Journal of Economic History*, 36; R. B. Outhwaite (1981) 'Dearth and Government Intervention in English Grain Markets 1590–1700', *Economic History Review*, 34. Much pre-industrial government intervention was, of course, designed to maintain public order rather than to implement any particular economic principles: see J. Walter and K. Wrightson (1976), 'Dearth and the Social Order in Early Modern England', *Past & Present*, 71.
27. See, for example, R. Ippolito (1975) 'The Effects of the Agricultural Depression on Industrial Demand in England 1730–1750', *Economica*, 42.
28. In an article that should become as influential as the one it undermines, see J. Mokyr (1977) 'Demand versus Supply in the Industrial Revolution', *Journal of Economic History*, 37; the original demand argument is in E. W. Gilboy 'Demand as a Factor in the Industrial Revolution' in A. H. Cole (ed.) (1932) *Facts and Factors in Economic History*. The idea that inadequate aggregate demand is unlikely to be a long-term problem for an undeveloped economy is also an underlying theme in a quite different context in J. Mokyr (1983) *Why Ireland Starved: A Quantitative and Analytical History of the Irish Economy 1800–1850*, p. 213.
29. Kirzner (1973), p. 99.
30. A. Alchian and H. Demsetz (1972) 'Production, Information Costs and Economic Organisation', *American Economic Review*, 62.
31. D. C. Coleman (1975) *Industry in Tudor and Stuart England*; J. Langton, 'Industry and Towns, 1500–1730' in R. A. Dodgshon and R. A. Butlin (eds) (1978) *Historical Geography of England and Wales.*
32. D. C. Coleman (1983) 'Proto-Industrialization: A Concept Too Many', *Economic History Review*, 36.
33. M. M. Postan (1954) 'The Famulus: the Estate Labourer in the Twelfth and Thirteenth Centuries', *Economic History Review, Supplement no. 2*; and (1975) *The Medieval Economy and Society*, p. 147.
34. For the idea that there has been a fundamental misinterpretation of medieval English history, see A. Macfarlane (1978) *The Origins of English Individualism. The Family, Property and Social Transition.*
35. H. R. Loyn (1962) *Anglo-Saxon England and the Norman Conquest*, p. 337.
36. For an impression of the diversity of 'putting-out' in time and place see the following: L. A. Clarkson (1960) 'The Organisation of the English Leather Industry in the late 16th and 17th Centuries', *Economic History Review*, 13; H. Heaton (1965 edn) *The Yorkshire Woollen and Worsted Industries*; E. F. Gay (1937) 'Putting-Out System' in *Encyclopedia of the Social Sciences*; N. S. B. Gras (1930) *Industrial Evolution*; articles by D. C. Coleman and J. Thirsk in N. B. Harte and K. G. Ponting (eds)

(1973) *Textile History and Economic History*; E. E. Rich and C. H. Wilson (eds) (1977) *Cambridge Economic History of Europe* vol. 5, Ch. 8; J. Hatcher and T. C. Barker (1974) *A History of British Pewter*, pp. 241ff.

37. This is not to say that the question of when wages actually emerged is not of interest, merely that it is not relevant to the question of the emergence of large firms in the expansion of 'putting-out' and the Industrial Revolution. As a separate income category reflecting specialisation, wages obviously predate, or at least are not necessarily connected with, the institution of money. But it seems that money must have been a powerful incentive to specialise for wages. The prospect of a money wage enabled people to sell a particular, specialised object in exchange for an extremely wide claim on goods. Moreover, unlike in barter, people with money were no longer obliged to specify when or on what character of goods they wished to exercise this claim. More interesting perhaps than when it happened is the fact that once it happened, once money was allowed into some primeval equilibrium situation, the individual choices of people could be deferred — they could suit themselves. The circumstances, resources and opportunities of individuals became much more difficult to know and to reconcile in the market. Enter the entrepreneur! See also H. R. Loyn (1962), p. 117.

The idea that wage-labour was a novel feature of large-scale factory industry has much in common — their source may be the same — with the claim that trade unions were necessarily a response to the same phenomenon. This too seems misconceived. Before the second half of the nineteenth century most unionised workers in Britain were to be found outside factory employment. It was the tradesmen, especially those with a long craft tradition, who took the lead in expanding trade unionism in the nineteenth century; their ancestors had been at least as active in this respect during the middle ages and were probably more effective in achieving their objects. As a recent study points out the notion that there were no durable combinations of workers during the eighteenth century and earlier, and that these had not extended by the time of the Combination Acts, makes the purpose of that legislation obscure: see C. R. Dobson (1980) *Masters and Journeymen. A Prehistory of Industrial Relations 1717-1800*.

38. See R. H. Coase (1937) 'The Nature of the Firm', *Economica*, n.s. 4; A. A. Alchian (1950) 'Uncertainty, Evolution and Economic Theory' *Journal of Political Economy*, 58; A. A. Alchian and H. Demsetz (1972), 'Production, Information Cost and Economic Organisation', *American Economic Review*, 62; A. A. Alchian and W. R. Allen (1974 edn) *University Economics. Elements of Inquiry*, pp. 281-308.

39. R. Milward (1981), 'The Emergence of Wage Labor in Early Modern England', *Explorations in Economic History*, 18.

40. F. H. Knight (1921) *Risk, Uncertainty and Profit*, p. 291.

41. Kirzner (1973), p. 78.

42. G. L. S. Shackle (1970) *Expectation, Enterprise and Profit. The Theory of the Firm*, p. 149.

43. A. Goodman (1977) *History of England from Edward II to James I*, p. 34.

44. On this point see S. N. S. Cheung (1973) 'The Fable of the Bees: An Economic Investigation', *Journal of Law and Economics*, 16.

45. A. P. Wadsworth and J. de L. Mann (1931) *The Cotton Trade and Industrial Lancashire 1600-1780*, p. 273. For the perfect type of the cross-entrant see K. H. Burley (1958) 'An Essex Clothier of the Eighteenth Century', *Economic History Review*, 11.

46. P. Mathias, 'Leisure and Wages in Theory and Practice' in Mathias (1981), Ch. 8.

47. V. A. C. Gatrell (1977) 'Labour, Power, and the Size of Firms in Lancashire Cotton in the Second Quarter of the Nineteenth Century', *Economic History*

Review, 30.

48. For example, see J. H. Hexter, 'The Myth of the Middle Class in Tudor England' in (1961) *Reappraisals in History*.

49. For some insights into this kind of problem with reference to the transfer of coal fuel techniques from England to France see J. R. Harris (1976) 'Skills, Coal and British Industry in the Eighteenth Century', *History*, 61.

50. Examples are rarely documented, but no better description of the type is known to me than the pen portrait of Caleb Garth in George Eliot (1871–2), *Middlemarch*, Ch. 24, final paragraphs.

51. A. Marshall (ed.) (1890) *Principles of Economics*, vol. 2, pp. 436–7.

52. P. R. Hyams (1970) 'The Origins of a Peasant Land Market in England', *Economic History Review*, 23.

53. Loyn (1962), p. 171.

54. See the discussion in P. O'Brien and C. Keyder (1978) *Economic Growth in Britain and France*, Ch. 5.

55. H. J. Habakkuk (1952) 'Economic Functions of English Landowners in the Seventeenth and Eighteenth Centuries', *Explorations in Entrepreneurial History*, 6.

56. Mokyr (1983), Ch. 4, who concludes that it was not an important factor in explaining Ireland's poverty either.

57. A. Smith (1776) *Wealth of Nations*, Bk. 3, Ch. 2, my italics.

58. Loyn (1962), p. 320.

59. E. Miller and J. Hatcher (1978) *Medieval England: Rural Society and Economic Change 1086–1348*, p. 176.

60. O'Brien and Keyder (1978), p. 135.

61. J. R. Wordie (1983).

62. J. H. Plumb (1967) *The Growth of Political Stability in England*, p. 158; see also J. Cannon (ed.) (1981) *The Whig Ascendancy. Colloquies on Hanoverian England*.

63. D. Landes (1969) *The Unbound Prometheus, Technological Change and Industrial Development in Western Europe from 1750 to the Present*, p. 357.

64. Rostow's work is probably most widely known and can be taken as typical; see, for example, W. W. Rostow (1975) *How It All Began: Origins of the Modern Economy*, Ch. 4.

65. R. Porter and M. Teich (eds) (1981) *The Enlightenment in National Context*, pp. 7–8.

66. W. Paley (1785) *The Principles of Moral and Political Philosophy*, p. 61.

67. In making use of the phrase 'entrepreneurial perception' it is not intended to suggest that it is entirely phenomenal in character, in the sense that there is nothing objective corresponding to it in nature. This is why it is considered part of a 'process', a concept that is as applicable to external events as it is to mental activity, and one which also maintains a distinction between them while allowing some contingency. The distinction is important, especially perhaps in considering the idea of time, where the mathematical concept in terms of distinct units is different from a person's direct consciousness of it. There seems to have been limited realisation of this kind of problem and its consequences in the study of history and the social sciences. But for some of the implications for modern science of the breakdown of classical (Newtonian) concepts of space, time, matter and motion since Heisenberg and Einstein, see M. Capec (1961) *The Philosophical Impact of Contemporary Physics*. If entrepreneurship is the most appropriate concept available for describing the active agent for change in a market process then, of course, any theory of that process which incorporated the entrepreneur could only be an explanatory, not a predictive, theory. What is more the only evidence that could be invoked in its support would have to be indirect, arising only after the events that mark the process have occurred.

68. Adam Ferguson (1978 edn) *An Essay on the History of Civil Society*, p. 183.

7 MARKETS AND DEVELOPMENT IN AFRICA AND ASIA

A. J. H. Latham

This chapter examines the role of the market in the economic development of Africa and Asia before the Second World War. It argues that the force of the market was crucial to the progress which took place there. To begin with, a simple African economic system is examined, and then the wider question of the nature of African and Asian economies in general is considered. Fashionable terms such as 'subsistence', 'dependence', 'mode of production', 'formalism', 'substantivism', 'reciprocity' and 'redistribution' will be avoided, in the belief that these terms only obscure our perception of African and Asian economies. The best way to understand these economies is simply to examine them, not dress up discussion with empty phrases.[1]

The question to be asked is to what extent was Africa a market in the pre-colonial period? This relatively innocent question has split economic anthropologists into two bitterly warring groups, and the economic historians of Africa into two equally feuding kinship groups. Without returning yet again to the tiresome detail of this dispute, it can be said that one faction believes pre-colonial African economies were mutual welfare systems in which people produced and shared their goods according to unspoken social obligations, rather as they do inside the family circle. People did not produce to sell to the market for personal gain, and because there were no market transactions, there was no need for money. The other faction is convinced that although goods were sometimes distributed within the extended family circle, they could have been sold through the market, and usually were. Because market transactions were widespread, money had been adopted to make exchange easier. The existence of money proves it was a market economy, and can be said to be the litmus test of its existence. The market can exist without money, but money cannot exist without the market.[2]

One way of tackling this issue, is to look in detail at a typical West African economy and see how it operated in the eighteenth and nineteenth centuries. The map on page 203 shows the Cross River area of Nigeria. The region was about 150 miles from north to south, and about 50 miles wide. Because of a diary kept in pidgin English by an African chief in the 1780s, and extensive material left by European traders, this district is probably better documented than any other part of Africa in these years. Yams were the basic food staple, but they were only produced in quantity in the north, where soil conditions were suitable. So if the downriver people wanted yams, they had to find other goods to exchange for them. To the south-west there were thick groves of palm trees, and the fruit of these provided a thick orange oil which was tasty, nutritious, and used for cooking. As the palm trees did not grow in such profusion further north, the yam growers were happy to swop their surplus yams for oil. In this way, the specialisation of production which resulted from the natural geographical location of resources, made exchange essential. But yams and palm oil were not a sufficient diet in themselves, and although there were eggs, chickens, goats and even a few dwarf cattle which were resistant to the tsetse fly, the region was low in protein supplies. So fish, prawn and shrimps were very important, and they were supplied by itinerant fishermen who lived in little communities along the estuary. In exchange for their fish, they received yams and oil. Again, the geographical allocation of resources determined the need for exchange. Fish, yams and oil do not make much of a meal without salt, and this vital commodity was only produced by the people of Tom Shotts, a town on the coast, where it was obtained by boiling seawater. These people supplied all the others with salt, and got back, in return the oil, fish and yams they needed. What is quite clear is that without the interchange of these basic commodities over the area, the people would have suffered from malnutrition and might even have starved. The people of each part of the region depended upon the supplies provided by the people of the other parts.

How was the interchange of these goods made? Throughout the region there was a network of markets, with major markets at Umon, Itu, Ikorofiong, Ikpa, Ifiayong and Calabar. Provision markets took place daily, but major market days took place on a four- and eight-day cycle. To these big markets were brought the craft products of the region; mats, baskets, ropes, nets, cloth made from the bark of the raffia palm, pottery, knives, hoes and other tools and implements. For there were specialist craft producers, and even particular craft villages, their location often determined by the natural location of raw materials. This specialisation of craft production is a classic feature of the market, as it enables people to concentrate on a particular task or skill, knowing that they can

Figure 7.1 Cross River Economy

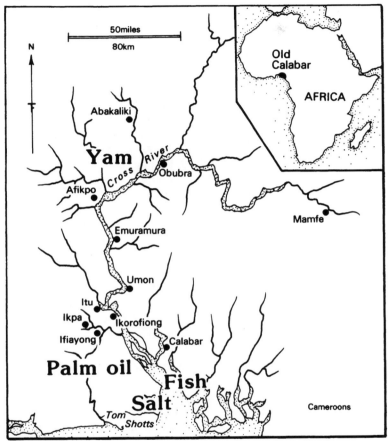

exchange their product for the food and other things they need. Blacksmiths were particularly important, and came from one Ibo clan. Some travelled from place to place, and others settled in villages under the protection of local leaders. Pottery making was very localised because of the availability of clay, the main production centres being at Ikot Ansa and Nkpara near Calabar, and at Ikorofiong, which was also a centre of cloth production. Another crucial skill was the building of canoes, for the region depended upon the river for transport. Again, nature determined that canoe production be very localised, as the largest were over 50 feet long, and the trees big enough for making them only grew at

Emuramura upriver, and down the far east of the estuary towards the Cameroons. At Emuramura the canoes were produced by mastercraftsmen, who sold their product to the other people of the region.

At the markets, exchange was made using copper rods as a form of money. It is the presence of these rods which is most difficult to explain away by those who believe the economy operated as a mutual welfare system. For if it was a mutual welfare system, like an enlarged family, why was money necessary? In trying to argue round the fact that these rods existed, it has been suggested that they were not really money at all, but a kind of coupon system by which status symbols were distributed. They could only be used for acquiring cattle, slaves, guns, medicine, magic, and official positions. They were not money, because they could not be used for small everyday purchases. Trying to buy a banana with a rod would be like trying to pay for a cup of coffee with a $100 note.[3] But it was precisely because of this difficulty that the local smiths split the rods into wires. These could then be used for small ordinary purchases, as is well documented. Rods and wires formed a proper monetary system, and operated as a medium of exchange, a unit of account, a store of wealth, and a standard of deferred payment, this last being made clear from their use in credit transactions. What is more, the use of this rod money goes back to our very earliest account of the region in 1668.[4]

So the Cross River was a monetised market economy, which depended on the interchange of goods determined by the geographical distribution of resources in the region. The exchange took place through the market, because it could not take place through family, clan, or tribal arrangements. For the yam producers were Ibo, the palm oil producers Ibibio, the fishermen Efiat, the salt producers of Ibuno, and the canoe makers, and pottery makers came from different tribes again. They even spoke different languages. The market therefore made the interchange of goods possible between people entirely separated by kith, kin and language. There wasn't even a dominant political overlord to bring them together, markets and trade existed happily without hegemony.

Not only was this a market system, it was a capitalist system. Canoes were major items of capital expenditure, and far from being communally owned, they belonged to individual traders. One nineteenth-century chief, King Eyo II, is said to have possessed over 400, which he used in his extensive trading operations. He was only one of many big traders, who expanded their canoe fleets with the profits of their trading operations. Canoes needed men to paddle them, and slaves were used. In a sense the slaves were capital goods, like the horses which used to tow barges, or like outboard motors. They were not wage earners, but did receive real wages in terms of food and housing. At the same time, the slaves themselves were petty capitalists, allowed to grow food for themselves and to sell at the markets, and they dealt in provisions when away on trading voyages for their master. In all but their legal status, they were peasant capitalist producers. This freedom to produce and trade gave them an incentive to maintain their allegiance to their master. Some acted as business managers for their masters, or agents for him at distant markets, and quite a few became successful traders in their own right. They legally belonged to their owners, and were members of his family, owing support and military service in times of war. Yet some were also substantial slave owners themselves, and Yellow Duke, a great trader and a slave, owned more than 3,000 in the late nineteenth century. Some of these would have been slave owners themselves! Indeed, the widespread internal slave trade shows this to have been more of a market economy than our own. For non-economic, moral reasons, human beings have been banned from the market in our own society, but they were openly available in the market places of Africa right into the twentieth century, when benevolent Colonial governments finally banned the trade. More goods therefore entered African markets then, than in ours today. What is more, the existence of slavery shows clearly this was not a communal welfare system, for someone who was taken into slavery and sold was not going to enjoy a mutual benefit with his vendor!

Substantial development took place in this market system over the years. One tribe near the coast, the Efik of Calabar, took advantage of their geographical position at the furthest inland deep water natural harbour to develop good contacts with the European traders when they began to come to the river towards the end of the seventeenth century. As the slave export trade developed during the eighteenth century, they established themselves as middlemen, trading European goods to the inland markets for slaves, and purchasing canoes, and the slaves to man them from their profits.

The European goods they imported stimulated the domestic economy, and added new items to local consumption patterns. Bar iron, for example, was a major import, and the local blacksmiths beat this into tools and implements, thereby increasing the efficiency of local production. Copper rods were brought in too, expanding the money supply and helping the flexibility of the local monetary system, to the benefit of the specialisation of production and division of labour. So much was this economy like our own, that in the nineteenth century, when substantial imports of rods led to over-expansion of the money supply, prices rose and the value of rods fell considerably. Copper rods were subject to the quantity theory! Imports of cotton textiles do not seem to have hindered local textile production, as raffia bark costumes continued to be produced for ceremonial costumes. Even the pottery industry was unaffected by imports of crockery from abroad, and continued to produce. The only industry which seems to have been adversely affected by European imports was the salt industry of Tom Shotts. About the beginning of the nineteenth century this industry collapsed, the fall coinciding with the import of large quantities of cheap salt from Cheshire, part of Liverpool's hinterland. This collapse is crucial in our understanding of the economy. If this was a mutual welfare system, then surely the people of the region would have resisted imported salt, because they knew it would destroy the livelihood of their neighbours and fellows. But, in fact, they acted as discriminating consumers, and chose the cheaper and superior imported product. They were making rational market decisions just as British and American consumers do when they buy imported Japanese cars, preferring the cheaper and better imports to the products of their own home industries, regardless of what it will do to the job opportunities of their friends. The destruction of the salt industry is the perfect example of consumer rationality in this economy, and proves clearly just how much a market system it was.

Although it might be assumed that the export of slaves from the region would damage the local economy, it is in fact difficult to show this. The British banned the slave trade in 1807, but the Spanish and Portuguese continued to take slaves away until the 1840s. This terminal period of the slave trade provides another example of the market rationality of the people of the region. As the slave trade waned, they did not just sit under the palm trees and beat their drums, but turned to look for new items to export to replace slaves. In Liverpool there was a growing demand for vegetable oils, as factory production gathered pace there. Lubricants were needed, literally to oil the wheels of industry, and oil was also needed for candles and soap-making. Some palm oil had reached Liverpool even in the heyday of the slave trade, and now the dense groves of palm trees provided the perfect answer to the region's need for a new export staple. With perfect rationality, the people increasingly shifted their efforts into developing the trade in palm oil, and so successful were they that tonnage of palm produce exports grew at an annual average of 3.11 per cent during the century. Paradoxically, slaves continued to be exported from the very region the oil was coming from, and even after the overseas trade finally ended, slaves were still provided for the internal slave trade, which continued throughout the century. How could this be? How could a region export both labour, and the product of labour simultaneously? The answer is probably fairly simple. The main business of the economy was the production of food and craft goods for the local market, and the supply of services such as transport, justice, medicine, magic, religion, music, dancing and masquerades. The export of slaves and the export of palm produce were both peripheral to this main business. Palm fruits were a seasonal crop, and grew on trees which grew wild. All that was needed was extra labour in the harvesting season, when men and boys cut the bunches of fruit from the trees, and women and children processed it and sold it to wholesalers. Slaves were not important in the production of oil, although they were used to transport it to the coast in the big trading canoes. The loss of people into slavery may have had little effect on the economy, as most of them were men, and men had only a small part to play in the production process. A wry comment on the African economy is that women did the unimportant things like growing the food, and men did the important things like deciding whether there should be a missionary or not! In any case, slaves were not normally captured *en masse* to be sold, although certainly some were prisoners of war. More usually men were taken into slavery after losing a legal case, or for adultery or theft. They were brought to the village markets here and there across the district, just as goats or chicken were. One source was the notorious Long Juju of Arochuku. This famous oracle was consulted from far and wide for judgement by litigants. After they had called their pleas into the yawning mouth of the oracle's cave, the deity would answer with judgement, and the loser would be led into the cave by the acolytes. The stream that issued from the cave would gush red with blood, showing that the guilty party had been eaten. In reality, the water was coloured with red dye wood, and the victim was thrown in chains, and sold down the river. The loss of people into slavery from here and there would not diminish the local economy any more seriously than the loss of goats into the pot. Even if these people had not been sold into slavery, there is no guarantee that they would have been available to the economy as workers or managers, because they might have been used as human sacrifices, or even eaten. Large-scale human sacrifice on the death of great men continued well into the nineteenth century, and a recent collection of oral testimonies referring to an adjacent region in the 1890s reveals beyond doubt that cannibalism was still practised at that time. War captives, criminals, and even unpopular relations were eaten! In sum, the loss to the region of people into the overseas slave trade was probably no more damaging than the loss to Britain of those who migrated to America.[5]

How typical was the economy of the Cross River, of Africa in general? A recent study of South Eastern Nigeria tells a similar story to the one already outlined, and further along the coast Ghanaian cocoa farmers have long been taken as a prime example of African peasant capitalists responding to market opportunities. Elsewhere in West Africa in the late nineteenth and early twentieth centuries peasants moved into peanut cultivation, showing that they too were used to organising their production for the market. In East Africa cotton and coffee became peasant cash crops, and right across East and Southern Africa maize was grown for sale. So much was East Africa a market economy that in some areas cattle were used for money, like copper rods, the small change being provided by goats. One is tempted to wonder if cattle would have been the money everywhere in Africa as they were in Asia in early times, had it not been for the tsetse fly! Everywhere Africa was permeated by the force of the market, even if the market economies which were operating were very simple.[6]

What was the situation in Asia, and how did Asian economies compare in their level of development with African ones? The existence of the copper rod currency system is a crucial part of the evidence that the economy of the Cross River was a market. As we have seen, other parts of Africa used cattle as money, and cowrie shells were also widely used.[7] In the distant past cattle had been used for money in India, and cowrie shells had been used there too, and in China. They were still used in Siam and Indo-China into the nineteenth century. So the implication is that money and markets date back far into Asia's history. The market requirement of an acceptable means of payment had led to the adoption of money at an early date. It is tempting to suggest that the level of sophistication of the monetary unit is a rough index of the level of development of the economy in which it operates. Thus an economy which uses shells as its money may be assumed to be less developed than one which uses gold sovereigns, minted to a specific weight and fineness, and stamped with a seal of authority. It is a moot point whether one which uses Bank of England notes instead of gold sovereigns is more developed or less! What is clear is that Asia had moved forward from shells and cattle money to proper coinage long before Africa, for both India and China had true coins by the fourth century BC. Even if Chinese currency was chaotic in the nineteenth century, by comparison with India's rupee it was still more advanced than Africa's.[8]

Certainly it is true that Asian economies were more advanced than African ones. India in the nineteenth century had a vast handloom cotton weaving industry, operated by individual craftsmen and their families. There were also spinners and dyers, and other craftsmen such as blacksmiths, coppersmiths, silversmiths, goldsmiths, carpenters, cartwrights, basketmakers, potters, leatherworkers, tailors, oil pressers, rice pounders, and so on. In China, Indo-China, Siam and elsewhere this multiplicity of crafts existed. These craftsmen were dependent upon the market for their livelihood, as the sale of the products earned them the purchasing power to acquire food, clothing and shelter. The relatively sophisticated monetary systems these countries possessed assisted this division of labour. Even when there was some communal distribution of crops as in some Indian villages, sales to the market were also made. The specialist centres of high excellence that existed were very clearly dependent on the market for the sales of their silks and fine cottons, carpets, damascene metal work, and gold and silverwork. What is more, there would have been no merchant caste if there had been no market, and there was certainly a merchant caste.[9]

It was this market oriented craft industry which received the severe shock of competition from British manufactured goods during the course of the nineteenth century. Just as imported salt knocked home-produced salt out of the African market, and proved that Africans responded to market forces, the fact that Asians chose to disregard the welfare of their fellow men and buy cheaper and better Lancashire cottons shows how effectively the market operated. The jibe that the bones of the Indian cotton weavers were bleaching the plains of India is open recognition of the responsiveness of the Indians to the force of the market.[10] That is why India was the fastest growing market for British cottons in the nineteenth century, and why China came next.[11] Those who rail against the ravages of British manufactured goods in African and Asian markets are merely recognising that Africans and Asians made straightforward market decisions, and preferred the superior and less expensive goods of foreigners to the inferior and more costly goods of their fellow countrymen. It was a matter of supreme unimportance to them what happened to the welfare of their neighbours. It was up to them to offer a better deal, or turn their hands to something else. In Siam, people turned from growing cotton to supply the handloom industry, to growing rice to sell for cash to buy imported cotton with. It was a market response which injected great dynamism into the Siamese economy.[12]

The development of Siam as a major rice exporting nation in the late nineteenth century is a superb example of the market responsiveness of Asian peasants. In Burma and French Indo-China too, peasants responded to the demands of the international market by bringing more land under rice cultivation to supply world needs. Burma was part of British India at this time, but the enterprise of her peasant cultivators turned her into the world's most important rice exporting region. Her peasants borrowed the necessary money from Indian Chettiar moneylenders, who themselves borrowed from the European banks. In Siam and French Indo-China, a similar process marked the expansion of rice cultivation, although in Siam the moneylenders were mostly Siamese and Chinese, and in Indo-China, Chinese.[13] The map on page 211 shows the pattern of Asian rice movements. Consumption of rice was growing both in Europe and in Asia, and Burma rice in particular went to Europe where it was used for making schnapps and beer, and the starch for Victorian petticoats and shirt fronts. An examination of the international rice trade between 1868 and 1914 shows that to begin with Bengal rice was sent to Ceylon, as this quality of rice was preferred by the Indian plantation workers there. But towards the end of the century Ceylon began to take more Burma rice, and so did Singapore and Malaya, where there were also many immigrant Indian workers. The rice was redistributed from Singapore up to Penang and the other ports of the Peninsula. It was at Singapore that the flow of rice from Bengal and Burma east met the flow of rice

Figure 7.2 Rice Trade c. 1910

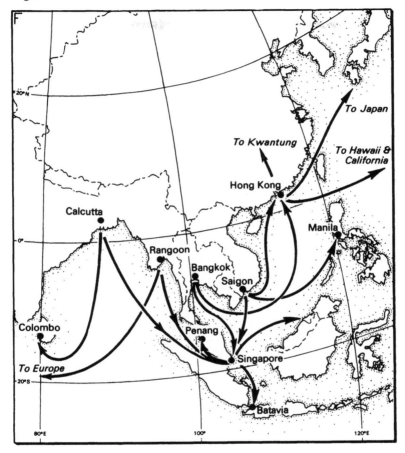

from Siam and Indo-China west. Rice from these countries was to the taste of the growing Chinese population of Malaya and the Dutch East Indies. Siam and Indo-China rice was also shipped east to Hong Kong, another major redistribution centre, to feed the grain deficient Chinese provinces of Kwantung and Fukien. Rice also went to the Philippines from French Indo-China.

Clearly there was an intra-Asian trade in rice, and further investigation shows that it was a true market, establishing a common price right across Asia. It is possible to construct a number of annual average rice prices of key exporting and importing countries, over the period 1868 to 1914. Simply by graphing these time series it is clear that annual fluctuations in all the series moved in the same direction, which is what one would expect if there really was a price-equalising market. To demonstrate this more clearly, the correlation between each pair of series has been calculated and placed in the matrix below. The matrix includes Bengal exports, Burma exports, Singapore imports, Singapore exports, Bangkok exports, Saigon exports, and China imports. The correlation between the pairs, with only two exceptions, was over 0.60. This implies there really was an intra-Asian market in rice. The fact that a commodity as basic to the Asian economy as rice was distributed through the market is overwhelming evidence that Asia was a market economy.

Having established that rice moved in an intra-Asian market, it can also be shown that the rice market was integrated with the wheat market to form one world market in basic food grains. By constructing similar price series for wheat in the West, it can be demonstrated that there was an international market for wheat. A comparison of the wheat series with the rice series reveals that the two markets met to form one huge international grain market in India. India was a producer and exporter of both grains, and Britain

Table 7.1: Correlation Matrix for International Rice Prices, 1868–1914

	Burma	Bengal Exports	Singapore Imports	Singapore Exports	Siam	China
Bengal	0.79					
Singapore Imports	0.69	0.37				
Singapore Exports	0.85	0.60	0.81			
Siam	0.88	0.66	0.72	0.91		
China	0.76	0.60	0.60	0.77	0.82	
Saigon	0.73	0.52	0.86	0.85	0.80	0.72

Source: A. J. H. Latham and Larry Neal, 'The International Market in Rice and Wheat, 1868–1914', *Economic History Review*, 36 (1983), p. 266.

took up to 18 per cent of her wheat imports from India in the early years of the twentieth century. India exported wheat west, and rice east. The correlation between the movement of annual average prices of wheat and rice across the Indian domestic market is 0.91. India was the transmission point between the two markets. To confirm that the two markets integrated, fluctuations in the price of Rangoon rice in London correlated with English wheat prices at 0.87, with American wheat in London at 0.84, and with US wheat exports at 0.81. They also correlated with Indian wheat exports at 0.77, and with Rangoon internal rice prices at 0.76. Rangoon internal rice prices correlated with Burma internal rice prices at 0.69. At the other end of the world Rangoon rice prices in London correlated with Chinese import rice prices at 0.61. The implication is clear. Not only did the force of the market permeate the Asian economy from the late nineteenth century, but it was fully integrated into the world market.[14]

The organisation of the international rice trade is still being researched, but one key factor linking the wheat market and the rice market was the telegraph. With this, prices and the state of supplies could be wired across the world instantly. Railways and steamships backed the information up with quick transport. The transatlantic cable was laid from Britain to North America in 1866, and another submarine cable was laid linking London to Bombay in 1870, India already having an extensive domestic telegraph network. Later that year Singapore, and Batavia in the Dutch East Indies, were linked into the international system, and Saigon, Hong Kong and Shanghai in 1871. The telegraph network was the nerve system of the international market.

The other market innovation of the late nineteenth century was the concept of futures trading. The first genuine futures market was the Chicago wheat futures market which began in 1848. It was not until 1883 that a genuine wheat futures market opened in Liverpool, and up to 1914 the futures markets in the great milling centres of Minneapolis and Liverpool dominated the trade. London did not have an important futures market at this time. Within 17 years of the opening of the Liverpool wheat futures market, a rice futures market opened in Rangoon. There were no exchange premises, and the dealings in spot and futures were done on the open pavements in Mogul Street, not far from the main Chettiar temple. Liverpool, London, Hamburg and Bremen trading firms had established themselves in Rangoon from about 1850, and Chinese merchants came too about the turn of the century. By 1907 Saigon had a futures market as well. There was no futures market in Bangkok, and dealings were direct between Chinese merchants and millers. The trade there was largely in the hands of one Chinese clan, the Teochieu, or rather certain Teochieu family firms. These family firms also controlled the trade elsewhere in South East Asia, including the great redistribution centres of Singapore and Hong Kong. There were few Hokkiens involved.[15]

If there was a united world market in basic food grains, rice and wheat, then certain implications follow. Rice prices must have been subject to supply and demand conditions in the East, just as wheat prices must have been influenced by supply and demand in the West. But the price of each grain must also have been affected by the price of the other, as clearly they were substitutes to some degree. If rice prices rose, then wheat prices must have risen, and vice versa. So the price of wheat in America would have been influenced by the price of rice in Asia. It follows that the returns of American farmers were affected by the price of rice. The incomes of western farm settlers provided much of the purchasing power for industrial goods in the United States, and were a basis for industrialisation. It follows that a collapse of rice prices would have grave consequences for the American economy. This was to have severe repercussions between the wars.[16]

The effect of the market in Africa and Asia before the First World War was not just to turn these countries into specialist agricultural producers. Where a particular country, like Burma, Thailand or Indo-China had a natural market advantage in a particular product such as rice, it was a sensible market response to base their development upon it. Britain in these years became more of a primary exporter herself, on the basis of her natural advantage in coal production. In other parts of Asia, such as Malaya, the Dutch East Indies, Ceylon and the Philippines, mines, plantations, and peasant crops provided a source of growth, again linked to the international market. Migrants from India and China flocked to several of these countries to seize their personal market gain of a better market price for their own labour in mine or estate. Their demand for rice was a source of stimulus for the international rice market. Right across Asia the peasantry underpinned economic advance by producing food for themselves and the village markets from their own smallholdings. From these farms too came a stream of coconut products, coconut oil being a vital element in Asian diets, and a welcome addition to the international market in vegetable oils. What palm oil was to African peasants, coconut oil was to Asian peasants, and there were many more of them! Meanwhile, in India and China the force of the market was encouraging the necessary specialisation and concentration of craft production which made modern factory production feasible. Industrialisation had begun! In 1875 there were 48 cotton mills in India, mostly under Indian ownership, and by 1913 there were 264 mills employing over a quarter of a million people. Local industrial cottons were already supplanting imports from Lancashire, and taking a toll of the local handloom industry. So successful was the production of yarn in India, that in the 1880s yarn from Bombay was being exported to China, and pushing Lancashire yarn from that market. In 1912 the first Indian steel mill was blown in at Jamshedpur, and it too was Indian owned. There was also a large jute mill industry. In China too a start had been made to factory production.[17]

After the First World War, development in Africa and Asia continued along the lines established earlier. But the war had seen a break in the free market system, and despite the return to normality, some hindrances to it lingered throughout the 1920s.[18] In India, fiscal autonomy led to the imposition of tariffs, and with their protection industrialisation advanced on the basis of the larger domestic market ensured. British goods were displaced, and so were the products of the local handloom industry. In China, too, industrialisation continued despite Japanese competition. But a greater success story is the continued market expansion in the rice-frontier countries of Burma, Thailand and Indo-China. This was partly a response to the even more spectacularly successful plantation and mining areas of Ceylon, Malaya, the Dutch East Indies, and the Philippines, and the less successful but ever hungry provinces of Southern China.[19]

It was this successful market expansion which led to the slump. As rice cultivation expanded in the East, wheat cultivation increased in the United States, Canada, Australia and Argentina. The market response of this increased supply was a gradual fall in prices from the mid-1920s. But farmers continued to add to their output as they sought to compensate for their falling incomes by growing more. 1928 was a good year, and bumper crops were harvested in both rice and wheat. Information supplied by the International Rice Research Institute in Manila suggests that the yield of rice can vary considerably according to the amount of cloud-free sunlight it obtains, and this may have been partly responsible for the good rice crop. When the 1929 crop was harvested, a quarter of the previous year's wheat crop was still in store in North America. The 1929 crop was not as good as the previous year's either in rice or wheat, but it was still a good crop. There was still storage space in the United States, but in Canada there was no room left, and the new crop had to go straight onto the market. It was a disaster and prices dropped like a stone. Farmers were bankrupted when the sales of their crop could not cover the repayment of loans they had taken out earlier in the year, and they brought the banks down with them.[20] In the United States alone over 5,000 banks went bust, more than a fifth of the total number of banks in the country.[21]

The impact in the east was immediate. On 29 January 1930 the Bangkok correspondent of the Singapore Free Press reported that the leading Bangkok miller, Lee Teck Aw, Chop Khoon Seng, was bankrupt. He had been handling 60 per cent of Bangkok's exports. The collapse of wheat prices had brought rice prices down. If the rice crop had failed at this point, the world market would have sustained wheat prices, and the agricultural collapse in America would not have taken place. What had happened is that expansion of rice and wheat had led to a market induced price collapse when providentially good weather conditions created a glut. In February there was an abortive rising in Indo-China against the French, and further trouble in May. The same month vicious race riots broke out in Rangoon, as the Burmese fell upon immigrant Indian coolies, and rioting continued intermittently until 1932. In June that year there was a bloodless revolution in Bangkok.[22]

So the great surpluses of rice and wheat caused the agricultural depression of these years. It is inconceivable that this agricultural crisis did not affect the industrial world. The collapse of grain prices impoverished farmers, and so they were unable to sustain their purchases from factories. The incomes of Western farmers were an important basis of demand for American industry, and American industrialisation. The decline in their incomes therefore must have reduced demand for industrial products. Whilst it is logically correct to argue that the income losses to farmers from the fall in prices must have been offset by the real income gains of non-farmers as food prices fell, the real income gains could not balance the losses, because the structure of aggregate demand was inevitably affected. Industrial workers were not going to buy more tractors because their real incomes had improved. An improvement in the real incomes of non-farm workers would have meant increased savings, and increased luxury expenditure, not a sustained demand for barbed wire. Inevitably those sections of industry that supplied farmers were to be gravely affected, with knock-on effects to those who provided these industries with raw materials and equipment, and those who were employed there. In the East, the decline in farm incomes had exactly the same effect on industrial demand, more particularly because the agricultural sector there was so much larger.

Sadly the response in both East and West to this natural and temporary market situation was panic. Rather than wait for a reduction in production through the effect of individual bankruptcies, and the return of less favourable weather, governments in East and West chose to assume the role of God themselves, and intervene in the situation. If Hoover's Farm Board was one of the most obvious manifestations of this interference in the market, by purchasing farm products at subsidised prices, it was by no means the first or only one.[23] One of the earliest inter-war attempts to manipulate the market in primary products was the Stevenson Restriction Scheme of 1922 which attempted to control rubber production in Ceylon and Malaya, as overplanting had led to oversupply and depressed prices. This Government-backed scheme failed because The Netherlands' government refused to join the scheme in respect to the plantations in the Dutch East Indies. Although the scheme was abandoned in 1928, it was an ominous precedent and in 1934, when a new Government control scheme was introduced, commodity control had become the order of the day.[24] The crisis from 1929 saw a collapse in demand for industrial raw materials like tin and rubber, and luxury items such as sugar. The sugar producers did not wait for Governments to agree but took matters into their own hands, and after a meeting in Brussels in 1931 introduced the Chadbourne Plan to restrict supplies by allocating export quotas to each participating country. The Dutch East Indies, as major producers, gladly participated in this scheme, as they were badly hit by the loss of the Indian market due to the imposition of tariffs, and the loss of the Japanese market through increased domestic production there and in Formosa.[25] Tin control schemes, with Government backing, were also introduced that year.[26] In 1932 the British empire moved to protection at the Ottawa Conference with reciprocal preference for each other's goods. Although Hong Kong and Singapore levied no tariffs of any significance to protect their entrepôt trades, this discriminatory system hit Japan in respect to India and Ceylon.[27] 1933 saw the introduction of control in tea.[28] The Dutch East Indies and the Philippines found their sales of rubber, tin and sugar falling, so they attempted to cut their rice purchases and pursue self-sufficiency policies.[29] These self-sufficiency policies were not always as successful as Governments hoped, however, as even in the worst years of the slump a smallholder could obtain more rice by growing rubber and selling it, and using the money to buy rice, than he could by growing rice himself. This demonstrates beautifully the rationality of the peasant producer, and suggests that the market would have readjusted to the situation in these years quickly if simply left to itself.[30] Attempts by the Government to restrict rubber production tended to discriminate against smallholders, who were more cost effective than the large estates and in consequence built up a legacy of resentment against Colonial authorities which was soon to make itself felt.[31]

So the grain crises of 1929–34 led to the collapse of the free market, and Governments in East and West were locked into interventionism, from which they were unwilling or unable to extricate themselves. The tariff barriers and controls which were imposed in the east created a particular problem for Japan for which a military solution seemed a natural outcome.[32] The fact that the market had been put in shackles meant that it could no longer be the motivator of development in Africa and Asia. Petty and destructive nationalism had taken over, and with it the intertia of bureaucracy to the loss of individual enterprise, and personal economic liberty. The peasant capitalists of Africa and Asia were the losers.

Notes

1. Early versions of this paper were delivered at Osaka City University, 7 February 1984; Institute of Developing Economies, Tokyo, 10 February 1984; Waseda University, Tokyo, 13 February 1984; Northwestern University, Evanston, 23 February 1984; University of Illinois, Urbana-Champaign, 24 February 1984; University of Western Ontario, London, 27 February 1984 and Bryn Mawr College, 5 March 1984.
2. A. J. H. Latham, *The International Economy and the Undeveloped World, 1865–1914*, (Croom Helm, London; Rowman and Littlefield, Totowa, NJ, 1978), pp. 165–8; Karl Polanyi, *The Livelihood of Man* (Academic Press, New York, 1977); Harold K. Schneider, *Economic Man. The Anthropology of Economics* (Free Press, New York, 1974), pp. 24–6; Douglass C. North, 'Markets and Other Allocation

Systems in History — The Challenge of Karl Polanyi', *Journal of European History*, vol. 6 (1977), pp. 703–16.

3. Paul and Laura Bohannan, *Tiv Economy* (Longmans, London, 1968), pp. 228–37.

4. A. J. H. Latham, 'Currency, Credit and Capitalism on the Cross River in the Pre-Colonial Era', *Journal of African History*, vol. 12 (1971), pp. 599–603.

5. A. J. H. Latham, *Old Calabar, 1600–1891. The Impact of the International Economy Upon a Traditional Society* (Clarendon Press, Oxford, 2nd Imp., 1978); A. J. H. Latham, 'Currency, Credit and Capitalism on the Cross River in the Pre-Colonial Ear', *Journal of African History*, vol. 12 (1971), pp. 599–603; A. J. H. Latham, 'The Pre-Colonial Economy of the Lower Cross River' in University of Calabar, *A History of the Cross River Region of Nigeria* (forthcoming); A. J. H. Latham, Review of E. J. Allagoa and Kay Williamson, *Jos Oral History and Literature Texts, vol. 4, Ancestral Voices: Oral Historical Texts from Nembe, Niger Delta* (Dept. of History, University of Jos, 1981) in *Journal of African History*, vol. 25 (1984), pp. 125–6.

6. David Northrup, *Trade Without Rulers. Pre-Colonial Economic Development in South-Eastern Nigeria*, (Clarendon Press, Oxford, 1978); Polly Hill, *The Migrant Cocoa Farmers of Southern Ghana. A Study in Rural Capitalism* (Cambridge University Press, Cambridge, 1963); A. G. Hopkins, *An Economic History of West Africa* (Longmans, London, 1973), pp. 128–9, 141, 214, 217–21; Cyril Ehrlich, 'The Uganda Economy, 1903–1945' in V. Harlow and E. M. Chilver (eds), *History of East Africa*, vol. 2 (Clarendon Press, Oxford, 1965), pp. 405–6; Harold K. Schnieder, *The Wahi Wanyaturu: Economics in an African Society* (Aldine, Chicago, 1970), pp. 65–8; Latham, *International Economy*, pp. 159–62.

7. Marion Johnson, 'The Cowrie Currencies of West Africa', *Journal of African History*, vol. 11 (1970), pp. 17–49, 331–53.

8. Paul Einzig, *Primitive Money in its Ethnological, Historical and Economic Aspects* (Eyre & Spottiswoode, London, 1955), pp. 100–5, 250–1, 253–8, 285, 311; Len-Sheng Yang, *Money and Credit in China. A Short History* (Harvard University Press, Cambridge, Mass., 1965), pp. 1–29; Jacques Melitz, *Primitive and Modern Money; An Interdisciplinary Approach* (Addison-Wesley Publishing Co., Reading, Mass., 1974), pp. 84–9; Alexander Del Mar, *History of Monetary Systems. A History of Actual Experiments in Money Made by Various States of the Ancient and Modern World*, 2nd edn (Augustus M. Kelley, New York, 1969), pp. 1–7, 16–17; Latham, *International Economy*, pp. 44–8, 168–9.

9. D. R. Gadgil, *The Industrial Evolution of India in Recent Times, 1860–1939*, 5th edn (Oxford University Press, Bombay, 1971), pp. 169–193, 325–37; James C. Ingram, *Economic Change in Thailand, 1850–1970* (Stanford University Press, Stanford, 1971), pp. 113–18, 128; Charles Robequain, *The Economic Development of French Indo-China* (Oxford University Press, London, 1944), pp. 243–9; Albert Feuerwerker, *The Chinese Economy, c. 1870–1911* (Michigan University Press, Ann Arbor, Michigan, 1969), pp. 17–31; Albert Feuerwerker, *The Chinese Economy, 1912–1949* (Michigan University Press, Ann Arbor, Michigan, 1968), pp. 10–12; M. N. Srinivas, *Caste in Modern India and Other Essays* (Asia Publishing House, London, 1962), pp. 63–9; Morris D. Morris, 'The Growth of Large Scale Industry to 1947' in Dharma Kumar (ed.), *The Cambridge Economic History of India*, vol. 2 (Cambridge University Press, Cambridge, 1983), pp. 668–76; G. C. Allen, *A Short Economic History of Modern Japan*, 8th imp. (George Allen & Unwin, London, 1966), pp. 17–19, 24.

10. K. Marx, *Capital* (Modern Library, New York, 1936), p. 471.

11. Lars G. Sandberg, *Lancashire in Decline. A Study in Entrepreneurship, Technology and International Trade* (Ohio State University Press, Columbus, 1974), pp. 165–70.

12. Ingram, *Economic Change in Thailand*, pp. 36–74; J. C. Ingram, 'Thailand's Rice Trade and the Allocation of Resources; in C. D. Cowan, *The Economic Development of South-East Asia* (George Allen & Unwin, London, 1964), pp. 102–26.

13. Cheng Siok-Hwa, *The Rice Industry of Burma, 1852–1940* (University of Malaya Press, Kuala Lumpur, 1968); Michael Adas, 'The Burma Delta', *Economic Development and Social Change on an Asian Rice Frontier, 1852–1941* (The University of Wisconsin Press, Madison, Wisconsin, 1974); Ingram, *Economic Change in Thailand*, pp. 36–74; Robequain, *Economic Development of French Indo-China*, pp. 38–9, 40fn, 44fn, 168, 308–11.

14. A. J. H. Latham and Larry Neal, 'The International Market in Rice and Wheat, 1868–1914', *Economic History Review*, vol. 36 (1983), pp. 260–80.

15. Latham and Neal, *International Market in Rice and Wheat*, pp. 273–4; A. J. H. Latham, 'Singapore and the International Rice Trade: Past, Present and Future', Lecture to the Rotary Club of Raffles City, Raffles Hotel, Singapore, 20 December 1983 (unpublished); Adas, *Burma Delta*, p. 117.

16. Douglass C. North, *The Economic Growth of the United States, 1790–1860* (Prentice-Hall, Englewood Cliffs, NJ, 1961), p. 103; Douglass C. North, *Growth and Welfare in the American Past. A New Economic History*, pp. 75–85.

17. Latham, *International Economy*, Chaps. 4, 5; Morris D. Morris, 'The Growth of Large Scale Industry to 1947' in Dharma Kumar (ed.), *The Cambridge Economic History of India*, vol. 2 (Cambridge University Press, Cambridge, 1983), pp. 572–92.

18. J. W. F. Rowe, *Primary Commodities in International Trade* (Cambridge University Press, Cambridge, 1965), pp. 78–81, 120–9.

19. A. J. H. Latham, *The Depression and the Developing World, 1914–1939* (Croom Helm, London; Barnes and Noble, Totowa, NJ, 1981), Chaps. 3, 5.

20. Latham, *Depression*, pp. 175–8.

21. W. A. Lewis, *Economic Survey, 1919–1939* 8th imp. (George Allen & Unwin, London, 1966), p. 54.

22. *Singapore Free Press*, 3 February 1930, p. 12; *Singapore Free Press*, 29 June 1932, p. 413; Rudolph von Albertini, *European Colonial Rule, 1880–1940. The Impact of the West on India, Southeast Asia and Africa* (Greenwood Press, Westport, Connecticut, 1982), p. 217; Adas, *Burma Delta*, pp. 197–200; Ingram, *Economic Change in Thailand*, pp. 2–3.

23. Lewis, *Economic Survey*, p. 109.

24. P. Lamartine Yates, *Commodity Control. A Study of Primary Products* (Jonathan Cape, London, 1943), pp. 119–21.

25. Yates, *Commodity Control*, pp. 58–9.

26. Ibid., p. 147; W. Fox *Tin. The Working of a Commodity Agreement* (Mining Journal Books Ltd, London, 1974), pp. 126–8.

27. Ian M. Drummond, *Imperial Economic Policy, 1917–1939. Studies in Expansion and Protection* (George Allen & Unwin, London, 1974), p. 429; Albertini, *-European Colonial Rule,*. pp. 51–2.

28. Rowe, *Primary Commodities*, pp. 149–50.

29. Latham, *Depression and Developing World*, pp. 164–6; V. D. Wickizer and M. K. Bennett, *The Rice Economy of Monsoon Asia* (Stanford University Press, Stanford, 1941), pp. 165–87; Lim Chong Yah, *Economic Development of Modern Malaya* (Oxford University Press, Kuala Lumpur, 1967), p. 175; J. S. Furnivall, *Netherlands India. A Study of Plural Economy* (Cambridge University Press, Cambridge, 194), p. 439; Albertini, *European Colonial Rule*, p. 173.

30. P. T. Bauer, *The Rubber Industry. A Study in Competition and Monopoly* (Longmans Green & Co., London, 1948), pp. 60–3.

31. Bauer, *Rubber Industry*, pp. 204, 209–11.

32. Furnivall, *Netherlands India*, pp. 430–3, 438–41; Lewis, *Economic Survey*, p. 119; Allen, *Short Economic History of Modern Japan*, pp. 157–60.

NOTES ON CONTRIBUTORS

B. L. ANDERSON is Senior Lecturer in Economic History in the University of Liverpool. His research interests lie in the field of the history of financial institutions and the development of capital markets. He is author of *Money and Banking in England 1694–1914* (1974), *Capital Accumulation in the Industrial Revolution* (1974), and *Commerce, Industry and Transport. Studies in Economic Change on Merseyside* (1983), as well as articles in the *Economic History Review*, the *Journal of Economic History*, and *Business History*.

A. R. BRIDBURY works at the London School of Economics, and is the author of *England and the Salt Trade* (1955), *Economic Growth* (1962), *Historians and the Open Society* (1972), *Medieval English Clothmaking* (1982), as well as articles in the *Economic History Review*; 'The Dark Ages' (1969), 'The Black Death' (1973), 'Sixteenth-century Farming' (1974), 'Before the Black Death' (1977), 'The Farming-out of Manors' (1978), 'English Provincial Towns' (1981), 'The Lisle Letters' (1982), and in the *Agricultural History Review*; 'Thirteenth-century Prices and the Money Supply' (1985).

ERIC KERRIDGE was educated at Ipswich School and read history at University College, London. Returning after six years in the Royal Artillery, he graduated with first-class honours in 1947. His discipline and inspiration he owed mainly to Professor Sir John Neale. He went on to research under Professor R. H. Tawney, but was influenced more by Professors J. U. Nef, J. A. Schumpeter and L. von Mises. After various temporary posts and six years of full-time research, he settled down to lecture in economic history at the University College of North Wales, Bangor, where he is now Professor Emeritus. His principal books have been *The Agricultural Revolution* (1967), *Agrarian Problems in the Sixteenth Century and After* (1969), and *Textile Manufactures in Early Modern England* (1985).

A. J. H. LATHAM is Senior Lecturer in International Economic History at the University of Wales, Swansea, and is Secretary to the Third World Economic History and Development Group. He has conducted research in Nigeria, India, Singapore, Thailand, Hong Kong and the Philippines, and has lectured in Japan, and at many American and Canadian Universities. In 1979 he was Visiting Professor of Economics at the University of Illinois, Urbana-Champaign. His publications include *Old Calabar 1600–1891: The Impact of the International Economy upon a Traditional Society* (1973), *The International Economy and the Undeveloped World, 1865–1914* (1978), and *The Depression and the Developing World, 1914–1939* (1981). He is currently working on the history of the international rice trade.

JAMES REDFIELD is Professor of Social Thought and Greek at the University of Chicago. His parents were ethnographers, and his own research, although conducted in libraries, is influenced by his early involvement with their work in the field. He was educated at the University of Chicago, where he worked with David Grene, and at Oxford, where he worked with E. R. Dodds, Antony Andrewes and John Gould. The year before he took his Chicago PhD in 1960 he joined the faculty there, and has remained. He is author of *Nature and Culture in the Iliad: The Tragedy of Hector* (1975), and, more relevant to his chapter in this volume, 'The Women of Sparta', *Classical Journal* (1978), 'Odysseus: The Economic Man' in Rubino and Schelmerdine (eds), *Approaches to Homer* (1983), and 'Herodotus the Tourist', *Classical Philology* (1985).

PETER SAWYER was Professor of Medieval History in Leeds University from 1970 to 1982, when he retired to live in Sweden. He now concentrates on medieval Scandinavian history, a development of his interest in the Viking period on which he has published two books: *The Age of the Vikings* (1962) and *Kings and Vikings* (1982). He has also worked on early English history and has published several studies on Domesday Book, *Anglo-Saxon Charters; An Annotated List and Bibliography* (1968), an edition of the pre-Conquest charters of Burton Abbey and a general survey, *From Roman Britain to Norman England* (1978). His contribution to the present volume reflects both areas of interest.

ROBERT SUGDEN has taught at the Universities of York and Newcastle-upon-Tyne, and is now Professor of Economics at the University of East Anglia. He is the author of *The Political Economy of Public Choice*, and (with Alan Williams) the co-author of *The Principles of Practical Cost-benefit Analysis*. Currently he is researching into choice under uncertainty, the economics of philanthropy, the supply of public goods through voluntary contributions, and proportional representation. He is also working on a book about the evolution of social conventions.

INDEX

Acton, Lord 81
Acts of Parliament *see* law
Adam of Bremen 69
Aethelbald of Mercia 62
Africa, markets and development in 201–8
agriculture
    archaic Greek 32–6, 38, 41–2, 44–51
    early modern 164, 165, 170, 174, 182–3, 197
    grain 210–18
    land tenure and 182–3, 186
Alchian, A.A. 175
Alingsåas 71–2
Alvastra monastery 70–1
Åmål 72
Anderson, B.L. 6, 221
    on entrepreneurship and industrial revolution 155–200
Anselm, St 89–90
Antwerp 136
arbitrage 158–60, 166, 172–3
    see also entrepreneurship
Argentina 215
Aristotle 48, 49
Arrow, K. 11–12
Arrow-Debreu general equilibrium model 11–13
Asia
    markets and development in 208–18
    see also individual countries
Athelstan 63, 66
Australia 215

Bakewell 66
Bampton 65
banking 83
Barry, B. 19
Barton on Humber 65
Beeston 66
Benveniste, E. 59–60
Berkeley, Lord 141, 142
Beverley 64, 66
Birka 73, 74
Black Death 93–4, 96
Bolingbroke 65
Bonham, Dr 127–8

Braudel, F. 41, 45, 50
Bridbury, A.R. 4, 221
    on Middle Ages 79–119
brigandage *see* raiding
Bristol 123, 179
Britain
    colonial trade 209, 210, 213, 217
    and North Sea oil 24, 26
    see also England
Bubble Act (1720) 127
Burma 210–16

Caesar, Sir J. 139
Canada 215–16
Canynges, W. 179
Cecil, W. 140
Ceylon 210, 211, 214–15, 217–18
Charles I, King 138, 140–3
charters 63–4, 71–2, 110–11, 140
Chilon of Sparta 52–3
China 208–9, 211–15
church *see* religion
cities
    fortified 62–3
    states 100, 103, 104
    see also urbanisation
class *see* social class
clothing industry *see* textile
coal 196–7
Coaley 65
Coase, R.H. 175
Cockayne, Alderman 138–9
Cockermouth 64
coins *see* money
Coke, Sir E. 125, 126–8, 138, 140, 142
Coleman, D.C. 174
colonies, archaic Greek 43–5, 47
common law *see* law
communication and transport
    grain trade 213
    industrialisation and 160, 161–2, 164, 166, 197
    in Middle Ages 91, 97, 117
competition
    entrepreneurial 166, 168, 170–1, 180
    equilibrium 11–12
    in Middle ages 87–8
    see also imports

225

Index

consumer society, emergence of 158, 161, 165–71, 194
Cookham 68
Cooper, W.M. 124–6
co-operation, social 22–5, 27
courts *see* law
craftsmen 167
   in Africa 202–4, 209
   expansion 160–1, 163, 170
   loss of influence 196
   in Middle Ages 109
   putting-out 174
creativity, entrepreneurial 169, 173
crime 114–17
   see also raiding
Cromwell, O. 143
Crown *see* royalty
'cultural system' 36
custom, law of 126
Cuthbert, St, Law of 64

Dalton, G. 60
Darcy, Lord 137
debt 51
   see also usury
decision-making, entrepreneurial 158, 179
Defoe, D. 189
demand 158, 171–2
Demsetz, H. 168, 175
depression caused by grain surpluses 216–18
disabled people 19
distribution of income and property 10–27 *passim*
Domesday Book 64–5
Douglas, M. 61
Dover 67
drainage of land 140–3, 182
Droitwich 62
Dunstable 64, 67
Dutch East Indies 211, 213–15, 217, 218

early fairs and markets 59–74
early modern English markets 121–53
Edward the Elder 63
Edward III 101
Efik 205
efficiency, labour 15–16
Egypt 46
Elizabeth II, Queen 140
Embsay 64
enclosures 135–8, 140–3, 183, 186, 197

England
   early fairs and markets in 59, 61–8
   early modern markets in 121–53
   entrepreneurship and industrial revolution 155–200
   kings *see* royalty
   in Middle Ages 96–7, 102–3, 105, 108–10, 115–16
   see also Britain
engrossing 108, 130, 134
Enlightenment 189–90, 191–2
entrepreneurship 155–200
equal division principle 23–6
equilibrium, competitive 11–12
Ethelred 66
Europe *see* individual countries
Eustace of Flay 66
Everitt, A.M. 159, 160
exports *see* imports; international
Eyo II, King 205

Ferguson, A. 189
feudalism 92, 94
feuding 102
Fielding, H. 189
firm, nature and function of 175–8, 180–1
Fleming, Chief Baron 126
Flew, A. 19
food trade 123
   laws 127, 134
   see also grain
foreign trade *see* international; long-distance
forestalling 108, 130
forests 141, 142–3
France 46, 216
   land tenure 183, 186
   wars 101, 103, 133
free market 123
futures trading 213–14
Fukien 211

Galileo 5
Geertz, C. 36
Geneva 136
George, H. 10
Germany 24, 203, 213
Ghana 208
Godfred, King 73
governments
   Middle Ages 79, 88–9, 99
   and primary product trade 217–18
   redistribution of income 12

grain trade 123, 210–18
  laws 127, 134
Greece, archaic, development of
  markets in 29–58
Greene, J. 44
guilds 131–2, 135

Habakkuk, H.J. 183
Hedeby 73, 74
Hesiod 41–2, 49, 51, 52
Hobart C.J. 126
Holt C.J. 143
Homer 29–39 *passim*, 43, 45, 52
Hong Kong 211, 213, 214, 217–18
Hume, D. 23, 24, 26

imports and exports 133–5, 138–9,
    165, 205–6, 209–13, 215
  see also international; long-
    distance
incomes
  decline 216–17
  demand and 171
  distribution 12, 14
  in Middle Ages 107, 117
  putting-out 174–5, 199
  redistribution 12, 14
  regulated 107, 132–3
  rising 164, 187
  taxed 15–18
India 208–13, 214–15, 218
individuals
  preferences and utility 14–15
  totality of 22
Indo-China 208–16
industrial revolution 155–200
  'yearly' 123
information and entrepreneurship
    159, 167, 168, 181, 188
Innocent III 88–9
international markets 59, 60, 123
  in Middle Ages 96–9
  see also imports and exports;
    long-distance trade
invention 139–40
Ipswich 67, 131
Ireland 183
irrationality of market 54–6
isomorphism 15
Italy 100, 103

James I, King 138–43
Japan 217–18
Jarrow 67

Jews in Middle Ages 90
Johnson, S. 189, 192
Jönköping 71
justice 17–27, 124
  see also law

Keble, J. 124
Kerridge, E. 4–5, 221
  on early modern English markets
    121–53
King, G. 92
kings *see* royalty
Kirton 65
Kirzner, I. 159, 168, 178
Knight, F.H. 177
Kwantung 211

labour
  abundant 97–8
  archaic Greek 33, 35, 48–9
  division of 192
  efficiency, index of 15–16
  for entrepreneurs 167, 174, 179,
    180
  markets 105, 106–7, 133
  in Middle Ages 105, 106–7
  mobility 185
  and property and morality of
    markets 9–28
land
  lack of 34, 51, 93
  markets 182
  reclamation 140–3, 182
  tax 10
  tenure 48, 92, 94, 182–6
  see also enclosures
landlordism 94
large firms 181
Latham A.J.H. 6, 61, 222
  on Africa and Asia 201–20
Laud, Archbishop 137–8
law
  common 124–32, 135, 137, 141,
    190–1
  courts 113–14, 127–9
  food trade 127, 134
  land ownership 184
  litigation 11–13
  in Middle Ages 106–7, 108–9,
    113–14
  Navigation 134–5
  statute 126–8, 132, 134–6, 139–40,
    142
  and textile industry 127, 135–6,

138–9
and usury 84
weights and measures 109
see also justice
Lee Teck Aw 216
legislation see law
Leighton Buzzard 65
leisure and fashion see consumer
Linköping 79
litigation in Middle Ages 111–13
Liverpool 213
loans see usury
local markets 59–60, 121, 159–60, 162
England 61–8
Middle Ages 96
Scandinavia 68–74
Locke, J. 9, 10, 117
Löddeköpinge 72
London 67, 74, 122–3, 162–3, 169, 213
long-distance trade
Africa 205
Asia 210–18
archaic Greece 31, 37–8, 40–4, 46–7
early modern 133–5
Middle Ages 97–9, 104–5
Scandinavia 73
see also imports and exports; international
Louth 65
Loyn, H.R. 182
Lund 68
Luton 65

McKendrick, N. 161
Maitland, F.W. 138
Malaya 210–11, 214–15, 217
Mandeville, B. 189
markets, defined 121
marriage in Middle Ages 87, 90
Marshal, A. 182
'maximin' theory of distribution 18
medical care industry 12
Merchant Adventurers' Company 138–9
merchants see entrepreneurship; middlemen
metals trade 36, 40–1, 217–18
metropolitan markets 122–3, 134
Middle Ages, markets and freedom in 79–119
middlemen
in Africa 205
in archaic Greece 47

and entrepreneurship 159–60, 163, 167, 170
Midgley, M. 23
Mill, J.S. 9–10
Milward, R. 176
Mirrlees, J.A. 14–17, 22
Mokyr, J. 171
money
coin finds 66–7, 69–71
controlled by people 129–30
debased coinage 137
in Middle Ages 82–3
in pre-colonial Africa 201, 204, 206, 208–9
seized by king 143
and status 60–1
see also wealth
monopolies 139–40
morality of markets, labour and property 9–28

Napoleon 96
natural primary goods 19
Navigation Acts 134–5
Neal, L. 212
Near East, archaic Greek trade with 37–8 40–1
Netherlands 103, 133, 217
see also Dutch East Indies
Newton, I. 5
Nigeria: Cross River region 61, 201–8
North Sea oil 24, 26
North, D. 129
Nozick, R. 2
Nya Lödöse 71–2

Odense 68–9
oil, vegetable 206–7, 214–15
Östergötland 71
Oundle 67

Paley, W. 191
Pareto-efficiency 11–14
Partney 65, 67
Paston letters 116
patents of invention 139–40
patronage Middle Ages 82–3
Paviken 72
Philippines 211, 214–15, 218
Phoenicians 30–1, 38, 40, 44
place-name evidence 66
Plato 45
Plumbe, J.H. 188
Polanyi, K. 60–1

politics 187–8
  see also governments
population
  growth 43–4, 164
  movements 96
  reduction 93–4, 96, 135–8, 208
  size in 18th century 181
  stable 171, 187
Porter, R. 190
poverty 82, 93–4
pre-colonial African market 201–8
pre-market economy 36
prestige *see* status
prices 11
  entrepreneurship and 159, 166–8, 170, 172, 179
  exports and 133–4
  fall 164, 171
  grain 211–16
  natural and artifical 123–4
primary products 18–19
  trade 210–18
privileges 81, 111, 114
profit and entrepreneurship 157, 159–60, 168–9, 172, 179, 182
property
  distribution 13–14
  freedom of 121, 124
  labour and morality of markets 9–28
  rights and entrepreneurs 181, 184, 195
  'proto-industrialisation' *see* putting-out
putting-out 173–7, 179–80, 199

raiding/brigandage
  archaic Greece 37, 43
  Middle Ages 102, 115
Raleigh, Sir W. 129, 143–4
Ramsbury 64–5
Ramsey 66
Rawls, J. 2, 17–23, 27
Razi, Z. 93
Read, L.E. 121
reciprocal advantage 22–3, 27
Reculver 67
Redfield, J.M. 2, 222
  on archaic Greece 29–58
redistribution *see* distribution
regional markets 121–2, 134, 162, 163
regrating 108, 130
religion
  archaic Greece 39–40, 49, 56

and common law 124
and local fairs and markets 64–71, 73
in Middle Ages 85–6, 99, 112
Ribe 73
rice trade 210–18
Ripon 64, 66
risks, entrepreneurial 168–9, 173, 178–9, 181, 195
ritual sphere *see* religion
Rochester 62
Roman empire 61–2, 95–6, 98, 99, 103
Rostow, W.W. 5–6
royalty
  and courts 113–14
  and early markets 63–4, 71–2, 73
  land ownership 141–3, 184–6
  licensing markets 108–11
  manipulation of law 137–43
  in Middle Ages 82, 84–5, 102, 102–3, 108–11, 113–14
  and taxation 133
rubber trade 217–18
Russia 46

Sackville Crow, Sir 142
St Ives 66
St Neots 66
Salisbury 110
salt 62
Salzman, L.F. 64
Sawyer, P. 3, 222
  on early fairs and markets 59–77
Scandinavia 24
  early fairs and markets in 59–60, 68–74
Schelling, T. 25
Scientific Revolution 188–9, 192
Scotland, attacks on 101, 143
Selby 64
self-sufficiency 218
Sen, A.K. 13
Settlement (1688) 184, 191
Settlement Law (1388) 107
Shackle, G.L.S. 169, 179
Siam 208–12, 214–16
Singapore 210–14, 216, 218
Skara 69
Skien 72
Skuldevig 72
slavery 49, 205, 206–8
Smith, A. 9–10, 183, 189, 192
Smollet, T. 189
Smyth, J. 142

social class
  archaic Greek 32–6, 39, 48, 52–3
  entrepreneurship and 161, 166, 169
  land tenure and 186
  in Middle Ages 81–2, 92–4
  mobility 161, 169
  see also status
social co-operation 22–5, 27
social pool, income and wealth in 20–1
social primary goods 18–19
social utility see utilitarianism
Socrates 45
Solon 52–3
Somerset, Protector 136–7
Southern, R.W. 112
Spain 133
specialisation 160, 161, 163
  in Africa 201–4, 209
  entrepreneurial 169, 173, 180, 189
  incomplete 164
  in Middle Ages 97–9
Spenser E. 83
stability 21–2, 187
status 112–12
  money and 60–1
  of traders 31
  see also social class
statutes see law
Stow 64, 66
Stratford upon Avon 68
Strömberg, M. 72
sugar trade 217–18
Sugden, R. 2, 223
  on labour, property and morality
    of markets 9–28
Sunday markets 64–7, 71
Svinnegarn 69

tailors 106, 131
taxation
  archaic Greek 48–51
  customs duties 133
  income 15–18
  land 10
  'optimal' 14, 15
Teochieu 214
textile and clothing industries
  Africa 206, 209
  Asia 215
  exports 135, 138–9, 165, 209–10
  guilds 131–2, 135
  and law 127, 135–6, 138–9
  size of firm 180
  tailors 106, 131
  wool 123, 127, 179

Thailand see Siam
Theognis 52–7
Thirsk 64
Threckingham 65
Thucydides 32
tin trade 217–18
tolls 62–3, 68
  in Middle Ages 109–10, 111, 116
'transaction, modes of' 60
transport see communication

uncertainty see risks
United States: agricultural trade
  213–17
Uppsala 68. 69
urbanisation
  in archaic Greece 29, 39, 48–9
  in Middle Ages 98
  see also citites
usury 136
  in Middle Ages 83–4, 107
utilitarianism 14–17, 21–2

Vallet, G. 46
Vasa, G. 71

wages see incomes
Walpole, R. 187
Walrasian general equilibrium model
  11–13
warfare 50, 55, 99–103, 133
Warminster 123
wealth 20–1
  in archaic Greece 48, 52–6
  in Middle Ages 84–5, 118
  see also money
weights and measures law 109
welfare maximisation 13
Westerfield, R.B. 159–60
wheat trade 212–18
Whitby 67
William the Conqueror 101
Williams, B. 23
Wilson, T. 92
Wolsey, Cardinal 136–7
Wolverhampton 63–4, 66, 67
wool see textile
Worcester 62

Xenophon 32

Yellow Duke 205
York 64, 66, 74
Ystad 72